Nourishing Routes

Your Compassionate Journey to Love Food, Adore Your Body, Become Yourself

Marissa Pendlebury

Nourishing
Routes

Published by Nourishing Routes 2016
www.nourishingroutes.com

© Copyright Marissa Pendlebury 2016

First edition.

ISBN: 978-1-911525-01-1 paperback
978-1-911525-02-8 ebook

Printed by www.beamreachuk.co.uk

Dedicated to
Graham and Marjorie Pendlebury:

Grandparents, best friends and the first Compassioneers who inspired me to fall back in love with myself and embark on my own Nourishing Routes journey.

You will forever be in my heart

Contents

Acknowledgements

This book was inspired by and made possible by the many Compassioneers I have had the fortunate opportunity to be supported by in my life. I couldn't have done it without the belief and encouragement from my late grandparents, who also happened to instigate and encourage my lifelong love for drinking tea. Speaking of which, this book would not exist it is wasn't for the many cosy and welcoming cafes that have allowed me to hide away and write for hours drinking endless pots of tea and mugfuls of frothy cappuccinos as well as lots of tasty and nourishing snacks.

This book has become a reality thanks to the endless mentoring and unconditional love from my parents and friends who have always been there to believe in my ambitions and passion to make the world a better and more compassionate place to live and thrive in. I also need to show my gratitude to Liverpool Hope University, Warrington Youth Centre and Warrington Disability Partnership for sparking my self-development and recovery, while making me believe that my life was so much more worthwhile that what I ate, weighed, looked like, or the grade I achieved on a piece of paper.

Finally, I give a sweet scented note to everyone who has ever took the time to listen to my philosophy, hopes and dreams with open ears and an open heart. Such genuine friendships are simply priceless and unforgettable.

"Being Compassionate is not only about giving and receiving love. It is also about trusting your own inner compass to lead the beautifully meaningful life you were born to live"

Foreword

This book was written with the huge passion and belief that our health and happiness doesn't solely revolve around the food or nutrients we eat, what we weigh, how much exercise we do, or what we look like.

Despite what we may have been manipulated into believing, the real truth lies in the fact that there are so many empowering and exciting elements to discover and integrate into our lives when it comes to experiencing happiness and health. A key part of this empowering discovery involves becoming compassionate beings who authentically love each and every part of ourselves – from the inside out.

By being compassionate beings, or what I like to call Compassioneers, this allows us to find a route to real freedom with food, mind and body, so we can go out into the world and be the amazing, inspiring and beautiful people we were born to be.

I created Nourishing Routes with a mission to empower you to *Nourish, Flourish and Thrive* through appreciating and tying together the many diverse and holistic elements of wellbeing. I want you to finally place a life filled with compassion, enjoyment, creativity, social connections, self-love and a positive relationship with food and body back on the menu. Sorry, no Calorie counts, faddy diets or detox plans are included. However, within this book, there are lots of extremely useful guides, tools and practical activities to get started and set you on the best path on your own journey forwards.

Why am I writing this book?

Blooming from decades of research and years of personally struggling from and eventually overcoming anorexia nervosa, orthorexia (an unhealthy obsession with healthy eating), depression and anxiety, I have uncovered that there are oh so many nourishing routes to wellbeing – around ten key elements to be precise.

It is no longer useful, or even non-harmful, for us as complex social beings to solely focus on our diet and exercise as the main fundamentals of a 'good', healthy or happy life. It is also no longer necessary for us to pursue faddy food and fitness regimens, and especially the ones that are forcefully pre-scribed to us by industries whose main motives are based on making a profit from individuals' vulnerabilities and insecurities. The time is now to bring a multitude of possibilities into our lives by appreciating and nurturing what we already have.

Within this book I will share with you my own Nourishing Routes jour-ney and how I finally became fully free and liberated to live a fulfilling life with food, mind and my whole body. This was made possible by learning to lead a more compassionately self-loving lifestyle, which is what I refer to as the journey to becoming a Compassioneer. More crucially, I am additionally going to offer you step by step guidance, inspiring quotes and your very own magic key to open up your own innate ability to love yourself, love food and love each and every part of your amazingly beautiful self.

I want to help you to integrate elements of Nourishing Routes into your own life in an empowering way while taking away the destructive thoughts and habits that have previously led to a life of limitations and self-loathing. There is even a whole section within this book on how to critically view dieting, stop Calorie counting and escape from any other restrictive rou-tines and unhealthy obsessions around food, body and exercise. I am here to enable you realise that it is completely possible for you to finally break free from these damaging thought patterns and behaviours for good. They no longer need or deserve to be a part of your current or future life.

If you are used to reading diet books, counting Calories and using your weight or appearance to measure and define your self-worth, then get ready to break free from those ties from this point on. I would like you to know in your heart that you CAN become the person you were born to be and learn to love your whole self. So, get ready to embark on an exciting step-by-step journey of a lifetime where you can *Nourish, Flourish and Thrive through becoming a part of the growing tribe of Compassioneers.*

Introduction

If you have stumbled upon or intentionally purchased this book I am eagerly excited to say that there is a good chance that you may be searching for a way to develop a happier, healthier you – someone who is free to love themselves and live a life filled with a sense of meaning and purpose no matter what they eat, what they weigh, how much they exercise or what they look like.

Fortunately for us both, Nourishing Routes is exactly that – a way of loving ourselves regardless of our diet, fitness, weight or appearance. Nourishing Routes ties all of the essential elements of wellbeing together so we can integrate them into our lives in a way that really feels empowering.

More specifically, the real pathways to wellbeing involve an empowering journey towards leading a more compassionate lifestyle, nurturing and nourishing the inside and the out using many creatively enjoyable methods – not rigid or self-punishing routines. I do believe that our diet and level of physical activity play an important role in the quest for happiness and health, but they only play a subordinate role and only really evolve when we firstly focus on many other essential elements of our overall wellbeing. Developing these essential elements, which we will talk more in depth about very soon, mainly involves creating and sustaining compassionate relationships with our mind, food, body and, inevitably, others and even the whole planet. This is because the way that we are able to love ourselves eventually plays out into the way we are able to show that love to everyone and everything around us.

What is Nourishing Routes and Who is it For?

No matter your age, gender, cultural background or state of health, what you and I may have in common is the ambition of seeking freedom with food, mind and body. Deep down we both want to experience health, happiness and wellbeing while being able to authentically love ourselves, follow our dreams and reach our full potential. Nourishing Routes is therefore for anyone and everyone who shares this positively life affirming ambition.

The answer to what we both seek is encompassed within our innate ability to lead a compassionate lifestyle, which involves learning to trust our inner compass – i.e. our intuition to live more compassionately with ourselves and others. This holistic route to wellness, or what I call the Nourishing Routes to becoming a Compassioneer, allows us to be nourished not only with nutrients in food, but also via loving ourselves while developing a positive relationship with food, mind and body. This holistic pathway additionally involves getting back in tune with our natural creativity, cherishing what we already have, making positive social connections with others and living in harmonious alignment with what we truly believe and value.

The life of a Compassioneer definitely does not involve any form of punishment, self-loathing or unnecessary restrictions on your life – far, far from it.

Completely unlike a faddy diet, fitness routine or disordered way of viewing food and our own bodies, the compassionate lifestyle of a Compassioneer is made up of lots of different elements of wellbeing. One of the best things, though, is that every single one of us has the permission, power and freedom to develop the elements that best suit our own personal needs. In theory this means that each of us has the ability to find our own unique Nourishing Routes to becoming a Compassioneer, without having to subscribe to someone else's rules or ideal way of living.

Living compassionately, as we shall explore together, can be described and experienced as a liberating expedition. Our ability to embark on this expedition – a journey of a lifetime – is deeply ingrained within our genes, not only to aid our own evolutionary survival, but also to better connect with, support and care for others as well as the whole planet. In simple terms, we were ALL born to be Compassioneers, and it is my mission to empower as many individuals as possible to pursue and fulfil this natural instinct.

Is Nourishing Routes Really For Me?

Perhaps you are sick of having quick fix ways to wellness shoved in your face, and if you see the next advertisement for any weight loss supplements, detox juicing plans, dieting trends, or new range of super food powders you might feel like punching a wall (I totally get you with this one!). You might know, deep down, that you are worth so much more than monitoring a number on a scale or logging your food intake with the sole purpose of living up to someone else's or society's expectations.

Perhaps you want to find freedom with your food and body or even recover from an eating disorder. This goal is completely possible, and a possibility I am all too familiar with. You might feel ready to begin contemplating and acting on the idea of being able to nourish yourself with the food that you enjoy and that allows you to feel energised – without feeling guilty, ashamed, or tempted to harm your body by starving yourself or binging on food. Similarly, you may want to break away from using maladaptive eating, toxic relationships or other harmful activities in your life that distract you from the real issues in your life that need to be faced by using more compassionate methods.

Perhaps you are trying to overcome a trauma, a physical or mental illness, or have become overly used to overworking yourself and trying to strive for perfection or live up to others' unrealistic expectations. However, despite your hardest efforts, you seem to be moving further away from happiness and wellbeing, instead feeling trapped in a negative spiral of low self-worth and poor health.

Perhaps you are just ready for change – ready to embrace the real, fun loving, compassionate person inside who cares more about their own health, happiness and the welfare of others than trying to be perfect, lose weight, be the best at something, or meet someone else's standard of what it means to be a good, beautiful or successful person.

Rest assured, you are beautiful, perfect and amazingly extraordinary just as you are in this very moment.

If you can relate to any of the above scenarios, I want you to realise right now that there is a way out, onwards and upwards. What I also hope is that we both have common understanding, deep in our hearts and minds, that happiness, health and wellbeing can be attained in so many more enjoyable, empowering and sustainable ways other than trying to improve and perfect what we eat, what we weigh, how much physical activity we do, what we look like, or even the type of career and income we pursue. However, we probably both know already that society or even our own friends and family very often tell us a very different story, along with setting their own ideal and unrealistic standards of what health and happiness should look like.

As I have learnt from first hand experiences and my own academic research from over a decade, our health, happiness and overall wellbeing involve so much more than a number on a scale, counting Calories, rigidly controlling what we eat, striving to be perfect, reaching a certain fitness goal, having a financially profitable career, or gaining ownership over as many valuable items as possible. There is a much more exciting adventure just waiting to be explored, and this adventure involves a nourishing and compassionate journey forward that swiftly weaves its way from the inside out.

In other words, if we are to begin to reach our full potential, the real work has to begin with our own minds and the art of learning to step into a loving relationship with ourselves just as we are.

Before we can even think about perfecting our diet, fitness and weight (if that were ever possible or even necessary), it is crucially important to firstly nurture our own minds and refocus the obscured perspective it currently holds. If we love what is already inside AND out, then optimal nourishment of the body and reaching our goals will happen naturally and become more sustainable. These are the Nourishing Routes that we were designed to journey upon, rather than the dark roads some of us are forced down in a way that leads to a path of self-hate, harm and an ultimate lack of life fulfilment.

Does the Nourishing Routes journey require me to live up to a certain standard?

Absolutely not. I have come to realise that, regardless of what we do or don't do in life, we don't deserve to beat ourselves up for not being perfect or quite good enough in relation to reaching a certain goal or standard. In fact, there is absolute beauty in many of our flaws and imperfections. Also, leading a more compassionate lifestyle while considering the many elements of happiness, health and wellbeing empowers us to realise this. We need to remember that we were born with an innate ability to show compassion to others and – most importantly of all – ourselves.

Nourishing Routes is based on these very realisations, and a thoroughly passionate mission to show you how becoming more compassionate in our everyday lives, including with our food and body, can have ever-expanding positive impacts on the happiness and wellbeing of ourselves, as well as that of others and even the whole planet.

Nourishing Routes is a Gift, not a Punishment

This book was ultimately created as an extra special gift just for you. If you are ready to place life back on the menu and discover your own Nourishing Routes towards happiness, wellbeing and gaining a greater sense of meaning in life, then you have already taken a huge step in this direction by the simple act of picking up this book. So, by continuing to read on with your own welfare in mind, I can say with absolute confidence that you are about to go on a nourishing journey towards self-love and compassionate living – a lifestyle where you can truly unleash your full potential in so many creative and enjoyable ways without ever needing to adopt any diet, follow a rule book or invest in any form of self-sabotaging method.

On our journey throughout this book we will explore how loving ourselves (including each and every part of our body), eating tasty nourishing foods that doesn't involve feeling guilty or ashamed, expressing our creativity, connecting with others, being grateful for what we have already, living in the present moment and taking action on matters that are in line with our values are key to finding freedom in mind and body while leading a happy, nourishing, flourishing and meaningful life.

Nourishing Routes is a Flexible Philosophy – Not a Rigid Regime or Diet Plan

You may have correctly guessed that the principles of this book and Nourishing Routes philosophy are definitely not about going on a diet, monitoring our weight or level of physical activity, attending an uncomfortably intrusive therapy session, or following any rigid routine to the point of obsession. Alternatively, Nourishing Routes, and therefore this book, provides you with a uniquely empowering way of finding and finally trusting your own 'inner compass'. This inner compass is the tool you can use in order to embark on a meaningful and compassionate journey that represents your own Nourishing Routes – ultimately enabling you to Nourish, Flourish and Thrive.

By inviting you to pursue your own Nourishing Routes I know that you can gain freedom with your food, mind and body in a way that involves the most optimal, enjoyable and liberating actions of nurturing yourself. Embarking on this journey is the fundamental route to becoming a Compassioneer. A Compassioneer, I believe, is the type of person we were born to be, as it largely involves living in harmony with ourselves and the many creatures we happen to share our beautiful planet with.

Firstly though, before I potentially confuse you with too many concepts to sink your teeth into, you might still be asking a few questions:

"What is in the name of Nourishing Routes and what does it really mean in the context of leading a more compassionate lifestyle?"

and also:

"What the heck is a Compassioneer?"

Well let me answer these questions right here.

❋ **Why Nourishing?** Nourishing is the word that I feel represents how our happiness, wellbeing and a fulfilling life is born out of being able to energise and replenish ourselves, not only with the energy nutrients we eat, but also through being able to live more compassionately – mainly by developing positive relationships with food, mind and our whole bodies, as well as other individuals, communities and the planet. In other words, Nourishment is about fuelling the mind, and body– not just about focussing on the exact types of foods we place into our bodies with the simplistic goal of meeting a certain nutritional need.

❋ **Why Routes?** Routes resembles the steps taken when embarking on YOUR own nourishing journey towards a more compassionate lifestyle, in whatever enjoyable and empowering way that may be for YOU. There are many avenues and winding roads to happiness and wellbeing – not just those that centre on nutrition, body weight and fitness regimens (especially if they involve dieting, counting Calories and loathing ourselves!). There are many other exciting elements to explore, whether that be learning to love ourselves, express our creativity, feel grateful for what we already have, connect with others, engage in pleasurable movement, be more mindful, act in ways that align with our personal values, and enjoy eating more plant-based foods that energise and replenish us while minimising the exploitation of other humans, animals and the planet.

❋ **What is a Compassioneer?** Compassioneer is a unique term and, as we will discuss in much more detail very soon, represents someone who is taking steps, no matter how big or small, to lead a more compassionate lifestyle. This could mean going on a journey to love yourself more, find freedom with food, and pursue lots of diverse avenues (i.e. Nourishing Routes) to wellbeing that don't involve rigid dieting or exercise regimens. The word Compassioneer is not yet another unnecessary label that you either are or are not. It is also not another type of faddy lifestyle you can fail at. Being a Compassioneer takes many unique forms and enables individuals to find ways of sharing their compassion with others, whether that be helping individuals to love themselves, reduce the exploitation of other beings or make behaviour changes that promote the welfare of the planet. Chances are, in many ways you are probably already a compassionate individual.

The aim with Nourishing Routes, however, is to take you even further on a journey to becoming someone with even more compassion – especially when this compassion is directed to yourself. On a positively important note, the world has recently been making huge positive shifts in terms of more and more individuals living as, or ready to become, Compassioneers. As I will highlight throughout this book, if there was ever a great or special time to think about going on a journey to become a Compassioneer yourself, the time is now.

If you really desire to seek a more compassionate lifestyle in all its amazing forms, while learning to love yourself and find freedom with your mind, food and body, I challenge you to delve further into this book and seek out your own uniquely Nourishing Routes to happiness, health and wellbeing. This decision in itself is the first and perhaps most fundamental stepping stone on your own Nourishing Routes.

On that note, I personally invite you on a worthwhile journey to realise your compassionate potential and follow your own Nourishing Routes to wellness, while joining a growing tribe of Compassioneers.

About the Author

The most important thing for you to know about me, other than having very curly hair and being an addict of drinking tea, is that I am truly 100% passionate about and 100% dedicated to empowering others to experience the far-reaching benefits of journeying towards a more compassionate lifestyle while finding freedom with their food, mind and body.

In my professional role I am a health researcher, psychologist, public speaker, wellbeing coach and specialist in the field of nutrition and eating disorders. However, this doesn't belittle the fact that I am a self-confessed addict of tea, seeker of quirky cafes, dipper of *everything* in hummus, nibbler of chocolate and compassionate lifestyle blogger. I also have an absolute love for cooking, yoga and following a deliciously nourishing lifestyle (inclusive of cakes and chocolate of course, because food is just as much about fun and enjoyment as it is nutrition!). These factors aside, my life mission firmly lies in leading a more compassionate lifestyle and enabling others to experience the benefits of pursuing this lifelong ambition too.

But, in order to be honest with you right from the start, on my own personal journey towards leading a more compassionate lifestyle I have been on each side of the love-hate spectrum. On one side of the spectrum, my life revolved around absolutely loathing myself, being hospitalised several times for anorexia nervosa, experiencing depression and being riddled with crippling anxiety that made me more or less house bound. On the other much more positive side, my journey towards a more compassionate way of living involved gaining an insight into the many elements of happiness and health, as well as learning to authentically love myself, thoroughly enjoy food, and become non-judgemental of what I ate, weighed or looked like. It was along this path, against medical opinion, that I was able to fully recover and begin living life to the very full. This positive side of the spectrum was and continues to be my journey to becoming a Compassioneer. Perhaps more crucially though, it is a journey that I can no longer repress from sharing, with my ultimate mission being to enable individuals like you to find their very own Nourishing Routes to becoming a Compassioneer.

My current reality seems far, far away from when I was the girl who 100% hated her body, felt guilty and ashamed about experiencing pleasure, thought she was ugly, only aimed for perfection, worked obsessively, restricted her meals to 'clean' foods only, obsessively counted Calories, spent countless hours reading nutrition research and health magazines, rigidly exercised, punished herself for 'failing' at things, and went to extremely unhealthy methods to live up to unrealistic expectations – no matter what the physical or psychological costs.

I was also the girl who was cripplingly anxious when speaking to new people, and could never be herself due to fear of negative judgement or failure. I felt unworthy of anyone's love, let alone my own.

Ultimately I was a person simply existing rather than living. And to me, that is no life at all. But surely it isn't possible for someone to be able to authentically love themselves, go through years of academic studying on positive wellbeing, nutrition and psychology if they once lived a life that can only be described as the exact opposite as the definition of living compassionately? Well, before I directly answer this question, let me take you with me to a time when I was physically shaking, heart pounding, standing lifelessly in front of an abundantly filled fridge looking at everything I had repeatedly told myself I couldn't eat.

I was usually shaking anyway, either because everything always seemed so icy cold or because I felt so grotesquely hideous after seeing myself in a mirror. But this time, looking at food in the way you might eye up your worst childhood enemy, I was shaking in absolute fear because I didn't know which apple to choose.

Which apple was the smallest and contained the least amount of Calories, fat and sugar? Which apple could I eat that wouldn't result in me feeling absolutely fat, worthless and grotesque soon afterwards?

I just couldn't tell, or be sure, mainly because my food scale (one of the only things I ever trusted to make decisions or my self-worth) was broken. I hopelessly stood there staring into space, feeling fat and disgusting, my hands quivering like someone on drugs, knowing that eating anything without knowing the Calorie or nutrient content would immediately result in being filled with crippling anxiety.

Like most other eating occasions, I was filled with a sense of utter self-loathing that felt as though someone was ripping a jagged knife throughout the bleak loneliness of my whole weak insides. The same feelings would arise when trying to shop for food, while trying to work out what was the best, healthiest, cleanest and lowest Calorie item to buy. Sometimes this would take well over an hour. Going out for a meal with friends and family was a complete impossibility.

Of course these situations are vast worlds apart from the current life I lead, where I now have a very positive relationship with my food and body. But, at the naive age of 14, after brutally falling out of love with my whole self, nothing I ever did felt good enough. I didn't have the confidence to speak up for what I really believed in. I was always trying to be perfect, make others happy and meet their expectations, never my own.

To try and achieve some sense of self-worth, I would stay up late into the early hours of the morning, perfecting an assignment, striving to achieve the best grade, even if it meant getting just 2-3 hours sleep and not eating. I would run on a treadmill or power walk in vicious circles around the block just to burn off more Calories than I had eaten. I would meticulously calculate my food intake on fitness pal while planning the next day's food intake to an absolute tee in order to eat just enough Calories to make it through the day, hopefully without falling unconscious.

There are many unanswered questions as to why an eating disorder became so deeply interwoven into my life for such a long time. Could this really by true of the girl who always seemed jolly, sociable and loved her food as well as having loving parents in her childhood? I guess so.

Perhaps my fate was a result of my genetic makeup, growing up in a competitive world of athletics and music performance? Or, perhaps its not worth worrying about the whys, ifs and buts at all. The reality is, it happened, and a huge part of the problem was growing to hate rather than love myself, just as so many of us are taught to do in the competitive, image focussed and materialistic society we live in. I wasn't alone in my experiences though, and like many others, I had grown deficient in vitamin C – Compassion

For nearly ten years I held the false belief that bouncing back from mental illness, recovering from anorexia nervosa and an unhealthy obsession with health eating, learning to love myself, being able to enjoy life and reaching my full potential were completely impossible goals. Or, if they were possible, I believed those goals could only be reached by a select few privileged individuals who were much more worthy of love than me – Individuals who were naturally beautiful, popular, slim, fit, rich and successful. However, I now know that the journey from self-hate to self -love is none of those things.

In fact, it is a completely possible process of liberation and empowerment to nourish ourselves in mind and body in many other ways than simply focussing on food and fitness.

So when did I really make up and start to become the compassionate and life loving individual that people know me as today?

Well, It wasn't in any of my 5 hospitalisations. It wasn't in a counselling session. It wasn't when my dearest family members told me that I was worth so much more than what i ate or weighed on a scale. No. My awakening happened on a cold November evening, looking out into a starry sky filled with bonfire night fireworks on the very day my granddad, my best friend, my lifelong mentor, passed away from this Earth. Gazing into the still emptiness of space, I knew that if I had anything left to lose, this was it.

Even in my darkest of times, when no one trusted me or could bare to see me so painfully thin, my granddad stuck by me. everyday visiting me in hospitals that were miles away from his home. Filling me with inspiration and never giving up hope. Reminding me that one day, perhaps one day, I would fully recover and that my experiences would be used to help inspire and empower our generation.

Of course I didn't believe him one bit. Not then anyway. I didn't trust anyone out of fear that their main motivation was to make me eat and gain weight But, on the night my granddad passed away very suddenly, I experienced a huge panic attack. A big bang that rattled my life and brittle osteoporosis ridden bones so enormously, I felt like running to the centre of the earth and curling up in a ball for all eternity. It felt as though the whole world was collapsing in on me, waiting to swallow me up into the darkest blackness in one big gulp.

All I could do was wait for that moment of impending doom. However, in darkness there is always a compassionate glimmer of light, and for the very first time in years, I found myself in my bedroom that evening, slowly wrapping my arms around myself holding on for dear life as tightly as a mother might do with her newborn baby. I was giving myself a hug. Something that felt so foreign and unreal that I wondered if the arms around me were that of a ghost and not my own. But those arms were my most definitely mine, and they sent a soothing sensation throughout my whole body along with an accompanying voice that emerged from inside the depths of my heart and mind. This voice, my own soul, said:

Marissa. This has to stop. You are worth loving.

You are not a number on a scale. You are not how many Calories you have eaten. You are not a grade on a piece of paper, You can't base your self worth on the quality of foods you have or have not eaten. You are not a fitness tracking app. You are not your eating disorder.

You are a beautiful human being, worth loving, who has so much potential to give back to the planet.

You weren't placed on this earth to hide away in a corner. You have a mission to share, but it will take a whole lot of self-love, self-care and self-development to realise how you can take action on it and go on to create an inspired tribe who believe in the art of loving yourself.

❊

These softly spoken words were loud and clear. Not like my usual whisper or harsh inner critic. On That lonely night, I didn't feel so alone anymore. I knew that although it would take a lot of energy and dedication to fully recover and really become more loving towards myself, it was actually possible.

Regardless of what medical professionals had said regarding the unlikeliness of full recovery, I knew that I had my own back, and that the journey from the self-loathing position I currently stood and where I wanted to be had to begin from the inside out. Not the other way around.

Although as anyone with a less than loving relationship with food or body might be able to imagine, recovery and self-love did not happen over night. Far from it. However, I did dedicate myself to learning more about the real science of health, eating disorders, psychology, health and nutrition. I also got involved in volunteering and creative activities where I could learn new things about myself and the world, meet inspiring people, and notice how amazing it felt to help others – time much better spent than on Calorie counting, obsessing about nutrients in food or weighing myself.

Eventually I completed college and began a quest to study health sciences, nutrition and psychology at university — topics that I studied in depth while developing my own research over the next 6 years . Over those years, I learned so much about the psychology of eating, the mind and body connection, and how they work in unison to influence our happiness and health. I also took up even more diverse volunteering opportunities and met so many interesting people along the way who gave me the inspiration and determination to carry on with my mission. These individuals were living their own life mission through living compassionately, not only by providing care and love to others, but also themselves.

A huge realisation on my recovery journey is that healing was not just about eating and weighing more, or getting to a so called healthy weight by following a recovery meal plan. Far from it. Instead, they involved stepping into a trusting and loving relationship with food, mind and body – in all forms, shapes and sizes. It was also about gaining opportunities to learn more about myself and develop personal skills rather than simply striving to achieve a grade marked in black and white ink on a piece of paper that I could falsely use to validate my self-worth as a human being.

Over time I gradually I learned to enjoy the pleasure of food without feeling guilty. I was also able to give up any unrealistic aspirations of being perfect or living up to the unrealistic expectations of others. Instead, the time I invested in getting involved in volunteering allowed me to realise just how gratifying and important it is to give compassion to myself as well as others.

Slowly but surely, and very surely, I began to trust my mind and body for the amazing things they could do. For the first time in years, I dedicated myself to nurturing both my body and mind with the nourishment it really needed, not just with food, but with self-love, expressing creativity, social connections, physically moving in ways that were enjoyable, and becoming grateful for everything I already had in my life. Instead of fearing the kitchen, it became my favourite and most energising place to be in my home, where I enjoyed following and creating my own deliciously nourishing recipes — which for the first time in years involved baking cakes and biscuits while eating the tempting mixture from my creative finger tips.

But, at the same time as I was recovering for real, I noticed that more and more people seemed to be becoming obsessed with counting Calories, losing weight, and following the next faddy dieting or fitness trend – the very things that my research had been showing leads to the exact opposite of health and happiness. Not that eating nourishing foods and engaging in physical activity to promote wellbeing isn't important, but I could see lots of individuals placing so much energy into these goals at the expense of time spent with friends, family and other creative pursuits that are absolutely crucial to wellbeing.

There were even individuals I knew who worked tirelessly at the gym, attacking themselves and pumping their bodies full of pills, powders and unknown chemicals in the pursuit to get leaner and more muscular. I couldn't bear that this was just deemed to be a natural and acceptable part of our society, and that change needed to happen in order for individuals to follow their own empowering routes to happiness and health – not those prescribed by a rigid meal plan, weight loss programme or fitness regime.

More importantly for the direction of my own life, I knew that I needed to be part of making that change happen. I also knew that I could help by using my experiences to show that creating change really is possible, especially when we choose to embark on our very own Nourishing Routes towards living more compassionately and finding many diverse ways to achieving happiness and health.

As part of this mission and my own personal experiences, I developed the idea that there are around 10 key elements that we can develop in our lives that will enable us to love more compassionately and experience authentic happiness and health. As I will soon explain and help you to understand, not only are these 10 key elements of Nourishing Routes supported by my own experiences, but they are also upheld by decades of rigorous scientific research from many fields of study – especially in the growing movement of positive psychology where there is a greater focus on mental and physical wellbeing rather than just ill-being.

I don't just believe in the 10 key elements of Nourishing Routes, but I live and breathe them in a way that allows me to feel like a real Compassioneer. Perhaps even more importantly for you though, I am thoroughly passionate about sharing the message that finding your own Nourishing Routes and becoming a Compassioneer is essential if you truly want to enter a loving and trusting relationship with food, mind, and your whole body. Ultimately, it has become my lifelong passion to share this message – a message to help more and more individuals to realise that we are each on our own unique roads to being able to flourish, thrive and reach our full potential, mainly through realising the strength in living compassionately and loving our-selves from the inside out.

How is this Book Set out and How can Reading it Allow You to embrace Your own Nourishing Routes?

This book is split into five main parts. In Part 1 I will firstly introduce you to the concept of becoming a Compassioneer, and then the 10 key elements of Nourishing Routes. Here I will cover, in depth, what it means to live more compassionately, along with supportive evidence in a fun, understandable and bite-size form. Most crucially, I will provide inspiration, key examples, empowering activities and step by step practical guidance on how to successfully welcome these vital elements into your life in a way that best suits your unique needs. Crucially, you can choose which elements are most relevant and important to yourself so that you can tailor your own empowering nourishing routes. There will also be opportunities for goal setting, so you can identify the elements of Nourishing Routes you would like to develop, how you can realistically do this, as well as successfully overcome any barriers that you might anticipate. I will then go on to show you why compassion is important, and how we evolved to live compassionately, with the idea of learning to love ourselves being of high importance. Once we have gotten a firm grip on compassion, we will look at how leading a more compassionate lifestyle, and becoming a Compassioneer, is about going on a life long journey rather than striving for perfection.

In Part 2 I will focus more specifically on applying the concept of Nourishing Routes and compassionate living to learning to love ourselves and journeying towards a place of creating peace rather than war with ourselves – where we can be our authentic selves, unleash our creative potential and living a life filled with a sense of freedom and purpose. We will also cover the importance of being able to integrate compassionate living into our work and relationships, while even suggesting practical ways that we can take time for ourselves in a truly nurturing and energising way.

In Part 3 we will apply the elements of Nourishing Routes and compassionate living to the very specific subjects the food we eat. To do this we will initially cover how, from birth, we step into a life-long relationship with food, and how we can nourish ourselves, stop counting on Calories and understand the benefits of eating flexibly and, against modern assumptions, even emotionally. Together we will develop a positive mindset that doesn't involve branding foods as 'good' or 'bad', fearing certain foods, or feeling guilty and ashamed for what we do or do not eat.

Further into Part 3 is about breaking free from any form of disordered eating or negative relationship with food so that we can begin to get back in tune and harmony with the way we were born to lovingly view food as more than simply nutrients and fuel. We will also look at what it means

✳

to eat more 'kindfully' as well as compassionately (novel concepts that we will define and explore) with the step by step guidance you can use to make your relationship with food and body as loving, enjoyable and energising as possible.

In Part 4 we will delve into how we can develop loving relationships with our whole bodies, no matter what we eat, weigh, how much exercise we do, or what we look like. This involves exploring ways that we can develop trust and send love to each body part, as well as how to carry out physical activity in a pleasurable rather than rigid or obsessive way. Throughout the whole of Part 4, our goal will be to nourish and not punish both our mind and body. As with Parts 1 and 2 and 3 of this book, Part 4 will offer you step by step guidance on the many topics we cover, so that you can successfully integrate what you have learned and want to attain into your own life – again in a flexible way that best suits you.

We will complete this book in Part 5 by reflecting on how to integrate the 10 key elements of Nourishing Routes and compassionate living into our everyday lives – while breaking free from the toxic relationships in your life that prevent this from becoming a reality. Finally, there will be a vital opportunity for you to take a life changing pledge to become a Compassioneer. This pledge states all the simple commitments you can make to yourself in terms of what you would like your life to look like by deciding to embark on a life-long loving journey to joining a growing tribe of Compassioneers.

Ultimately, by writing and encouraging you to read this book, I would like to help you believe, 100%, that your ability to experience happiness and health while reaching your full potential can become a completely possible reality. All it involves is being open to the intriguing idea of becoming a Compassioneer, while developing loving, nourishing and freeing relationships with our mind, food, body and the planet. If you think you are ready, then let's get going by firstly questioning whether there really is more to happiness and wellbeing than food, body weight and exercise.

"Your body is an abundant vessel to fill with compassion, which you can use to fuel your own mission and purpose to help and empower yourself, others and the planet"

PART 1:

A Compassionate Road to Authentic Happiness and Health

More to Happiness and Wellbeing than Food, Weight and Exercise

As we begin our journey to living more compassionately, you may already be starting to understand that there is perhaps much, much more to our wellbeing than just what we eat, weigh and how much we exercise. Yet the fact remains that we live in a culture where there is an assumption that the weight, shape and fat percentage of our bodies, how much we exercise as well as the nutrients and Calories we consume are key indicators of health. Not only that, but we live in a time where we are morally judged on being able to successfully, or unsuccessfully, embark on a journey of self-improvement, This journey usually involves moulding ourselves into something that is expected or idolised according to society's or someone else's standards. In other words, we live in a world of 'healthism', where our bodies and food intake have been subjected to the following:

❊ Increased surveillance by the media, medical professionals, workplaces and even family and friends. These communities now often have rights to assess our physical measurements, food intake and nutrient profile too

❊ Pressure from profit making companies to ensure that we buy into the latest weight loss, fitness or healthy eating products

❊ Advances in profit making technologies that have been designed to help monitor and control what we eat, weigh and look like

❊ Undermining messages from magazines, TV shows, social media and public health campaigns that make it acceptable and morally obligatory to eat less food, lose weight and exercise more in order to be perceived as a worthy citizen who takes care to reduce costs in health care for the rest of the community

❊

For a long time, individuals who have gone against the 'healthism' culture have been shunned, negatively judged, stigmatised and outcasted – not exactly helpful in terms of promoting happiness and health. However, even though we still live in a world where 'healthism' strongly prevails, times are rapidly changing...

It is no longer appropriate to view food, weight and exercise as the main pathways to health – which is ultimately being able to live a life where you are able to experience optimal physical, psychological and social wellbeing. In addition, the famous saying that 'nothing tastes as good as skinny feels' is increasingly leaving a bitter aftertaste in people's mouths. It definitely does in mine!

When we come into contact with messages about 'improving' what we eat, weigh and how we exercise, there is an assumption that simply coming into contact with these messages will make us instantly spring into action in terms of 'achieving' weight loss, eating a 'cleaner' whole food diet, or improving our physical fitness in order to obtain a 'perfect' physique. In reality, behaviour change is a much more complex process than this, and messages that do have such a focus often have the very opposite impact to their intentions. Many such messages also make us feel unworthy of love and lacking in confidence or the right quality of motivation to take suitable action that really will lead to positive changes in terms of our happiness and health.

I don't disagree with the common saying that 'health is your wealth'. After all, wealthier individuals, in terms of finances and personal resources, do tend to be in better conditions of physical and mental health with a longer life expectancy. However, what I do disagree with about the 'health is your wealth' mantra is that, more often than not, it is associated with changing our food intake and exercise at a substantial cost (expensive superfoods and running away on a treadmill without enjoyment spring to mind) or some form of negative experience. There are so many magazines that portray individuals eating fruits and vegetables, promoting rigid diet plans and detoxing, or exercising with a big smile on their face, usually along with a slim waist and a before and after picture with one looking notably sadder than the other.

As we will soon discuss in more detail, food, weight and exercise are not the only or main pathways to wellbeing. Even commonly used indicators of health, such as an individual's body weight, body mass index (BMI) or waist circumference are now being viewed much more critically in terms of how accurate and reliable they are at gauging our current or future state of health and, just as importantly, our happiness, and overall life satisfaction.

At one end of the health spectrum, we are bombarded by messages through various forms of media, suggesting to us that we are not a 'good enough' or worthwhile person just as we are. The answer they give us to our apparent inadequacies involves being pushed to get off our 'lazy bottoms' and undertake some (usually expensive) form of self-improvement. This might be related to changing our diet and exercise routine, or perhaps even buying into a certain type of beauty product, superfood, weight loss aid, medication or even surgery.

Although many of us would like to think that the routes to wellbeing were as simple as eating 'clean', exercising more, or buying the most scientifically advanced beauty product, I can tell you right now that there is so much more to health and happiness than this. It may have taken me too many years of my own life to realise this, but it is a realisation that I have used to propel my passion for Nourishing Routes and helping others to realise it too.

So what is the problem, if any, with focussing on diet and exercise as key route to health? Surely this can't be a wrong idea as a large majority of the population – especially those who are already health conscious – place a great weight on how much and what they eat, as well how they carry out physical activity?

Part of the answer lies in how this simplified focus can lead us away from being self-compassionate and taking time to share with others and express our natural creativity. Instead, such a focus frequently leads towards a life filled with obsessions around food, exercise and appearance as a way of externally seeking self-worth. Sometimes this can happen in a disordered way, while allowing less attention to be placed on other huge, and I do mean huge, determinants of wellbeing.

Some of these mighty determinants include:

❉ Feeling socially connected and part of a community

❉ Experiencing deprivation or inequality

❉ Encountering discrimination

❉ Feeling stressed

❉ Having a sense of meaning and purpose

❉ Having opportunities to be creative

❉ Spending moments being in the present moment and accepting what 'is' without negative judgement

❉ Feeling connected with nature and being grateful for what we already have

❉ How much kindness we show ourselves and other beings

You could also add in how an individual's wellbeing is largely influenced by a mix of their genetic makeup and environmental circumstances that are beyond their personal control.

The fact of the matter is that the elements that make up health are widely diverse, and although they do partly involve exercise and nutrition, this is by no means the whole story. Nevertheless, this doesn't stop how flicking open near enough any health-orientated magazine, book, journal or news article usually involves becoming intrusively faced with written, spoken or visual messages that incessantly sing about the benefits of eating certain types of foods, purchasing the next new 'superfood' or carrying out a specific form of exercise. Many messages that we read, even within the same day or media source, can even often conflict with one another, leaving us feeling more and more confused so that eventually we become a bit like a rabbit stuck in

❉

the headlights, not knowing what messages to believe, trust or take action on.

I am not discrediting that food and fitness are important, especially as both have contributed to my own recovery and wellbeing. But – and a big but – I do believe that our focus is very much unbalanced when it comes to food and exercise. Take the diet and fitness industry as a prime example. Despite these companies heavily investing in marketing, manipulating customers and promoting services that apparently aid weight loss or build muscle mass, most individuals who actually invest in them end up experiencing no benefits at all. Some individuals even experience the very opposite of what they were promised, whether that involves weight gain, unhealthy weight loss or poorer health in the long run. Even well-known diet companies have openly said that individuals who follow their programmes can expect a 5% weight loss, even when most individuals who do invest in their services aim to lose much, much more. Is this something that should be supported by a society who really wants to promote happiness and wellbeing among all of its community?

A key message here is that the diet and fitness industry are out there to make a profit – not promote health. If their concepts didn't fail for individuals buying into them, then they wouldn't have a valid business model. Full stop. This might be a completely acceptable goal for companies involved in this model, but is it really acceptable for us to let our society get caught up in it to the point where our own sense of self-worth becomes based on what and how much we eat, weigh, exercise and look like?

Even companies that don't necessarily promote changes in weight or muscle still promote the idea that there is some form of 'perfect' eating out there that can magic away life's problems or any chances of future illness. For the individuals who buy into that idea, the concept of healthy or 'clean' eating can quickly become a way of gaining control. However, rather than improving wellness, a person is encouraged to venture along a pathway that very much spirals out of control, usually into the depths of disordered eating patterns where a person's daily routines and sense of self-worth become caught up in a web of restriction. This often comes at the expense of not being able to invest time and energy into many other important elements of health and happiness.

Instead of getting caught up in the latest vitamin or 'superfood' we should be consuming enough of, or pursuing the latest exercise trend that will apparently extend our lifespan, it crucial to view the much bigger picture of wellness by asking ourselves:

- Do most of the individuals I interact with accept me for who I am, and are they supportive of my beliefs or hold similar values to me?
- Do I carry out creative activities that are feel freeing, enjoyable and fun?
- Am I currently on a journey that will allow me to reach my full potential in both mind and body?
- Does part of my life involve having opportunities to help others or give back to the community?
- Do I have enough financial and social resources to feel as though my basic needs are being met?
- In my work and personal life, do I feel like I have a choice over the type of activities I engage in and how I do them (e.g. rather than feeling controlled by others)?
- Do I regularly venture into or get to see natural green spaces and places of natural beauty?
- Does my current lifestyle enable me to 'take a step back' and see the amazing things in my life that I already have?
- Am I able to genuinely be kind and loving towards myself without being critical and feeling 'not good enough' or having low self-worth?

❋ Do I view my health and wellbeing as being based on many more things other than what I eat, how much I weigh, or the amount and type of exercise I carry out?

❋ If you feel that you have never or very rarely asked yourself the above questions, then you are not alone. There are many individuals spending hours planning exactly what they are going to eat, counting Calories, exercising excessively and going to various extreme efforts to lose weight or 'eat clean' with only perfectionist standards to live up to.

Instead of viewing meal times as an opportunity to enjoy and spend time with the people we love, there are individuals who would rather stay at home to eat a lonely meal that meets their Calorie quota – even when it does not bring them any pleasure or opportunities for social interaction.

Ultimately, although there are many benefits from eating a nourishing diet and engaging in regular physical activity, individuals who base their lives around self-restricting activities with little room for self-exploration and life fulfilment are likely to be trekking down the wrong path. This unfortunately leads them to significantly lose out on developing and enjoying many other vital elements of health and wellbeing.

But what really does matter for our happiness and wellbeing?

As research in the field of psychology and nutrition are increasingly showing, it is possible that the benefits of being able to love ourselves, have positive connections with others and have both creative and meaningful activities in our life are worth so much more in the health equation than any vitality boosting vitamin or 'superfood'. This book also highlight findings, and places a large emphasis on the relationships we have with ourselves, what we eat and who we share the planet with – not just diet and exercise alone.

As yet though, the health and fitness industry don't seem to think this way or promote a more holistic perspective of wellness – at least not yet, anyway. If they did, there would be huge losses to be made in terms of financial profit. A potential consumer who is already content with loving who they are while finding other routes to wellbeing other than food and fitness aren't exactly an ideal target for selling the latest self-improvement product or program...

If we are to go about authentically promoting health and wellbeing, then I wholeheartedly believe in and recommend the idea of starting to take notice of the other vital elements that promote longevity, happiness and a good quality of life – especially when it involves leading a more compassionate lifestyle.

In practice this means helping individuals to reduce the proportion of importance they place on nutrition and exercise and redirecting our attention onto appreciating what we already have, loving ourselves as we are, engaging in creative and meaningful pursuits, making positive social connections and helping others and the planet to flourish and thrive.

There are vast amounts of research evidence that focussing on these elements of wellness has positive implications for the way we nourish our bodies and the way we move. In other words, nurturing the many holistic elements of our wellbeing can improve the mindset we have around optimally nourishing and energising ourselves.

For example, individuals who have a more socially connected life with a positive relationship with food and themselves, tend to describe feeling happier with their lives. Perhaps unsurprisingly, they also tend to be at a reduced risk of anxiety, depression and disorders related to eating, exercise and body image (e.g. anorexia nervosa, bulimia, binge eating, body dysmorphia, exercise addiction etc.). The reason for this partly lies viewing health in a flexible and balanced way rather than black or white terms.

Of course I am not saying to throw the idea of healthy living by utilising food and exercise out of the window. This really would be throwing the baby out with the bathwater, as there is much evidence to support their importance. Also, what we eat and the way we exercise feeds into the way we socialise and our ability to live compassionately (e.g. through ethical dietary choices), so there really is a complex maze to venture through when thinking about how the elements to happiness and health dynamically function across our lives.

With the unique direction of Nourishing Routes, though, I would like to highlight that food and exercise are only a couple of elements that contribute to the much bigger picture of wellness, which does not simply manifest in an input equals output model. Instead, I am strongly suggesting that we can come to feel OK, supportive and even enthusiastic about the idea of not trying to aim for a perfect diet, exercise, weight or personal image related goal. Alternatively, what we really need to do is place an equal if not greater amount of importance on the compassionate relationship we can develop with ourselves, others and the planet while considering many other elements of wellbeing. Ultimately, by allowing compassion to be at the heart of our lives, as we were all designed to do, then I truly believe that this is the key to finding our own inner compass that will direct us towards the real routes to health and happiness.

The 10 Key Elements of Nourishing Routes

With the philosophy of Nourishing Routes, it is my mission and passion to empower you to experience a greater sense of compassion, and also to reach your full potential.

As we have recently described, Nourishing Routes is based on 10 key elements that are the keys to happiness and wellbeing. Each of the 10 elements is, as I have also experienced myself, interconnected with the others, and together, they fuel our ability to become empowered and the amazing people we were born to be. What's even better is that none of the 10 elements involve food restriction, weight monitoring, or rigid exercise regimens!

Below is a brief outline and description of the 10 elements that make up our Nourishing Routes. These elements are all strongly evidence based, and although I won't be discussing all of them individually (as that might require me to write an additional 1000 pages with lots of references), they will all be interwoven between most sections of this book in a way where they can be understood in real life terms with personal examples and practical applications. A key theme running throughout the 10 key elements is about compassionate living, which is a topic we will delve into throughout the rest of this book.

1) Compassion for the Self and Others

The first steps towards reaching your full potential comes from being kind and loving to ourselves without negative judgement and self-comparison. Compassion is also the key foundation that each other element of Nourishing Routes is based on, as without compassion we become really limited in terms of our self-development.

By becoming more self-compassionate, we can accept ourselves as beautiful unique creatures who also have the capacity to be kind and compassionate to others – both in human and non-human form, as well as the environment.

This may involve taking time away from work and other people's expectations to nurture yourself, as well as eating and exercising in a way that fills you with joy.

Being self-compassionate can also help us to become more open to new ideas and ways of living.

Compassion for others can involve taking time to be supportive to friends, families or even strangers, while placing yourself in their shoes and trying to help alleviate their suffering. Compassion for others can also involve following a lifestyle where you aim to use or consume products that minimise the exploitation of other animals (e.g. eating less meat or other animal products) and the planet (e.g. connecting more with nature and developing more environmentally friendly behaviours).

As the most fundamental step in Nourishing Routes, self-compassion is the most important aspect of compassion to develop. There is no obligation to follow any particular lifestyle, but on my own journey and also from meeting many others on the way, I have found that being more self-compassionate naturally leads to the desire to be more compassionate to others and even the planet. All we need to do is be open to the positive possibilities that compassion can bring into our lives and the way we choose to live it.

2) Nourishment Not Numbers

Food is a core part of our identity, culture, memories and pleasurable experiences we encounter as human beings. What we eat is not simply a bundle of Calories, macronutrients or a method of weight control (despite the constant lies we are told…). Food is also definitely NOT about dieting, and viewing it in such a rigid way can even lead to more harm than health benefits. We simply aren't designed to diet, and I'm sure as you have possibly experienced yourself, a life of constant dieting is not exactly a lifestyle filled with joy, unlimited energy and feeling your best.

Food, or your body for that matter, is not something to be looked upon as a negative item that we need to rigidly regulate, either by pre-planning, calculating or logging every single item we consume.

By looking past the numbers, and instead valuing a more 'kindful', intuitive and even spontaneous philosophy of eating – without harshly judging ourselves for what consume – we can learn to view food as an integral part of our life, way of connecting with others and optimally nourishing ourselves in both body and mind.

By viewing food as nourishment for the mind and body, we can place a greater focus on the quality of our food (e.g. where it comes from and how it contributes to promoting a better world) while seeing food as a resource for becoming optimally energised to go out into the world and become more compassionate and life-loving individuals.

3) Health at Any Body Size

Health is not simply a number on a scale, a certain body mass index (BMI), or what we look like in relation to societal expectations. Unless our body weight or shape severely restricts our ability to move and engage in meaningful activities that we enjoy or allow us to reach our full potential, health can be obtained in a variety of beautiful sizes – from those that are bigger, smaller, and every intriguing dimension in between.

Our bodies are vessels that we use to enjoy and do good in the world, not simply objects used for negative self-comparisons and beating ourselves up for not being quite 'perfect' or 'good enough'.

In their own unique way, everyone is body beautiful right now – we just need to realise it and see past the constraint of what others say we should look like.

Arguably, we become less healthy by focussing so much of our time on being a certain size, even if we are so-called 'overweight'. Health encompasses our ability to be creative and find a sense of purpose and greater meaning in the world – all things that don't require us to be a specific weight or body size.

4) Creative Expression

Health not only depends on what we eat or how much physical activity we do. As human beings we have an innate urge to be creative, in whatever form that may be.

Investing in your creativity is not a waste of time, energy, or something to feel guilty about. Even colouring in a picture, knitting a scarf, writing a poem, playing an instrument, choosing an outfit to wear, engaging in gardening, and putting a piece of furniture together all qualify as amazingly creative and health promoting activities.

By engaging in creativity we can take the time to think outside the box, express and communicate our deeper feelings, learn to live life in the moment, realise our amazing abilities, and also feel proud of what we have made or achieved. Acts of creativity can also inspire others to be creative and become more in tune with themselves and their own ambitions.

5) Freedom and Autonomy

In a world full of expectations, pressure and social influences, it can sometimes be hard to act in ways that align with what our true values are. Going with the flow isn't necessarily a bad thing, but when our lives are dictated by the rules and expectations of others, this is not the best route to take when aiming to reach our full potential.

Valuing freedom and autonomy requires us to take time to sit back, be present and notice what we really value in life – what do we want to achieve, do we have a mission, and can we alter the way we go about learning, recovering, or achieving ambitions in a way that suits us best?

✳

The best of our actions truly come from within, so it is important to develop the strength of mind to override negative social influences and expectations, and instead become more in tune with your intuition – what you feel and know is right.

6) Gratitude

Being grateful involves gaining satisfaction from even the simplest of things – usually those that we take for granted. Gratitude is a key element to promoting long term happiness, as it enables us to feel fulfilled and satisfied with our lives.

We can often forget to be grateful for what we already have when we live in a culture that constantly reminds us of the things we haven't got, or how we are not quite good enough in comparison to other people.

Many of us also live in expectation of achieving the next best thing – a better grade, academic status, job, or body weight. Rarely are we provided with opportunities to accept ourselves and our lives for what they are. We are rarely reminded that many of us are faring really well already!

Being grateful can simply involve taking note of a beautiful day, the support of a close friend, or the unconditional love of a family member. It can also involve appreciating how we live in a culture where the majority of people have a roof over their heads and access to clean water and education.

To up our grateful game, we can also learn to live more minimalistically, by letting go of the materialistic items that no longer serve us, and instead taking time to treasure the possessions that really do bring us joy to look at, use and cherish. Whatever you are grateful for, making a short amount of time for it on a regular basis can be a fundamental predictor of how happy we feel and can become.

7) Mindfulness

We can never appreciate what we have if we never live in the present. Mindfulness is about consciously embracing the present moment, appreciating the here and now without negative judgement. It is also about connecting with all of our senses – sight, smell, taste, touch and sound.

By embracing our ability to become more mindful of the present moment, we can harness our psychological resources in ways that allow us to see anxiety for what it really is. We can also become more able to take control of our lives and overcome stress.

We can be mindful almost anywhere, whether that involves noticing the colours of some beautiful flowers on a walk, the aromatic flavours of a meal, the softness of your bed covers, how you are feeling emotionally, or the subtle sounds in your everyday environment – the list is amazingly endless.

Ultimately, being mindful allows us to be grateful of the present, connect with our inner emotions and values, feel free in our minds and appreciative of who we are right now – not who we think we 'should' be.

8) Making Connections and Sharing Stories

Life is not an individual matter where only our own goals, feelings and behaviours are important. Without quoting from a famous Disney film, we are all part of the circle of life, and are all quite beautifully interdependent with one another. Our connections with others are what make us human beings.

Without friendship, love, or even the simplicity of touch, our brains and capacity to socialise would be severely impaired. Feeling connected and sharing our experiences with others allows us to develop a sense of identity, meaning and purpose in the world.

Few of us laugh or go through our emotions without the presence of others, and even when we do, part of dealing with our emotions often involves seeking the reassurance and support of others – whether they be human or animals. Without connecting with other people or even animals, it would be impossible to live an enriched life, as well as share information in ways that would allow us to educate and protect our own and future generations.

9) Pleasurable Movement

Movement is vital for wellbeing. It keeps our muscles and bones strong, boosts our mental wellbeing, protects us from stress and chronic disease, and allows us to remain fit and healthy in order to carry out activities to the best of our abilities. However, movement does not need to come in the form of running on a treadmill or joining a gym. These are enjoyed by many people, but for others the thought of getting onto an exercise machine fills them with dread – yet they continue to harshly push themselves to do it anyway.

There are many individuals who pursue physical activity in a self-hating manner – pushing themselves to the limit, following a rigid fitness regimen, and punishing themselves if they don't reach a particular goal or burn a certain amount of Calories… This can be a very unhealthy side to physical activity, as such pressure can lead to physical injury, fragile self-esteem and even disordered behaviour around food and exercise.

Movement does not have to be any of these things, as one of the most health promoting benefits of movement is the feeling of enjoyment of freedom – exploring activities that feel fun and allow us to move in the ways that we want to. It is a magical thing when we pursue physical activity because we already love and want to nurture our bodies, rather than trying to make ourselves love a body that we currently dislike. We need to flip and overturn the idea that self-love only happens when we exercise the 'right' way or have a fitter and 'better' body.

Pleasurable movement can be undertaken in a way that is enjoyable because of where it takes place. For example, taking a walk in a beautiful green area rather than lifting extra heavy weights and pushing yourself over the limit in a dreary looking gym filled with individuals competing to exercise and look the best.

Pleasurable movement can also come in the form of an enjoyable brisk walk, relaxing yoga session, playing with a child or pet, and even cooking! Ultimately, physical activity, ideally involving pleasurable movement, is essentially an opportunity for creatively expressing our unique personalities and abilities – not just jumping on the next fitness fad or activity that is likely to make us feel more punished than physically and psychologically energised.

10) Empowerment

Empowerment is what connects the 10 elements of Nourishing Routes together, as we need to feel empowered enough to follow our own routes to wellness.

Empowerment can be in the form of anything and everything that allows us to experience freedom, reach our full potential and be the amazing people we were born to be.

Empowerment might involve critically questioning and challenging what we have been made to believe or think a certain way, so it allows us to search for the real truth and make informed decisions based on our own intuition and values.

Examples include the way we have been made to think that certain foods are 'good' or 'bad', that we should embark on the latest diet or ritualistically count Calories, as well as that being overweight will inevitably lead to poor health. If you believe in empowerment, then you ultimately believe in yourself and your own ability to challenge the status quo for the good of humankind.

Empowerment is what makes us enlightened, energised, and determined to go out into the world and be effective human beings – developing your connections, identity, way of living, creativity and ability to make the changes you want to happen.

Overall, each element is founded on the concept of living more compassion-ately, as they involve taking time to nurture ourselves from the inside out. They also interlink with one another, so developing each element naturally has a positive influence on another, and so the positive cycle continues to a point where we become empowered to reach our full potential in both mind and body.

For myself, taking time for myself to nurture each of these elements has been one of the most, if not the most, life changing things I have ever done. It has been the magic key to overcoming years of hating myself and recover-ing from an eating disorder, depression and severe anxiety. Perhaps you can experience a similar journey too, no matter what you are currently trying to overcome or achieve in your life.

Whoever or wherever you are, I 100% believe that these elements are the true nourishing assets to becoming empowered, living a meaningful life, and sustaining authentic happiness and wellbeing.

Compassioneer Activity: Identifying your Own Key Elements of Nourishing Routes to Pay Attention to

The 10 key elements are all worth paying attention to and developing in our lives, as ultimately they all interlink. However, you may have noticed that some elements resonate with you more than others. For example, you might feel that the element Nourishment and Not Numbers is a more key element for you to develop compared to Pleasurable Movement.

Before moving on any further on our journey through this book, a useful activity is to note down the key elements that most resonate with you. This simply involves making a note of which elements you have already developed in your life, as well as those you think need working on further or need to take a greater priority for the time being. By doing this, as you read this book, you can keep the elements you most need to develop further in mind, which can help you to understand the concepts we discuss in more specific relation to your own needs. It can also help to develop more specific plans about how to begin and move along your journey towards becoming a Compassioneer. For this activity, simply place a tick next to the relevant elements.

Elements that I already have developed well in my life:

❋ Compassion for the self and others

❋ Nourishment not numbers

❋ Health at every size

❋ Creative expression

❋ Mindfulness

- ❉ Gratitude

- ❉ Making positive connections

- ❉ Feeling freedom

- ❉ Pleasurable movement

- ❉ Empowerment

Elements that I think I need to focus on more/further develop:

- ❉ Compassion for the self and others

- ❉ Nourishment not numbers

- ❉ Health at every size

- ❉ Creative expression

- ❉ Mindfulness

- ❉ Gratitude

- ❉ Making positive connections

- ❉ Feeling freedom

- ❉ Pleasurable movement

- ❉ Empowerment

Before we can really understand how the 10 key elements of Nourishing Routes apply to many areas of our lives, it is important to understand the concept of compassion as this is what each of the 10 elements is underpinned by. To help you understand this in a bit more depth, I will define and outline what compassion really is, how it might have evolved as a human trait, and how we can begin to utilise it effectively within our own lives.

Compassion – The Foundations of Your Nourishing Routes

What does compassion really mean?

By definition compassion means 'to suffer together', and to experience compassion for another person involves being able to experience or deeply understand their suffering in addition to being motivated to help them and alleviate their suffering.

Although some individuals may view compassion as being the same as empathy (being able to experience or deeply understand how another person is feeling), altruism (helping others without conscious expectation of a beneficial return) or showing kindness, there are a few distinguishing features to bear in mind. Firstly, compassion not only involves feeling empathy, but it also involves an authentic desire to help others. More specifically, compassion involves a highly attuned sensitivity to suffering, whether that be in relation to ourselves or others, with a deep commitment to try to prevent or relieve it. Empathy on its own only involves gaining a deep understanding about how someone is feeling, but it does not necessarily involve taking action to alleviate suffering.

When engaging in an opportunity to reduce a person's suffering this does not necessarily come from a place of compassion, such as placing yourself into the position of someone else's shoes. There are many instances where acts of kindness occur, which may seem compassionate, but are actually carried out with an underlying motive to get something in return – or simply engage in a task that is in line with what is expected of them (e.g. when helping others is part of a healthcare professional's job role).

To simply be kind or empathic does not fit the bigger picture that compassion encompasses.

�֍

But now we have defined compassion in a bit more detail, let's talk a little more about self-compassion.

Self-compassion, as the name suggests, is an extension of compassion in a way that involves showing compassion to your own self. You can demonstrate self-compassion when you already love yourself, but it is especially powerful in instances where you feel inadequate, ashamed, guilty, upset, or when experiencing general emotional or physical suffering.

With self-compassion you treat yourself with respect and positive encouragement, just as you would do with a close friend, family member or a young child.

Whether you currently do or do not show compassion to yourself, it is key to remember that you were born with a compassionate mind, where you can learn to understand and accept the pain you experiencing, while having the motivation to take care of yourself in ways to alleviate it. It is perhaps even more important to note that the view we have of ourselves will be the mirror that reflects onto the world. In other words, by being self-compassionate, we can also treat others and the world in a similar way – the way we would wish to treat ourselves. Negatively judging or criticising others, or comparing ourselves to others, also becomes much less of an issue – perhaps even not existing at all. This is because such things become unnecessary once we realise that each and every one of us is worth loving just as we are.

Researchers such as Kristin Neff (a renowned researcher and one of the founders of the concept self-compassion) have proposed that self-compassion aligns with the following 3 core elements:

* **Self-kindness:** Being understanding towards ourselves when we suffer (physically or psychologically), fail, or feel inadequate, guilty or unworthy, while altering our thoughts and actions in a way that can alleviate suffering.

* **Common humanity:** Appreciating that all humans suffer and that we cannot be perfect or good at everything we do. Everyone shares their experiences with other human beings, and we are naturally vulnerable

and imperfect. We also have the capacity to share these experiences in order to help one another feel understood and eventually move forward with their lives.

❋ **Mindfulness:** To be present in the moment while accepting and being non-judgemental about our thoughts, emotions or life circumstances. Mindfulness involves being able to observe and accept our thoughts and feelings as they are, regardless of whether they are more positive or negative. Being mindful allows us to let our thoughts and feelings come and go, without trying to suppress, deny them or obsess over them.

Some misconceptions around compassion stem from how it is seen as being at odds with the individualistic culture and achievement mind-set of most western cultures – one that has limited time or resources to help others in need if it might place our own resources or goals at risk. Put more simply, in a highly competitive society, many of us are trying to get noticed and be the best, regardless of whether that comes at a cost of pushing ourselves to the limit, damaging or own health or even not noticing the needs of other beings around us. It seems as though our fast paced culture has left little room for being compassionate beings when most of us are taught to pursue an impossible goal – that we all have to be number one.

Similar to the misconceptions with compassion, with self-compassion there is a common misunderstanding that showing this is a symbol of weakness or a form of self-indulgence that might actually veer us further away from our goals rather than closer to them. There is also a misinformed belief that self-compassion is the same as being egocentric and neurotic, where we view ourselves as being superior to others. However, this is because most people don't fully recognise the huge importance of appreciating and taking steps to appreciate and solve our own human vulnerability and suffering.

99.99% of the time, if someone loves themselves, this comes from a place of wanting to become a person who is able to live in line with their values, reach their full potential and also care for others. In stark contrast, individuals with an egocentric mindset are more likely to sing their own praise due to having an insecure self-esteem – which they mask by engaging in behaviours that they think will make others like them more.

❋

Being self-compassionate is not egocentric

Being egocentric is the opposite of self-compassion and, unlike the common myth, will not lead to being overly laid back, indulgent or lazy. In fact, self-compassion can be a tough task in itself, but can positively spring us into action to reach our goals rather than laziness.

In many ways we can view self-compassion as being a form of fuel for the mind and body, which involves accepting who we are, right now, while not aimlessly trying to live up to societal standards or even our own expectations to be perfect or the best. Instead, by becoming more self-compassionate, this can breathe life into our everyday actions in a way that allows us to follow our passions, live in line with what we truly believe and become more motivated to take action in ways that can help ourselves as well as others.

Unlike self-indulgence, self-compassion allows us to nurture our mind and body in the most optimal way. So, rather than self-compassion being an excuse for you to indulge in excessive quantities of food or alcohol for example (yet another silly myth), self-compassion offers a supportive hand that enables you to look after your own wellbeing, allowing you to feel nourished and able to flourish without any form of self-punishment.

Self-compassion shows our inner critic the fire exit

When being self-compassionate you treat yourself as you would do a close friend, young child or family member. This means that we can become more stubborn to the harsh inner critic (what I call my mean girl) that many of us have lurking inside our minds telling us that we just aren't good enough. By being self-compassionate we can show our inner critic where the fire exit is, because we no longer view their opinion as worthy of our time and energy. In a way, becoming more self-compassionate is similar to breaking away from an abusive relationship while embracing a much more trusting and loving one that allows you to flourish – rather than hide away in a corner.

No matter how tied down to that abusive inner critic we may have learned to put up with over the years, we CAN still break away and learn to be compassionate beings. At the end of the day, this is the way that will allow us to do what we do best in the world while promoting multiple physical, psychological and social benefits for ourselves and others too.

The evidence-based benefits of being self-compassionate

Regardless of my own view that self-compassion is not a sign of weakness or self-indulgence, there are many other researchers who have repeatedly demonstrated how strengthening our ability to show compassion towards ourselves can positively impact several physiological and emotional systems that are essential for our happiness and health. In practical terms this research has shown that becoming self-compassionate impacts the biological functioning of nervous systems, including the neuronal networks of our brains and how they respond to our internal and external environments. Self-compassion has also been shown to promote many prosocial behaviours that not only benefit the self, but others too.

Individuals who have more compassion for themselves, as well as others, tend to be more optimistic, grateful and mindful of the present moment – ingredients which are key to happiness and health. Self-compassionate individuals also tend to be more willing to forgive others rather than holding grudges, which on their own can lead to significant stress and poorer health. There is also a significant link between self- compassion and being at a lower risk of anxiety, depression, stress and physical health complaints.

These examples can help to explain part of the reason why self-compassion enables individuals to be more resilient in the face of adversity, including physical or mental illness, as well as being resilient to stress and associated outcomes.

Another important aspect of being self-compassionate is the way it enables individuals to be in a better position to be compassionate to others, helping to affirm the idea that love really does grow from the inside out.

Although people with limited self-compassion often do have compassion for others, individuals with greater self-compassion tend to be more authentic in the way that they are able to relate to others and help alleviate their suffering. Research has shown, for example, that individuals with greater self-compassion are more likely to be altruistic, such as looking after other colleagues at work, volunteering, and being less likely to take their own stress or anger out on others.

In the workplace, self-compassionate employees are shown as being less likely to experience burnout, while self-compassionate workforces, overall, tend to have better functioning and more engaged teams with lower rates of sickness absence and presentism. Since these factors can have substantial health and financial implications, there is growing evidence to demonstrate that developing self-compassion, especially within organisations like the workplace and academia, is significantly cost-effective.

In the context of this book, we will be looking at how we can apply self-compassion to how we holistically relate to mind, food and body, where we can love ourselves just as we are and enjoy pleasures in life without unnecessary feelings of guilt, shame or unworthiness.

In a brief summary, self-compassion can take many diverse forms, and can be applied to several life domains, including work, study, relationships, eating and exercise, body image and the general way you set out what you would like to achieve and how.

At this point a key question you might have be asking is how can you benefit from becoming more self-compassionate?

Perhaps you can make up your own mind if you consider one or more of the following to be true for you:

❋ You beat yourself up over making mistakes and ruminate about them in a way that makes you feel bad

❋ You often fear failure or not living up to certain standards

❋ Rarely is something you do 'good enough'

❋

❋ You tend to think of things in black and white, where something is either viewed as good or bad with no grey areas in between

❋ You find it hard to take time to relax, take a break or look after yourself (either physically, psychologically or socially), often due to thinking that time spent away from other priority tasks or looking after others is lazy or unproductive

❋ You have an inner voice that frequently tells you to push yourself more, try harder, work longer or that nothing you do is ever good enough

❋ Experiencing pleasure (e.g. eating nice foods, taking a bath, having a break from work) is often followed by feelings of guilt or shame – you don't feel as though you are worthy enough or have worked hard enough to gain the right to experience pleasure or positive things in your life

❋ You seem to always be looking out for the next new diet or fitness regimen as a way to feel better about yourself

❋ You tend to focus more on the things you have done wrong or could do better rather than the positive things you already have or can achieve

❋ You frequently deflect or avoid compliments about you and feel uncomfortable about receiving them, regardless of whether you give them to others

Thoughts about failing (e.g. at work or school) fill you with an enduring sense of dread – you feel you wouldn't be able to cope with not achieving what you had set out to achieve

Regardless of how many questions you have said yes or no to, I can guarantee that most individuals reading this book have noticed that their lives would become much more enriched if they were able to be a bit – or a lot – more self-compassionate. But if you are still feeling unsure, let's look a bit more into the evolutionary roots of why it is essential that human beings are able to show and experience compassion.

❋

Evolutionary Roots of Compassion

Self-compassion might help us lead a happier and healthier life, but is it really essential? Or, perhaps as a more appropriate question, is compassion an evolved trait that has helped our human species to survive and thrive on our planet?

If we look to some of the views of one of the most famous evolution theorists, Charles Darwin, he argued that one of our strongest instincts is one of caring and ensuring that our children or siblings have their safety maintained. Also, communities that included the greatest number of the most caring and supportive members would flourish best, as they would be better able to trust one another, work together, provide support and ultimately protect the group from danger. This allowed such groups to acquire the greatest number of resources in order to survive.

As with many other human traits, compassion has its roots set deep into our evolutionary history, so it must surely have some benefits if it has allowed us to survive, as Darwin suggested, by passing our genes onto the next generation.

It is also interesting to bear in mind that compassion can be shown to and by both humans and animals, and that it can function as a way of encouraging a sense of social connectedness between members of a group.

There is a large body of evidence to support that connecting with other beings, both human and animals – in a positive way can promote wellbeing via psychological as well as physiological mechanisms. For example, research findings strongly suggest that interventions to improve our compassion can lead to reduced depression, anxiety and feelings of isolation, as well as increases in positive emotions, optimism, hopefulness, and experiencing a greater quality of life.

At a more biological level compassion, including self-compassion, is also shown to reduce stress, cellular inflammation and blood pressure while even having a positive impact on the functioning of our immune system. This is thought to be because when we are kind to others and ourselves, there is a 'hard wiring' within each us that sparks into action. Such hard wiring involves alleviating suffering, which engages our nervous systems in ways that create a sense of calmness and a desire to connect and cooperate with others. By showing self-compassion, or compassion to others, we ultimately enter into a state where our whole physiology is working at its best – allowing us not only to survive but also to thrive.

From an evolutionary perspective, when we show compassion we are demonstrating our innate motive to make positive connections with others, work as a team and pass on our genes. Originally, for humans this meant using compassion as a tool to be aware of and take care of vulnerable children who, unlike many other non-human species, are very reliant on being fed and supported by a carer for a lengthy period of time.

It is unlikely that we would have survived for very long if we left our children to fend for themselves alone – our (un-compassionate) genes would have stopped right there.

However, as humans began to live in groups, mainly to share caregiving practices and other resources, compassion took on another role. As we mentioned before, this role involved being able to obtain support from others and gain more resources to aid our survival.

When we are compassionate towards others, even those who are not genetically related to us, we communicate that we genuinely care and want to nurture them towards a positive state of wellbeing. What we often get in return is a similar level of support and attention, which creates a positive cycle that enables species to overcome challenges, get through the tough times and, ultimately, survive.

Broadly speaking, by assisting and being compassionate to others, even those who are not genetically related, we (often subconsciously) communicate that we are 'good' people who also 'deserve' to be helped when in need. What this means is that being compassionate allows others to be more willing to reciprocate and help us when our own resources, wellbeing and lives are at stake.

With compassion breeding even more compassion, we are in effect building up our own support resources so that we too have a greater chance for optimal wellness and survival when the going gets tough. This is partly the reason why humans evolved to live in social groups. Being compassionate promotes acts of social support to other members of our group, who might not have otherwise survived if faced with a crisis on their own.

With the survival benefits of showing compassion, it makes sense that being compassionate needs to be experienced as a positive thing so that such behaviours can be reinforced – i.e. carried out again when necessary. In relation to this idea, research has shown how acts of compassion are positively associated with an increased production of feel-good hormones (such as dopamine in the brain) and social bonding hormones (such as oxytocin) that allow us to experience a range of positive emotions and a sense of psychological wellbeing from assisting others. In theory we are hard wired to be able to take on board the perspective of other humans and animals (empathy) and respond to their suffering (compassion). This is also why many of us experience psychological discomfort to see other humans and animals in pain or distress.

There may be a view that showing compassion can be a drain on our own time and resources, but the reality is usually the very opposite. For example, much research

has shown that an act of compassion, such as volunteering or providing a gift to someone, evokes more positive feelings when compared to receiving help or being given a gift from others. In this way, there is often more to gain from being compassionate compared to when we expect to receive it from others.

But what about being compassionate to yourself and why would this be beneficial?

The act of being compassionate to yourself is not about being able to view ourselves as better than others or being self-indulgent – this only leads to fragile self-esteem and pursuing materialistic goals that have no real long-term impact on our wellbeing and sense of meaning in life.

Instead, self-compassion has evolutionary benefits by encouraging us into action. The act of being kind and loving towards yourself is often much more motivating than giving yourself a good telling off and being your own worst critic. You would unlikely act this way to a young child in order to encourage their success or even acknowledge an unsuccessful attempt. Yet, it is often acceptable for us to be un-compassionate to ourselves. By growing a greater sense of self-compassion, though, we are likely to become more motivated to pursue the goals that are in line with our true values and ambitions, rather than those that originate from meeting the expectations of others.

Although westernised societies seem to view being self-compassionate as something negative or unproductively self-indulgent, we are still by nature self-compassionate creatures.

It is just unfortunate that many of us live in a society where it has become the norm to place individualistic goals of being the best or perfect at something on the top of our priority list. Not only does this lead to feeling comparatively unsuccessful and weaker than other individuals in most circumstances, but draws us away from feeling part of a wider supportive community with a need to show compassion to others.

For example, we might become more concerned with getting the best grade at college or university, or trying to climb the ladder in a particular career. Similarly, we might try to spend excessive amounts of time reading health and fitness magazines and tiresomely working out at the gym to lose or gain weight in order to mould the 'ideal' physique. Although there is nothing wrong with such goals, they generally draw us away from our community values while also setting us up to feel ineffective in comparison to the rest of the world. Not exactly a formula for self-compassion.

There is also a general tendency to disregard compliments and put ourselves down when we don't achieve something or live up to our own or others' expectations of us. Such a lack of self-compassion can lead us to feeling disconnected from others, unworthy of support and generally lacking in motivation to pursue our goals. Even our hardest efforts might not seem good enough for any form of affection or compliment.

Overall, our ability to show compassion to ourselves and others is deeply rooted in evolutionary history through its use in helping to aid our own and others' survival. In modern times, self-compassion produces optimal circumstances to effectively realise our dreams, stay in touch with our inner values and set goals that resonate with these and enable us to reach our full potential. With this in mind, it is fundamental that our society begins to value both compassion to others and ourselves, so that, rather than viewing compassion or self-compassion as a sign of weakness or a waste of time, we can cultivate them as significant strengths that are viewed as beneficial investments for the human race, other animals and even the whole planet.

Compassionate Beings in a Non-Compassionate World

We are all born as genetically diverse individuals. Yet, as we have just outlined, there is one fundamental human trait that most of us share. This is not a physical characteristic that we can visibly identify or compare on a quantitative scale, but a fluid way of thinking and feeling that sets us apart from many other creatures. The shared trait I am talking about is compassion, of course – including the kindness and love we direct to others and ourselves.

We are born with the capacity to love, share, develop friendships, show empathy, live in harmony with nature, and provide kindness and affection to others. Even if compassion is not yet valued by the whole human race, we cannot dismiss the positive outcomes that everyone can benefit from when it comes to expressing compassion – whether that be to ourselves or others.

Although I have just discussed compassion in more detail, I would like to go a bit deeper here by questioning whether the society we currently live in promotes our ability to express it in different areas of our lives.

Are we provided with opportunities to think fondly of ourselves without negative self-comparison with others?

Are we fully supported to help others, and are we trained by society in ways that enable us to put priorities of sustaining important relationships above striving for some materialistic object, unrealistic standard or way of gaining approval from others? Current circumstances suggest not, at least in most western cultures...

As I also similarly described in the previous chapter, from a very young age we are taught to strive for becoming the best, or at least very good, at something in comparison to our peers. We develop motives to get good grades, get a good job, earn a high wage, live a wealthy life made up of expensive or prized possessions.

We are also taught to value our sense of self-worth on the appearance of our skin and the contours of our body, as well as how healthy and wealthy we are in terms of exactly what we eat and exercise. If we are not in line with societal standards, or have too many lines for that matter, then we are simply not good enough to compete in a materialistic world that values materialistic wealth and beauty in its physical form. Yet, in an ideal compassionate world, this is a very limited perspective on the beauty that lies around us in so many different forms.

Not many of us grow up to fully experience and value the nature around us. We might sit in our office away from the natural environment during lunch time, or even exploit, knowingly or not, the other animals of the earth with which we co-inhabit it.

We might view ourselves as superior to other life forms, just because we happen to have the weapons and machinery to kill, cook and eat them, even when this is not necessary. Or, we could even be overly concerned with how many Calories we have eaten over the last 24 hours rather than directing our attention on how many positive experiences and opportunities preparing and eating food brings us.

Of course such actions don't draw away from feeling happy per se, but they do draw away from experiencing the most authentic and long-lasting of happiness. This form of happiness allows us to feel fulfilled in ways that are not simply based on what we look like, how powerful we seem, or what items we possess. However, leading a life without compassion at the centre inevitably leads to spending overly large amounts of time focussing on work, looking better, eating better, and spending more on materialistic resources – while ultimately losing sight of the real key elements that can lead to true happiness *and* health.

We might neglect time with friends and family, or even talk negatively towards ourselves if we don't feel like we are meeting societal expectations.

✳

We can get lost in an endless cycle of competition and self-comparison, until we begin to feel the effects of chronic stress, anxiety, depression and other severe forms of mental or even physical illness.

Some people do benefit from these experiences, but these individuals are usually those employed in businesses that thrive on making individuals feel inferior and not good enough – unless they buy into 'x' product or 'x' way of living. If lots of profit is involved, then the likelihood is, compassion will take a second best and be left behind in the race to attain self-worth and a sense of superiority based on materialistic goals and trying to meet the expectations of others.

I personally feel that this is quite sad, since I do strongly believe that most of us possess the amazing abilities and skills to live more compassionately and in harmony with ourselves, others and the world around us. There is no longer a legitimate need, if there ever really was one, to get caught up in a world of worrying about what we have not yet got or what we 'need' in order to fit in with societal standards.

If only someone could get us to believe that we really are good enough just as we are right now and that the real key to happiness and health lies within our hearts and in front of our very noses. But would we even listen? Would we take action to become the compassionate beings we were born to be?

My aim here is not to answer these questions for you, but I do want to help you realise that you have a choice in the matter of whether you live compassionately or not. You have the power to get back in tune with your own innate compassion, regardless of what society we live in. What is even more exciting is that choosing to go on a journey towards living more compassionately is not something that feels draining or stressful, but something amazingly energising that draws a wealth of vitality, love, self-worth, happiness and fulfilment into our everyday lives.

Without much effort, many individuals find that one form of compassion in their lives leads to another. For example, they might start with taking time to help others or making more ethical lifestyle choices that minimise the exploitation of animals, but then realise that they themselves are equally worthy of being shown compassion. Their self-worth is no longer based on striving for the next best grade, diet, job, salary or status, and they gradually learn to value more important things in life such as the quality of their relationships, their ability to nourish their bodies in enjoyable and flexible ways, while also taking time to become more connected to green space and nature.

There is no real cost to show compassion to others or ourselves. The cost only comes when we choose to be deceived into believing that humans can successfully live without it. My real hope is that you choose the more empowering option, by realising that you have compassion imprinted in your genetic makeup, ancestral history and your current abilities. It only takes a compassionate genius like yourself to unlock the code.

Changing Times for a More Compassionate World

Not all of us may have realised it yet, but the world is rapidly changing. Not just on a physical level, but also on a psychological level.

Many of us have grown up in a culture consumed by a need to base our health on seeking the best new pill, diet, fitness regimen, or even a cosmetic product. As for now, however, our culture is becoming ever more critical of what society sets out as being an ideal way to live and the true meaning of happiness and health.

Many of us no longer want to be caught in the turmoil of basing our self-worth and capacity for reaching our full potential on a Calorie count number, specific body weight, nutrient intake, or an ideal physical appearance. More and more of us each and every day are realising that happiness, health and our contribution to the planet as a whole goes much, much deeper than this. It's almost as if we have been engaged in a really long telephone call for most of our lives, but now realise that the topic of conversation and people we need to be engaging with are on another line – we are in the transitory process of finding a new wave length to tune into.

Perhaps not all of us are ready to hang up our phones and realise the true meaning of compassionate living, but things certainly seem to be changing in a forward facing direction.

Many individuals are now realising that their health is based on what they are able to 'do' and give to others and themselves, rather than how they can be manipulated or moulded into a certain shape or eat in a perfect way. They are also realising that one part of authentically growing as a person, and finding our true meaning and purpose, means slowing down and being mindful of the present moment. This means that a life lived in the fast lane and constantly pursuing a future version of the self is becoming less and less desirable.

As we are all creatures of an intricately connected community, no matter how far we live away from other human beings on the planet, there is becoming a gradual breakdown of the usual tendency to view ourselves as being an independent walker on a journey along our own path. Our paths are all connected and, as you may have guessed, one of the connective elements that string these paths together involves compassion.

There is no doubt that our world is entering a positive transition towards a more holistic model of wellness, where community, mindfulness, gratitude, social connectedness, kindness and compassion thrive at the centre.

I truly believe that we are all brought to this planet to live compassionately so that we can continue to create, rather than destroy, a more united world for the next generation to live and thrive in. We are not placed here to destroy our world, or live in a way that allows us to feel superior over other human and non-human beings.

Unfortunately, this shift in the way we think and behave doesn't mean that the world will instantly change overnight. We are far from that being a reality, but rest assured we are on an enlightening journey that is occurring at a quickening pace. For those of us who are ready to embrace this journey, it is one of excitement and ongoing learning.

From my own personal experience, stepping into this journey has meant becoming aware that my own focus on nutrition and health was once very far apart from the real deeper meaning of wellbeing.

Finding my own self-compassion and developing it in a way where I could also show compassion for others through my actions, including what I eat and how I view my body, work and relationships, has been revelational.

What might you encounter on this compassionate journey?

The first steps for you on this journey might be small, and they can include learning to be critical of your own negative thoughts towards yourself.

They can also be choosing relaxation over vigorous exercise, and even choosing to eat differently to how you might normally do just because you want to give yourself some freedom from an otherwise rigid dietary regimen.

In terms of being compassionate towards others, you might start with a simple kind act each day, or gradually cutting down on the number of products you use that involve the exploitation of animals.

Trying to dive in at the deep end and try all these activities at once might be too much, but becoming more confident with one, and then another, soon enough you can become more confident and aware of other compassionate steps you can make.

As I am also currently becoming aware of, the journey towards a compassionate lifestyle is not one with an end point. I think as human beings we will always be learning through trial, error and success, but I think of this process as an exciting adventure rather than a burdensome chore.

For many people I have met along my own journey, becoming more compassionate has led them to see the world and themselves in a completely new light. For example, their renewed perspective about life and themselves has led to taking up new hobbies, finding things that they are truly passionate about, feeling more connected with others and nature and discovering a greater overall meaning within their own lives.

As you can probably grasp, unlike any specific diet, fitness regimen, or medical pill, it is clear that showing and receiving compassion is revitalising for the body, mind and even the planet. Compassion also brings joy and self-acceptance, as opposed to self-comparison and hate when alternatively pursuing a path where we base our self-worth on how we fare in relation to the expectations of others and society.

To summarise some of the key points within this chapter, I truly believe that our world is making a transition in a new compassionate orientated direction. We may not have made the whole conversion yet, but the seeds of change are growing fast, and the roots are becoming ever deeper and ever stronger.

Each of us has the passion and power inside to help to world move even further in the right direction, no matter how small their actions might be. If it isn't us who are going to make the changes the world so needs to see and experience, who will? It's up to us now to create the world we want to live in. If not us, then who? If not now, then when?

In the grand scheme of our lives, each of us is creating ripples of influential movement. With each small step, in time, each of these ripples will become waves of powerful change. This is something so amazing and extraordinary, and it makes me feel that each and every one of us has the opportunity to make a transformative difference, not only to our own lives, but the lives of others and the whole planet both within and beyond our own life times. Now is the time when we can begin to really grow our tribe of Compassioneers.

"Imagine the most empowered and best version of yourself, while letting go of any part of you that doesn't believe in that vision"

Becoming A Compassioneer

A Compassioneer is a whole new concept of being and thriving that does not involve temporarily following yet another rigid diet, reaching a certain Calorie quota or carrying out a strict fitness regimen. It is by no means another faddy lifestyle, and it also doesn't involve obsessively counting Calories, unnecessarily trying to be perfect or buying into expensive products, superfoods or cosmetic services. Being a Compassioneer also isn't simplistically based on one element of wellbeing.

Instead, being a Compassioneer *brings multiple holistic elements of physical and psychological wellbeing together*, in a way that suits many different people's needs and life circumstances. It also deeply values the multiple connections that link the mind and body, while ensuring that we live a life that feels enjoyable, fulfilling, socially connected and meaningful.

Becoming a Compassioneer is a *lifelong tool* of wisdom that allows us to become more in tune with what our bodies and minds really need in order to feel nourished, fully flourish and thoroughly thrive. Being a Compassioneer is a way of getting back in touch with our own inner compassion, where we can develop a powerful voice that stands up against how we have been told (mostly by organisations motivated to make a financial profit through exploiting others) how we 'should' and 'should not' live our lives.

At its core, becoming a Compassioneer involves learning to love ourselves as we are now, as well as others and the planet, while regularly taking part in self-care by nourishing our bodies AND minds in a variety of exciting, creative and enjoyable ways.

The word Compassioneer, alike to compassion, also contains the word Compass. This might just be a coincidence, but the Nourishing Routes philosophy happens also to be about learning to trust and get back in touch with our own inner compass. I believe that our inner compass is the part of ourselves which intuitively knows how to master the art of self-love and compassionate living through pursuing goals that will lead us along a path towards authentic happiness and wellbeing.

Throughout this book, you will see that just about ANYONE can be a Compassioneer, and that there are oh so many ways to happiness and well-being – without dieting, counting Calories, or trying to mould your body into something 'perfect' or that appears to be in line with someone else's standards.

Becoming a Compassioneer is enabled by integrating the 10 key elements of Nourishing Routes.

Compassioneers ultimately seek to develop any one or a number of these 10 key elements, which I will soon describe in more detail in a way that is easy to understand and practically integrate within any lifestyle.

But has becoming a Compassioneer been scientifically evidenced to provide any real benefits?

Although the concept of a Compassioneer is new, the idea to create it and what it is based upon has been born out of a wealth of evidence-based research from the fields of positive psychology, health and nutrition. Another huge part, as I mentioned at the beginning of this book, is based on my own personal experiences of battling and overcoming mental illness as well as a negative relationship with food, mind and body for nearly a decade.

For myself, the benefits of becoming a Compassioneer couldn't be clearer.

My Nourishing Routes to becoming a Compassioneer

Just a few years ago, I was so caught up in leading a life of striving for per-fection, overworking to the point of obsession and exhaustion, punishing my body, and feeling guilty for experiencing any amount of pleasure. To me, health was exactly what type of foods and how many Calories I ate, how much exercise I had carried out, the grades I had achieved at college and university, and my level of progress on a career ladder.

In many ways, the relationship I had with food and myself played out in other areas of life, so nearly everything I did was carried out with the extreme aim for perfection. Unsurprisingly, from everything I tried to do, the end product always seemed to be not good enough. With a sense of failure, emptiness, shame and continued dissatisfaction, I would continue to place my interests in another ambition to see if perfecting that would help me feel better about myself. Unfortunately, no activity – other than eventually being willing to step into a whole new world of compassionate living – actually made a spot of difference where my self-worth and overall happiness and health were concerned.

These times seem so far removed from how I live now that it is hard to fully describe how they made me feel – other than depressed and housebound by physical weakness, stress, anxiety and a fear of failure. There was nothing I could do at that time to feel like I was worthy of anyone's affection, let alone my own. As long as I didn't allow compassion to flourish in my life, I remained in a pessimistic world where I was destined to remain in a vicious cycle for far too long.

Forwarding to the time of writing this book, where I have integrated the concepts of following my own Nourishing Routes to leading a more compassionate lifestyle by becoming a Compassioneer, my beliefs and ethos of living a healthy, happy and meaningful life couldn't be any more different. I no longer obsessively strive for perfectionism or gaining someone else's approval rather than my own. I genuinely appreciate myself, take time for self-care, and my relationship to food and my body has flourished into something really beautiful. I value how I think and feel much more than how I physically appear, what I weigh or what I have eaten.

Part of this revolutionary shift has involved coming into contact with many inspiring individuals who were able to share their own experiences and powerful stories of leading a more compassionate lifestyle. This mainly includes individuals and communities who had taken steps towards being kind and nurturing towards themselves, others and the planet. By hearing their stories and seeing the abundant benefits first hand, I gradually came to the understanding and truth that recovery from an eating disorder and finding real happiness and health was completely possible.

This strong belief soon became a life mission, and it wasn't long before I expressed the ideas and concepts I was thoroughly passionate about by creating my own website and blog – Nourishing Routes. I knew in my heart that our society was destined to find a more holistic route to achieving happiness and wellbeing, and that there are so many elements to uncover without basing our self-worth and health on nutrition, exercise and weight.

Through my own experiences of the 'ups' and 'downs', which are inevitable on any Compassioneer's journey, I learned to believe in the art of self-care. Gradually, I invested more and more time in myself by fuelling my body and mind in the way that nourished rather than deprived them. At the same time, I decided that it was about time I said a fond farewell to allowing myself to accept that feelings of shame, guilt and self-loathing were a normal part of eating. I also had many eye-opening opportunities to thoroughly study, research, work and volunteer within many different realms of health, psychology and nutrition. These experiences massively opened my eyes even further while allowing me to understand, at a deeper level, the many complex determinants of our happiness and wellbeing.

Instead of being driven by achieving the perfect diet, Calorie count, body shape, or career, my Compassioneer lifestyle is now centred on finding more nourishing ways to relax, cherish the present moment, enjoy food (including chocolate, biscuits and cake of course!), feel grateful for what I already have, spend time with friends and family, volunteer for organisations that are in line with my values, engage in creative activities, rekindle old hobbies, find new quirky cafes to drink tea and coffee in and be physically active in ways (usually just simply walking my dog or practising yoga in my own room) that are both pleasurable and energising. I now have a much deeper understanding and intuition that our wellbeing is much more dynamic than anything we can quantifiably measure in terms of nutrition, Calories, body weight or appearance.

There are not many words to fully describe how awesomely amazing the journey towards becoming a Compassioneer has been, but it has enabled me to finally find and follow my own nourishing routes towards living a meaningful life filled with compassion, happiness, health and the most revitalising energy you could ever experience. This feels miles apart from the life I once felt wasn't worth living, or even existing for.

As my perfectionistic standards and self-punishing lifestyle have gradually tumbled away over the last several years, Nourishing Routes has become such a positive and passionate part of me. It has been such a powerful driving force, and has been the fuel I needed to thoroughly research and develop my ideas in a way that has helped me to transform the concept of becoming a Compassioneer into a reality. It is how I live and breathe. But now it is the time to help empower others to embark on their own Compassioneer journeys if they are willing to accept the quest.

Becoming a Compassioneer is quite honestly one of the best and most fulfilling things I have ever done for my health and happiness, and I can't waste another minute keeping the secret to living this lifestyle to myself. I know that your own story won't be the same as mine, but that is part of the beauty of being a Compassioneer – the ways of living as a Compassioneer can be tailored or adapted to anyone's and everyone's unique circumstances and dreams of how they would like to live a life that enables them to flourish and thrive.

I now wholeheartedly believe that it is time for individuals and groups open to the idea of becoming a Compassioneer, perhaps individuals like yourself, to see and feel the benefits for themselves – in mind, body and soul. Now is the time to create your own Nourishing Routes.

Isn't being a Compassioneer just another faddy lifestyle or label for individuals to unnecessarily categorise themselves by?

This question might be a common one, and is one that I initially thought about when coming up with the term Compassioneer. However, hopefully you will soon understand why being a Compassioneer is in no way faddy.

Also, unlike many unnecessary labels that society places on individuals, a Compassioneer can be absolutely anyone – in any shape, form, age bracket, social status, culture or religion.

Being a Compassioneer is not a right or wrong way of being or doing things. Uniquely, being a Compassioneer is a personal choice that involves going on a positive journey towards becoming more compassionate. As being a Compassioneer does not require us to think in black or white terms of what it mean to live a 'good' life, pursuing this lifestyle does not involve being 'bad' or 'good', 'falling off the wagon', failing, being inadequate or feeling guilty for not being good enough when unable to live up to a certain standard. In fact, being a Compassioneer involves the very opposite, as its ethos simply involves living in accordance with our authentic values while taking relevant action without negative judgement of ourselves. All you need to do is make a commitment to try taking gradual steps, no matter how big or small, to lead a more compassionate lifestyle in whatever form that may be.

But what do we even mean by a compassionate lifestyle as a Compassioneer?

A compassionate lifestyle involves acting, wherever is appropriate and when is practically possible, in the art of being kind and loving towards others, but equally towards yourself and the planet. It is a practical way of living in line with our own values, rather than meeting external expectations that often involve harming ourselves, others or the planet.

Compassioneers are individuals on a journey towards becoming more compassionate beings, but they also understand that compassion lies at the heart of our whole humanity. Being a Compassioneer lies within our genetic code and has been ingrained within us since birth and even the whole history of our human species.

As you will soon hopefully uncover, to find meaningful ways of giving and receiving to yourself and others is one of the most effective and enjoyable ways for optimal and long-lasting happiness and wellbeing. It is the way we were born to Nourish, Flourish and Thrive.

✤

70

Compassioneers, unlike many individuals following faddy lifestyle regimens that set out their own unrealistic standards to reach, have a shared sense of common humanity. This simply means that our experiences as well as our so-called flaws and faults are viewed as an inevitable part of our human nature – we all experience similar events and feelings, and no one is perfect. In reality there is so much beauty, and even a sense of reassurance, in our own imperfections

Compassioneers are more concerned with being able to appreciate their actions and personal progress in relation to their own values and goals rather than trying to compete to be the best. Can we really aspire to or imagine a world where everyone tried to be the best? How practical or enjoyable is that?!

Although I have already spoken about the origins and importance of living more compassionately, I will restate that there is an extensive body of research evidence that shows how compassion for others and yourself is a very powerful tool to stimulate positive emotions, alleviate stress and anxiety, make positive social connections, and lead an extended life filled with authentic happiness and sustained physical and social wellbeing. The evidence is distinctively clear that compassionate living brings a wealth of benefits at a physiological, psychological and social level. We could choose to ignore this evidence, but would you really want to?

But signing up to a Compassioneer as a lifelong lifestyle choice might sound a bit of a commitment, right? Like I initially did myself, you may question whether being a Compassioneer means being in compassionate 'mode' 100% of the time without any slip ups.

To answer the first question, being a Compassioneer is a commitment, but it is a commitment that becomes so much a part of our everyday lives, often without conscious effort, that you will likely begin to wonder how you ever lived any differently.

To answer the last question, the short and simple answer is no. It is unlikely that we can ever feel compassionate all of the time. Sometimes we will feel 'not good enough' or like we need to attain the next best thing, beat someone else or live up to a certain standard in order to feel like a worthy person or better about ourselves. However, this is again part of being human, and Compassioneers respect that they too can't live a life completely filled to the brim with compassion. Striving for perfectionism with compassionate living, just like anything else, is an unrealistic goal.

What a compassionate lifestyle does allow room for, though, is for us to be open to experiencing negative thoughts, feelings and even behaviours towards ourselves and others. As long as we know that we are still on a journey towards becoming more compassionate beings when and where possible, we are still Compassioneers at heart. That way, we also won't feel emotionally exhausted when trying to act as though we are being compassionate, when in reality we are not.

There are so many different ways that you can become a Compassioneer. There are no distinct levels, ladders or snakes to climb or slide down. There are no ceremonial ways to be initiated or become cast out.

Compassioneers appreciate that they will always remain part of a deeply connected community who share similar values and, while not aiming to be perfect, realise that we are all on a journey forward regardless of any feelings of having a setback. In other words, being a Compassioneer is part of consciously being on a life-long journey, rather than dangling off a cliff waiting for the moments when we lose our grip and fall deep into the darkness of failure. It is not about keeping on the straight and narrow, but it is about finding a wide spanning and exciting road with endless opportunities. This is a journey of a lifetime that won't involve falling off a wagon.

Ultimately, the journey and life of a Compassioneer is an enlightening road that awakens us to the reality that we are all naturally and strongly connected with one another – ourselves, other people, animals and the fine balance of nature that exists on our planet.

Key Examples of Being a Compassioneer

✶ Taking time to nurture yourself:

The time we spend looking after others, meeting certain expectations or taking care of many competing priorities can leave us feeling anxious, stressed and with little energy left to direct attention towards number one – i.e. ourselves. However, a crucial component of becoming a Compassioneer involves developing compassion for ourselves and engaging in self-nurturing activities.

Nurturing ourselves is in no way selfish or egocentric. This is a very common myth as we outlined earlier, but there is more truth in the art of nurturing ourselves. Just like you probably wouldn't deprive a young child from trying to calm itself by being close to a parent or comforting object, it is not of any value to deprive ourselves of the comfort, nourishment and love we need to give to ourselves.

Compassioneers value the importance of trying to be our own comforting best friends, rather than letting their mean inner critics to take the steering wheel. Compassioneers also recognise when to not trust or listen to their inner critic, who would otherwise belittle us into live a life escaping fear rather than pursuing positive opportunities.

Self-compassion through nurturing ourselves leads to being able to spend more time in the present moment and feel more energised to create even more compassion. In other words, the self-love that we have on the inside also shows in the energy we create on the outside, which more likely than not attracts other positive energies towards us – whether that be in terms of people or opportunities. This inevitably leads to the compassion we give to ourselves being able to positively impact those around us, which is yet another reason why nurturing and spending time on ourselves is so important and not selfish at all.

Nurturing yourself can come in many other forms, such as taking time to pamper yourself, putting a relaxing candle on, bathing in a bubbly bath, reading a favourite book, taking up a new hobby, trying out a new enjoyable form of physical activity, treating yourself to your favourite meal without obsessively counting Calories or just about anything that makes you feel relaxed. Nurturing yourself can also involve eating nourishing foods that are enjoyable in abundance without feeling guilty or classifying certain foods as 'bad'. Even by spending time alone to appreciate what you have in life can be a form of self-nurturing, as can taking a break from work, your usual exercise routines, or any other obligations that you don't find genuine enjoyment or fulfilment in.

By nurturing ourselves, we can begin to create some much needed time just for ourselves, and not to please someone else.

The underpinning concept of self-compassion and nurturing ourselves is absolutely key to Nourishing Routes, and you'll find that we discuss it frequently with lots more practical applications and examples throughout the whole of this book.

✳ Exploring a passion:

Exploring a passion is quite fundamental when being self-compassionate in a way that allows you to invest energy in your strengths. Yet, in the fast paced and overly competitive world many of us live in, we can often forget that there are many important things we can choose to focus on in our lives other than succeeding at school, college, university, or in a certain career. Spending time on these pursuits isn't necessarily a bad thing at all if we really are passionate about them and they allow us to experience authentic happiness in the long run, but putting all of your time and energy into trying to obtain the 'best' grade or career will likely leave you with less time and energy to spend enjoying the activities you are truly passionate about.

A huge part of our lives is about exploring the many unique gifts each of us was born with, or the gifts we don't yet have but still have the magnificent potential to develop. Other than progress in your academic life or career, this might involve exploring creative passion for painting, writing stories, playing a musical instrument, learning a language, cooking and baking, or developing a new skill. It can be absolutely anything. You don't have to be an expert, but just a person willing to explore themselves, from the inside out, and unearth the creative and enjoyable pursuits they are passionate about. Passion really is a prime fuel for empowering us to feel energised within our lives. Without investing time in yourself to develop the strengths you have a passion for, then you really can't head in the direction that allows you, as the uniquely beautiful person you are, to flourish, thrive and reach your full potential.

✵ Being grateful for what we already have:

Appreciating what we already have simply refers to feeling grateful for the many things we already have in our lives. These 'things' don't have to be material possessions, but can include the simple fact of having a loving family, a roof over our heads, going on a beautiful walk, or having organs and limbs that allow our body to function. The things that might seem the most insignificant to us or go unnoticed are often of great importance in terms of our health and wellbeing.

Unfortunately there are many individuals spending much of their time ruminating about the things they haven't got, yet no matter how much material wealth they gain, the story of not feeling like they have enough or that they are good enough remains. The more we look to get, the more we haven't got.

These types of thoughts generally lead to poor self-comparison, which draws us further and further away from appreciating the real beauty in what we already have. Instead we feel like inferior individuals, and so continue to strive trying to achieve some form of 'ideal' standards.

Even if you have no material possessions that are worth a penny, or a body that seems far away from those seen slapped on the front of a magazine, simply knowing that you are loved, and can give love, is very powerful in terms of being able to experience authentic happiness and wellbeing. This is significantly shown in research in economically deprived countries, where individuals who lead a very 'poor' life by western standards still have greater wealth in terms of happiness and both mental and physical health compared to richer countries like the UK and America.

✵

By taking a step back and looking at the bigger picture, most of us already live a life filled to the brim with wealth that is well worth appreciating and feeling grateful for right now.

❄ Appreciating natural beauty:

Getting back to nature and experiencing natural green space is one of the most instinctively and quickly uplifting activities you can do. By being in environments of natural beauty – think green parks, tranquil waters, open spaces, rolling hills or even mountains – we instinctively feel safe that there are nourishing resources close by that will aid our survival.

We also can use nature as a way of being mindful of our surroundings and getting back in tune with our feelings, all the while being able to reduce any levels of anxiety or stress.

Other than the environment, being self-compassionate could mean appreciating your own natural beauty – accepting yourself for who you are right now. No matter what you look like, weigh, eat or how much you exercise, Compassioneers recognise that true beauty lies within, and in what we do – not how we unnaturally appear on the exterior.

❄ Helping others:

Being compassionate doesn't have to be in the form of what we give to ourselves or another person. It can also involve the steps that we take in order to alleviate the suffering of other humans, animals and even the whole planet. This can come in the form of volunteering or helping a cause that you believe in, or even adopting a more sustainable and cruelty free lifestyle.

As a personal example, taking up volunteering in my local community, actively supporting a charity and eating more vegetarian and vegan foods (foods that have not been made with the intentional exploitation of animals or other beings) has helped me to realise the many diverse ways we can show compassion. Volunteering especially has made me feel so much more socially connected, meet inspiring individuals, feel grateful for what I already have, understand of the many issues that need to be changed in the world with a greater sense of meaning and purpose.

In relation to helping others with food, I do not follow any rigid or strict rules in relation to what I eat. Instead, I aim to have a very balanced approach to food rather than obsessively striving to adopt any unnecessary diet labels. For me this often means going to my favourite cafe (with tea and cake of course) and socialising with close friends and family who can also benefit from positive social interactions while eating.

My mission within this book is not to make you follow a vegan, vegetarian or plant-based lifestyle. You do not have to follow any particular diet, eat 'clean' or eat a certain type of food in order to help others or become a Compassioneer. As we recently discussed, living more compassionately and being a Compassioneer isn't something you either are or are not just because you do or do not engage in a certain type of behaviour - including what you eat. Alternatively, I would simply encourage you to think about how eating more vegetarian and vegan food can be a powerful way of enhancing your understanding about the bigger picture that food plays in everyone's life, as well as your own ability to show compassion to yourself, others, animals and the planet.

It is important to recognise that any diet-related choice is best pursued with reasons for compassion, rather than because it encourages you to be like someone else, live in line with a particular ideal standard, label yourself, or feel 'safe' from adopting a regime that feels restrictive and more in control.

From personal experience, trying to be completely vegan, vegetarian or plant-based can mask many forms of disordered eating and low-self esteem, as well as drawing individuals into very rule-based and, ironically, non-compassionate ways of living. However, if pursued for reasons of compassion, eating more plant-based foods can make up an amazingly balanced and enjoyable way of living that enables you to nourish yourself, help others and the whole planet without feeling deprived, suffering from disordered eating, or remaining trapped in a vicious cycle of control.

As I have found along my own journey towards becoming a Compassioneer, developing a positive relationship with food, while knowing that the way we eat significantly contributes to the welfare of others, has been really satisfying, fulfilling and freeing. By doing this I have been able to continue letting go of all my restrictive routines around eating, while making it completely OK to eat more processed forms of foods, such as cakes, biscuits and sweets when and as I want to.

No amount of dietary lifestyle labels or knowing exactly how many Calories or nutrients are in specific foods can ever complete with our own natural physical, psychological and social intuition (which we will talk about in much more detail later on in in this book).

❋ Being understanding and forgiving of others' circumstances:

A Compassioneer is open minded in a way that allows them to see how some people's actions do not align well with their actual intentions. Sometimes it may seem that people are acting against us, with their own best interests as the main motive. However, this is often a misinterpretation of the fact that others who appear this way have a bundle of issues of their own. More often than not, their attitudes or behaviours towards us or others reflect an inner turmoil that they have with themselves, such as a lack of self-compassion.

As Compassioneers we can look beneath what we see visually, even in the most negative of circumstances, and ask ourselves why a person may be behaving in a particular way. The likelihood is that there is a whole host of reasons to be uncovered, the majority of which are not driven by motives to hurt or demoralise you. In such situations, unleashing your compassion in action might simply mean ignoring other people's hurtful comments, or offering your help and support to someone who might actually need to better develop their own sense of self-compassion. At other times, if harm has already been done, being compassionate involves forgiving others rather than holding a grudge. In the grand scheme of things, grudges actually do more harm to ourselves rather than the person we are holding a grudge against, since it is us who carries the corresponding anger and stress around with us. True Compassioneers realise this, and also that forgiveness is a remedy for many of life's difficult circumstances that involve conflict with others.

✴ **Take up volunteering opportunities that resonate with something you value:**

Volunteering can take place in many forms and for as little or as long as you are able with any population group. The key to the benefits of volunteering is to do something that resonates with your values, not because you feel like you 'have' to in order to please someone else or be seen as a 'good' person.

Becoming part of a voluntary organisation can allow you to gain a sense of community, feel connected to something meaningful, engage in relaxing and/or creative activities and even find a new sense of purpose in your life. There are honestly so many benefits from knowing that we can be of help to others, and in my own experience, volunteering was the key element that led me on a journey to not only being compassionate to others, but eventually to myself too.

Volunteering was one of the main ways I was introduced to a compassionate way of living. At first this was mainly through the way I tried to volunteer more alongside my work at college and university, and eventually find a nourishing way of eating that allowed me to enjoy food in abundance (no guilt included) while minimising exploitation of other animals and humans.

You don't need an initiation ceremony to become a Compassioneer

Many activities we have mentioned that might be pursued by a Compassioneer can fit into almost any lifestyle, and they highlight that anyone really can become one in their own right. There may be no initiation ceremony for when you begin to follow your own Nourishing Routes to becoming a Compassioneer, but I am confident that choosing this empowering path, in whatever form this looks like, will bring you and others joy in so many forms. The positive possibilities are literally endless, and they are just waiting to be uncovered by us all.

✴

To reinstate some of the main points we have covered, being compassionate through becoming a Compassioneer is not an all or nothing game. Compassioneers don't try to think in black and white terms. As long as you are ready to take steps towards a more compassionate lifestyle, while accepting our human flaws, then you really can't fail.

There is honestly no better decision in my life that I have made that comes close to the benefits experienced from following a more compassionate lifestyle, and it is a key mission of mine to promote the concept of becoming a Compassioneer on a positive, loving and empowering journey forward.

By becoming Compassioneers, I believe that each of us become musketeers on a quest to nurture ourselves and others and stand up for what we believe in while inevitably enhancing the welfare and happiness of those around us. Being a Compassioneer is deeply embedded within our genes, and I feel passionate about sharing with you this knowledge so that you too can step foot onto a journey of a lifetime while realising your full potential and just how beautiful and perfect you already are.

Can Nourishing Routes Help Me to Heal My Relationship with Food and Body?

With the philosophy of Nourishing Routes and leading a more compassionate lifestyle, happiness and health is much, much more than just eating a specific way, becoming a certain weight, or carrying out a particular exercise regimen. However, at this point on our journey some of you who are currently pursuing certain health goals, suffering from an illness, or experiencing a disordered relationship with eating or your own body might be wondering whether your journey to a happier and healthier you can be aided by the Nourishing Routes philosophy.

To answer questions related to pursuing other health behaviours, you may be surprised to know that leading a more compassionate lifestyle can naturally lead to leading a healthier lifestyle. The more we love ourselves and express our natural compassion both inwards and outwardly, the more we are able to identify with our life purpose and nurture ourselves. Also, the ways that we choose to nurture ourselves are unlikely to centre on faddy quick fix methods. Instead we choose activities that are enjoyable, in line with our values and are ultimately more sustainable over time.

Specifically related to recovery from disordered eating and healing a poor relationship with food and body, Nourishing Routes can definitely help you to journey towards these goals if you are ready to pursue them in a self-loving way. Although in many cases recovery partly involves a focus on increasing a person's food intake and weight, which might seem against the Nourishing Routes philosophy, it is important to remember that such goals are for the benefit rather than the detriment of a person's physical and psychological wellbeing. For example, when recovering from an eating disorder, a focus on food and body may be for the purposes of restoring essential fat stores, feeling more energised and getting back in tune with natural intuition and hunger around food – so they can ultimately lead a life that allows them to reach their full potential.

The problems happen, however, when the focus on food and weight during recovery become the primary focus, while further down the line of important issues to tackle is learning how to address how individuals continue to use food and weight as a way to feel more control in life. This of course isn't always the case, but when it does happen, while medical professionals continue to monitor a person's weight and eating behaviour, this can perpetuate the idea that individuals' self-worth and health are based on what they eat and how much they weigh. I can completely resonate with many of these experiences, and walking into a psychologist's office with the first activity involving standing on a weighing scale before telling someone exactly what I had eaten that week didn't exactly instil positive feelings or hope that real recovery was possible. Instead, I was left feeling that what I ate or how much I weighed would continue to dictate my self-worth and the quality of my life for many years to come. Thankfully I was wrong in my predictions, but this point highlights that a focus on food and weight as a means to recovery from disordered eating or a poor relationship with food and body really isn't going to create a magical ending at the end of the dark fairytale someone feels they are currently living in.

As many individuals with experience of an eating disorder can understand, a focus on weight and food can in one sense be helpful for recovery, but on the other hand half the demon they have to battle. It takes you so far, but trying to plan every morsel of food, Calorie and weight change can be hugely time consuming and a heavy burden to manage. Quite ironically, a focus on nutrient intake and weight can inadvertently reinforce the idea that self-worth and wellbeing are based on numbers – whether they be Calories or what appears on a measuring scale. In reality though, empowering forms of recovery should ideally help individuals view health as so much more than this.

In my own experience, recovery was alike to a full time job (especially the meal planning and ensuring that I ate a certain number of Calories and snacks at a certain time). I was so used to my eating behaviour being so pre-planned, coordinated and orderly that the idea of recognising hunger or being able to eat 'intuitively' seemed like a myth, or at least a darn right impossibility. It is only years later, after having explored additional avenues to health and wellbeing, I have realised just how wrong I was.

Even if individuals in recovery do achieve the goal of becoming physically healthy in terms of the food they eat or how much they weigh, the same core disordered thought patterns around food, body and life in general may still remain. There is also the concern that looking a 'healthy' weight means that individuals' psychological issues around their food and body go unnoticed, which in itself acts as a barrier to recovery as many individuals feel that they will not be given the support they continue to need if they finally achieve a 'healthy' weight or are seen to eat a 'decent' amount of food. Put more simply, a focus on weight and food tends to hinder a person's ability to flourish and thrive in both mind and body, partly because time invested in being able to show self-compassion or live more compassionately in general has been a relatively neglected activity.

Nourishing Routes takes on a much more holistic perspective when it comes to recovery. Altering your food intake and/or weight may be important, but you will find that the main ambition when using the Nourishing Routes philosophy is to place a focus on how you think and feel around food, body and your whole life – not just how much you eat and weigh.

For myself, this holistic focus was a huge driving force behind my own recovery. I realised for the first time that recovery wasn't just about trying to find the perfect recovery meal plan or weight I felt comfortable at. Recovery was about being able to finally love myself and develop a positive relationship with food and body. It was also fundamentally about discovering my life purpose and following the dreams that were in line with my own goals and values – rather than what I thought was expected of me in order to feel like a successful or healthy person by society's standards.

I must point out here, though, that eating disorders cannot simply be 'snapped out of' in a matter of minutes, days or even weeks. Recovery is not about simply 'getting a grip'. From personal experience I can only empathise with and show genuine compassion for just how difficult it can be to put up with the unnecessary stigma and ignorance that still surrounds eating disorders as well as any form of disordered eating or body dysmorphia.

Rarely have I come across anyone, myself included, who personally asked to have or remain suffering from these life threatening issues. Dissimilar to popular belief, individuals suffering from an eating disorder do not 'choose' a lifestyle of restriction, binge eating, or anything on the spectrum of disordered eating purely out of vanity. There are many biological, social and psychological factors involved, and in no way should individuals with an eating disorder or any form of disordered eating or way of viewing their own body be seen as attention seeking or lacking in willpower.

As with health in general, there is a much, much more complex picture to be explored, including elements of genetics and neurological functioning that are beyond individuals' control, especially at the height of an eating disorder. Also, just like everyone else experiencing poor mental or physical health conditions, individuals experiencing an eating disorder are compassionate human beings who want to get well and reach their full potential – only they have lost the ability to express compassion for themselves.

Society and the nature of the medical profession can sometimes bracket individuals into boxes – providing individuals with physical or mental health problems with a label, a meal plan, a Calorie count to abide by, a medication, or a specific weight target as being the ingredients to recovery or improved wellness. Of course, as with any holistic treatment plan, this is part of the way forward. We need optimal nutrition to physically function, and to think clearly in a way that directs us to reaching our full potential. However, if we only focus on these specific elements, then we are losing sight of the person we are trying to help and nurture through their recovery journey.

In more simple terms, I have realised that if focussing on food becomes the main priority during recovery, then it is not really helping individuals to see that their lives are much more meaningful beyond what they eat and weigh. We have our own Nourishing Routes to discover!

Adopting the philosophy of Nourishing Routes and leading a more compassionate lifestyle does not mean giving up on the idea of initially having a meal plan, a structured routine or weight management goals to aid recovery from an eating disorder. They can each have their place, and at the end of the day we need to eat and breathe in order to live and reach our dreams. However, adopting the philosophy of Nourishing Routes and leading a more compassionate lifestyle can additionally help you realise that there is a life worth living beyond food and weight. More specifically, individuals with experience of an eating disorder can be empowered by the philosophy and guidance of Nourishing Routes in a way that enables them to focus on the many essential elements of their wellbeing. As we talked about earlier, this can involve being able to express creativity, show compassion to ourselves and others, socially reconnect, love what we already have and feel free to be whoever we want to be.

On my own recovery journey, I decided to alternatively focus my time and energies on the new activities I had learned to love, even though this initially meant taking the gas pedal off academic work and my career. Sometimes in life we need time to stop, and take care of our real needs. The real need to grow, learn about ourselves and become able to show compassion.

Through learning to ride on the colourful ropes of Nourishing Routes, whether the reason be improved health and wellbeing or recovery, you can go out there and realise your true potential. No one can stop it from happening if you truly believe it. Regardless of whether you have or have not experienced an eating disorder or disordered forms of eating and relationships with your body, nothing can take away from the fact that you are an awesome human being who has a reason to live, express your creativity, connect with others, and show you compassion in all its beautiful forms.

This is why I passionately believe that Nourishing Routes has the potential to change lives, not through only altering what individuals eat or look like, but by empowering the energising life force that lives. This life force can be of huge benefit to enabling us to pursue certain health goals in our lives or successfully cope with and recover from a trauma or illness.

If you believe that there are Nourishing Routes to recovery, happiness and health, then you also believe that you can journey towards a compassionate lifestyle that involves authentically loving ourselves, others and the planet. We can become our very own Compassioneers.

A Journey of Compassionate Discovery – Not Just Recovery

Leading a more compassionate lifestyle does not necessarily just involve recovering from something in your life, whether that be from a physical illness, psychological trauma, or recovering from a mental illness such as depression, anxiety or a form of disordered eating or body image. If that was the case, all a compassionate life would accomplish would be to heal us rather than help us to grow, flourish and thrive. However, many people's lives have become centred on recovery rather than discovery of who they really are and what they can offer themselves, others and the world other than their stigmatised identity of a medical diagnosis.

In an attempt to regain what part of us we have lost through an illness or trauma, many of us set out on a journey of recovery with a limited mindset – trying to patch up, puzzle together and restore who we once were. But this is not the full story of getting to a place where you can genuinely reach your full potential by being able to nourish, flourish and thrive.

In the grand scheme of our lives the process of recovery or overcoming a trauma is great. It is certainly a huge step in a positive direction. Whether that be starting to gain support from someone, learning to eat food in a way that nourishes the mind or body, or successfully undertaking some form of therapeutic activity, it can be a great help in terms of finding an enlightened perspective on our personal issues and learning to directly deal with the problems life has challenged us with.

However, recovery is not the end point of your story when finding your own Nourishing Routes to becoming a Compassioneer. The reality is that recovery only repairs something that was faulty in order to get to a static place of restoration. Recovery is a bit like trying to plaster over a crack in a crumbling wall without looking at what caused the hole, or how you can make the foundations of that wall even stronger.

In other words, a sole focus on recovery prevents rather than enables us to become open to changing shape and being transformed into something that reflects our true beauty, strength, purpose and potential. To do this, we must see the recovery journey as a process that leads us not only towards restoring ourselves to something that once was, but to transform ourselves into something even stronger and wiser than before.

What we really need to do is to set out on an alluring adventure of discovery, not just recovery, where we can use our negative life experiences to learn new things about ourselves, gain a new perspective and embark on a whole new exciting path forwards. In relative terms, recovery is similar to erasing a pencil mistake with a rubber, whereas discovery is more about using that mistake as a way to form new ideas and write a whole new story. Discovery is also about viewing your life experiences – both negative and positive — as something that can transform you for the better rather than aiming to remain in a static place that feels familiar and safe.

For example, when recovering from an eating disorder, a person may spend a large part of their time trying to avoid maladaptive behaviours, while trying to seek out the best meal plan in order to regain a healthy amount of weight and attain an 'optimal' BMI. They might also engage in multiple therapies, or even be rehabilitated in a hospital setting. All these would be deemed as recovery, but yet they all lack a crucial element to their effectiveness – they are not able to fully help a person break away from the person they once were, or the eating disorder identity.

Actions solely geared towards recovery may only fill a hole, and leave little room for creative thinking about who you really are or could become. A primary focus on recovery and restoration could also leave few opportunities to reconnect with your core values and find out what other exciting adventures life now has in store for you.

Without actively engaging in opportunities for discovery, a person may become labelled as 'recovered' without actually feeling as though they have reached their full potential. A person might also feel that they are still at risk of falling into the same trap. They may even still be caught up in following rigid recovery routines and rituals that feel familiar and safe, while not being able to visualise themselves as a stronger person with a greater understanding about the world and themselves than ever before.

This is why a journey of discovery, and not just recovery, is so important. But what crucial ingredients does a recipe for discovery contain?

Well firstly, it involves using your experiences of illness or trauma as lessons to learn more about yourself. By looking at how we have coped with or overcome certain issues, we can gain a great sense of confidence in how far we have already come. Even in the most negative circumstances where you have fallen to your feet multiple times, I can guarantee that there have been parts of those experiences that required a lot of physical and mental strength to stand back up again and face the music.

You can also go about recovery as an opportunity to engage in activities other than those aimed at getting you physically well. By that I mean trying out new hobbies, getting involved in volunteering and taking time out for yourself to relax doing the creative or engaging activities you enjoy doing. Enjoying these things is important, and there is absolutely nothing to feel guilty or lazy about. It is certainly not a waste of time, and you can think about it as a positive personal investment in your long-term happiness and wellbeing.

With discovery as well as recovery you can claim the freedom to choose the inspiring opportunities life offers to you, while not viewing recovery as a linear road of rigid routines. By venturing on this path, you can also become more open to different ideas, ways of reflecting on who you are and what you really enjoy, as well as learning to see the beauty in the simple things in everyday life. With discovery, you embark on a more authentic journey that enables you to grow beyond what you originally were, as you take new experiences in your stride and learn to assess the positive meaning in even the most negative of situations.

For myself, embracing discovery as well as recovery has enabled me to personally grow in a way I could have never imagined.

Illness and trauma may be there to partly break us down, but only so that they can help build us back up as well as transforming us into something new and even more beautiful.

If you too choose discovery, and not just recovery, I have every belief that this will lead you to learning more about yourself, becoming more self-compassionate, and being well on your way to becoming a Compassioneer so you can truly nourish, flourish and thrive.

A Step by Step Journey to becoming a Compassioneer

When considering any new way of thinking, feeling or behaving it can be easy to jump into black and white thinking – I am either living a particular way or I am not. This leads us down a road, usually a lonely and overly critical one, where we either feel like we are winning or losing a battle. Yet, in reality, any step in the right direction is a success to be noticed and celebrated.

For me, compassionate living, whether this be towards loving myself more, nourishing my body, not harming animals, or taking more consideration of the world around us is not a journey with a specific end point. Like many other things in life, there is no standard for perfection. Being compassionate is not about taking a huge leap into the unknown and setting ourselves up in an all or nothing, win or fail, situation. Instead, living compassionately grows from each and every small step that we can take – day by day and even minute by minute.

In practical terms, this means not expecting to instantly heal your relationship with food and body with the click of a finger. Yes, these scenarios would be ideal if they were possible, but for most people they are not, no matter how strong their motivation or proactive they may be. The human mind is very complex, if not a very frustrating piece of equipment to get our heads around! Sometimes we can wake up in the morning and want to change our whole perspective, our lives and even the whole world. But the truth of the matter is that long term sustainable change starts small. This is why I view compassionate living as a journey rather than a win or lose situation.

Whether we want to become free of disordered eating patterns and ways of thinking about ourselves, or just about anything that allows us to live more compassionately, our goals inevitably involve learning lots of new things.

At the very least, this requires time and room for trial, error and success. We simply can't expect to be experts at living the life we want to live overnight. But we can take delight in our small triumphs, no matter how small or infrequent they may be to begin with.

When we do reach our initial goals this does not mean we have to stop there. Motivations for beginning our compassionate journeys may change and our awareness of all different aspects of that lifestyle can dramatically increase – driving us to learn more, set new goals and create new ambitions. This is part of the fun and lifelong adventure of compassionate living, rather than viewing our journey an exhausting expedition with no end point.

Before I began to appreciate this perspective myself, I continued to believe that my journey would be a simple linear process towards recovery. However, I soon came to realise that I needed to accept that there would be many bumps and unexpected turns along a lengthy road. At first I just wasn't ready to allow myself to be open to the unknown. Anything unexpected or stepping outside of my strict recovery plan made me feel like a failure, which frequently led to me giving up and falling deeper into the trap of a self-destructive mind-set. That is, until I discovered the art of being more compassionate to myself and understanding the weird yet wonderful psychology of the human mind.

Slowly but surely I began to grasp that the idea that we weren't made like machines – to work in one specific functional mode without fail or room for taking a different move than originally intended. What started off as a recipe for disaster turned into a compelling journey of discovery – an exciting journey that I am still happily venturing along today.

To summarise these ideas in a little note of wisdom I would like to say that we can achieve the great things we set out on a journey of self-exploration. By picking a realistic and optimal pace to challenge ourselves, we can fully explore, integrate, and learn from each little step we take.

By jumping too far ahead of the game or expecting to reach our goals in an instant without fail, we may miss out on vital learning opportunities. Out journey to being more compassionate beings involves appreciating that we

*

are all human, and cannot expect to be perfect or a completely different person in a matter of days, hours or minutes. Long lasting change is a life-long journey that involves setting specific and realistic goals, but allowing room for setbacks and changes in direction as well as destination.

Through each small change, and accepting that our journey might not have a distinct start or finishing line, we will become more able to seek new learning experiences, develop more specific and realistic goals. Overall, our journey towards reaching our goals will be leading us to become ever closer to being the compassionate beings we were born to be, which is more than enough reason to celebrate and allow yourself rooms to break free from an 'all or nothing' or perfectionistic mindset.

Progress – Not Perfection

Before continuing any further in our journey towards living more compassionately, it is really crucial for me to highlight that one of the best things you can do is to strive for progress – not perfection. When aiming to achieve anything in our lives, whether that involves recovering from a physical or mental illness, nourishing ourselves better, or developing positive relationships with our mind, food, and body, it can be easy to throw ourselves into the deep end – expecting ourselves to be perfect with no slip ups.

While this might seem a great way to get our new mind-set and behaviours off on the right foot, what we are really doing is setting ourselves up for disappointment and ultimately a lack of self-compassion.

I have been guilty of the very same. I was so used to acting on my goals with too many positive intentions and strict rules, without any flexibility to be able to make the occasional slip up without regarding this as an ultimate failure and reason to stop trying to recover or live more compassionately.

However, as I have learnt over the last several years, any life change is about slipping up or veering off course sometimes. These occasions are feared by a lot of us, as we feel that they will make us feel stupid, worthless, guilty, ashamed and like the ultimate failure. In reality however, tripping up is a positive sign that we are only human. Any mistakes that we make are an important part of a lifelong journey forward, and all of them act as crucial points in our lives that we can utilise to learn, grow and become stronger.

From my own experiences, my journey towards recovery and a more compassionate way of living has often been hindered by my own unrealistic expectations and lack of self-compassion. If I didn't meet all my goals for that day, I felt like giving up. What was the point in continuing if I already had proved myself to be a failure? However, thoughts about failure are the biggest failures of all, not the act of occasionally tripping up. Our trips are there to help us learn more about ourselves. No one is superhuman, and no lifestyle change is especially easy to follow in an instant. These things take time – they are a matter of progress and ongoing learning – not striving for instant perfection.

Perfection in itself is not a realistic goal for any sane person. Part of being human is about accepting that we cannot be the best or reach certain expectations 100% of the time. By accepting our imperfections and learning from our slip-ups, this is one essential way of being self-compassionate.

To turn my own unrealistic expectations for perfection around, I eventually learnt to take action on my goals with the willingness to make more room for mistakes – thinking of them as guiding friends rather than evil enemies. I was able to appreciate that mistakes are important milestones rather than mountain peaks to fall from, whether that be recovery from illness, coping with trauma, or embarking on a journey towards a new way of living. These principles can apply to anyone and most of the challenges of opportunities we face in life.

Despite wanting to change into the best possible version of yourself overnight, there is a much better reason to expect progress rather than perfection. Not only will this help cushion our falls by treating these as inevitable, they can also be used as events to stimulate the self-nurturing rather than self-hating part of ourselves. In this way, we can truly grow from our life experiences, with the added bonus of being more self-compassionate and understanding that our downfalls are just part of the wider human experience – definitely not your own lone personal failures.

So with these points in mind, I encourage you to take the leaps of faith that will allow you push fear of failure aside and go forth to embark on the journeys that will create a fulfilling and more compassionate you. But, when planning your adventures and the goals you would like to achieve, cherish your slip ups as well as your triumphs.

By doing this you will open yourself up to experiencing lifelong adventures of self-love and learning – not getting stuck in a bottomless pit or venturing right back where we started. We happen to live in a society that might not be ready to completely accept the idea that perfection doesn't exist, but I can 100% guarantee that progress and not perfection on your own Nourishing Routes to living more compassionately is one of the key magical ingredients for being able to flourish and thrive.

"By realising and living in alignment with your real beliefs and values, you can feel free and energised enough to fulfil your purpose in life – not other people's or society's unrealistic expectations of you"

Ideal Goal Setting

Before we can embark on our beautiful Nourishing Routes to become a Compassioneer, we firstly need to vividly picture ourselves in the place we want to be and set goals that are realistic, achievable and in line with our personal values and deepest desires.

There is absolutely no point in venturing any further along our journey if our main reason for being here is not for ourselves. The key element of being a Compassioneer involves learning to do things for yourself because they align with your own values, rather than meet external expectations or trying to please others. If we can step onto our journey from a place of wanting to help and show compassion to ourselves then we are already halfway there.

It saddens me that there are literally hundreds and thousands of health and wellbeing books that have been passionately written with an important message to share, yet less than 10% of individuals reading them actually take actions on what they have learned. Apart from prolonging the process of individuals getting to a place where they want to be, it can also lead some to feel like a failure through their own fault, and perpetuate feelings of low self-worth. These aren't exactly the type of feelings that fuel further readiness and action for change, or leading a more compassionate lifestyle for that matter...

This really is such a shame as most individuals who pick up health and wellbeing books are in a state of readiness to change. What I would like to do, through this book and the philosophy of Nourishing Routes, is to harness that opportunity to its full. For you, this means that I am NOT prepared to let you slip through the pages of this book back into your old routine, where not liking or loving yourself becomes the acceptable norm.

But why do so many other health and wellness books lead to the similar outcome of providing inspiration without action? Well, the answer is partly in the question. For one, there are no practical guidelines of how to integrate the lessons learned into a person's actual lifestyle. Even if there are tips, the way that they are written can seem difficult to place into a reader's own reality. Secondly, and perhaps most crucially, most health and wellbeing books don't look into the type and quality of motivation that drives individuals' goals.

Take for instance a self-help book on overcoming anxiety, depression, chronic illness, an eating disorder, or even books based on following the latest dieting and fitness trend. One of the main reasons individuals pick up these types of books is because they don't feel happy with the way that they currently are, and also that no one else accepts or loves them either. A key reason for buying such books is driven by wanting to meet our essential needs to feel accepted and loved, but mainly by other people rather than ourselves, whether that be a partner, family member or a colleague. If we look into these motivations a little deeper, you might be able to see that they are driven by an external factor – mainly a need to meet the expectations of others.

What we know from years of psychology and health research, though, is that motivations to change that are driven by external forces are NOT the best ingredients for success – especially in the long term. This is mainly because pursuing goals for reasons that involve external pressure from others to change does little to improve our own self-worth. Without external pressure, for many individuals, the motivation to continue engaging in 'self-improvement' behaviours dwindles.

On the other hand, when an individual recognises that changing their attitudes and behaviours is in their own best interests, values and also because they fully deserve the right to accept and love themselves, this is when the gears of change really spring into action. In psychology we term this type of motivation 'intrinsic motivation', and it has been consistently shown to lead to the best results where behaviour change and improving our health, happiness and wellbeing are concerned. In many ways, intrinsic motivation is a compassionate form of motivation, as it usually involves wanting to fulfil our deepest, most authentic and important desires for reasons that aid our own happiness and health.

Despite this evidence, we are left with many self-help books that allow their ambitious readers to continue flicking their pages with the main motivation of pleasing others. A simple mistake, but thankfully one that can easily be avoided or overcome.

As we will now go into, avoiding or overcoming this challenge in relation to Nourishing Routes involves me and you thinking about the real reasons why leading a more compassionate lifestyle is important. This will crucially involve delving a little deeper into the reasons why you are actually reading this very page, and recognising that setting goals that are intrinsically ori-entated is based on the idea of wanting to become a Compassioneer, and is not solely dependent on a need to please other people or some ideal standard of success.

An example might be that you are wanting to heal a negative relationship with food and body, whether this involves jumping on board with faddy diets, experiencing an eating disorder, or feeling sick of seeing yourself in the mirror because you hate the reflection staring back at you.

For some of you, a reason for change might be wanting to develop a pos-itive relationship with food and your body, have enough energy in work or family life, or allow yourself to flourish and thrive in a way that makes you feel authentically happy and bursting with life. Alternatively, from a more extrinsic motivation perspective, you might be reading this book in the hope that it will help you feel safe through adopting another lifestyle choice that you can use to make you feel in control or like a worthy individ-ual. There isn't anything completely wrong with these extrinsic forms of motivation, but because they are usually based on meeting the expectations of others while not being driven by self-compassion, they will be unlikely to be successful when compared to motivations that are intrinsically driven by a desire to please yourself.

In an ideal world, and hopefully from reading this book, you might realise that being able to nourish, flourish and thrive while developing a positive relationship with food and your body will be achieved through basing these goals on intrinsic rather than extrinsic motivations. For example, such goals might be driven by a desire to have more energy to pursue your life purpose and fulfil your dreams – and not the ones that are based on meeting a certain ideal standard. You might also be motivated by knowing that you fully deserve to go on your own Nourishing Routes while appreciating all the amazing things you have to offer this world and yourself.

Creating and applying motivations that come from within and are open to a world of unknown exciting opportunities, rather than external expectations or rigid rules, are therefore much more likely to succeed. This is why in the next part of this book we are going to take a little time to ensure that you can learn to base your goals around more intrinsic motivations. Believe me, it is one of the best chances we can make for ourselves in order to really experience long-term success, and I can use my own experiences as a real-life example. For years I tried to recover from an eating disorder for other people. I also wanted to pursue a PhD and attain a prestigious place as a top researcher just because I thought it would make me seem like a worthy successful person. Without it, I convinced myself that I would be nothing. As you may have may noticed, these goals were not fuelled by a need to please myself. They were completely extrinsically orientated as they were driven by my need to allow myself, so I thought, to seek approval and acceptance from others rather than myself. Getting the 'best' research position or becoming qualified with a PhD might have been a form of success, but in reality they would also be a way of me trying to gain a sense of self-worth by living up to the expectations that society places on us – i.e. getting a good job or becoming an expert within a certain field of work. My motivations weren't about leading a happy or healthy life, which says it all about how successful they were in terms of actually promoting 'real' recovery.

Years and years went by before any change really happened in terms of my recovery journey. It was only when I eventually realised that my own self and happiness needed to be at the centre of my goals that the real magic happened. And thank goodness that I was able to realise this, otherwise I might not be here writing this book and living a life that I am truly passionate about.

Through setting intentions and goals that are based on accepting and loving yourself while being able to reach your full potential, I have full faith that you can step into a life that is filled with exciting opportunities to nourish, flourish and thrive. So what are we waiting for? Let's get the gears moving in the right directions so that you can truly begin to become the beautiful Compassioneer you were born to be.

✳
102

Compassioneer Activity: Ideal Goal Setting

The first step we will take in terms of promoting the ideal motivation to change will be visualisation and orientating our goals to be in line with our own values rather than other people's expectations. Only then can we get started on the real specifics of how we can make our goals and a Compassioneer lifestyle become a reality. For these goal setting activities all you will need is your own open mind as well as a pen and paper (as colourful or as beautifully designed as you like, but that might just be my obsession with stationery speaking).

Step 1:

Find a calm and quiet space, and begin by asking yourself what the words compassion and self-compassion mean to you. After finding your own definitions, close your eyes for a few minutes and imagine yourself stepping into a blissful world of self-love and living more compassionately.

Step 2:

In a sentence or brief paragraph, what would living more compassionately involve and feel like and how might it relate to your own life?

"If I were to apply the concept of living more compassionately in my own life, it would involve 'x,y and z'."

This could be a number of things, but for me it was about being able to love myself, eat anything I wanted to without feeling guilty, feel more energised, and be able to use my experiences or expertise as a tool to help others.

Step 3:

Find a quiet and calm space, while making yourself feel comfortable. Perhaps you could even light a candle or snuggle up with your favourite cup of tea. Now close your eyes and try to imagine what an ideal day would look like for you if you were to lead a more compassionate self-loving lifestyle. Ask yourself:

"How would I want my mornings to start and feel like in order to step positively into my day?"

Are there any things that you would like to happen, such as being able to give yourself the time and freedom to enjoy a nourishing breakfast, while not feeling a need to measure your self-worth by what you have eaten, weighing yourself or scrutinising yourself in the mirror?

"What type of work would I like to be doing, and where would this take place? Would I prefer to be working at home, or be in a job that provides me with a sense of purpose or a lifestyle that enables me to spend more time with friends and family?"

"What hobbies/activities would I engage in that make me feel happy, 'in the moment' and as though I am really alive?"

This might be something like writing, yoga, going on walks, cooking a nourishing meal, baking a cake, taking up a new craft – almost anything that makes you feel great.

"Are there any activities or behaviours that I currently engage in that are actually holding me back in my life?"

For example, you may find that you always say yes to everything and other people's requests. Or, you may be in a negative cycle of weighing yourself each morning, obsessively counting Calories and logging food, skipping meals, binge eating, or saying no to opportunities that will allow you to relax and nurture yourself.

"How would I like to enjoy my evenings?"

❈

This might involve an ideal form of relaxation for you, such as making yourself a bath, going out for a meal with friends/a partner, reading a child a bedtime story, curling up with a book of your own, or simply being able to easily go to sleep without discomfort or excessive worry.

OK, now you've completed the first and fundamental steps. The next step is about getting a little bit more specific about what living compassionately involves and what it will be able to do for you in terms of reaching your full potential.

Step 4:

If you have contemplated what you would like a more compassionately life-style to include in your own life, you can now ask yourself the following questions before noting your answers down on a piece of paper that you can keep to refer back to.

"What areas of my life would benefit most from being more self-compassionate?"

"How will my life be positively different if I were to lead a more compassionate lifestyle?"

"How will living more compassionately make me feel, and are there any specific emotions that I might expect to experience?"

"What ongoing issues or negative experiences in my life might following a more compassionate lifestyle help to address or resolve?"

"What would it feel like to be someone who truly understands that health and happiness are based on so much more than exactly what and how much I eat and exercise, as well as what I look like, my academic qualifications, my career success or how many valuable/materialistic items I own?"

"How might other individuals I love and care about benefit if I led a more compassionate lifestyle?"

❖

"On a scale of 1 to 10, how much would I rate the overall benefit that I might experi-ence from learning to lead a more compassionate lifestyle?"

"By considering the benefits of leading a more compassionate lifestyle, do I now feel ready to follow my own Nourishing Routes to becoming a Compassioneer?"

Step 5:

As a final yet crucially important step, write a list of at least three reasons why you are a worthy person who fully deserves to love yourself more and lead a compassionate lifestyle. Following this, read the encouraging sen-tence shown below:

"I was born to be a Compassioneer and now it my time to shine while embarking on a journey towards living a more compassionate lifestyle – not because it will please others, but because I deserve to experience love formyself and others, as well as reach my full potential in mind, body and soul."

Well done! You have now completed the first stage of becoming a Compassioneer by making your goals more intrinsically orientated and in alignment with your values.

This is a fundamental step forward in terms of being able to believe that you do deserve to lead a more compassionate lifestyle while being able to gen-uinely love and respect yourself, regardless of what society or other people think and expect of you.

All that is left for you to do now is get ready to embrace the journey of a life-time to find your own Nourishing Routes. To do this we will now delve a bit deeper into the art of self-compassion, where we can accept ourselves as we are now while learning to genuinely love ourselves from the inside out. We will also briefly look at how we can apply the concept of compassion, including self-compassion, to our work and relationships. Only then can we begin to get into more specific, empowering and utterly life-changing details about how to apply the concepts of compassionate living to the way we think, feel and behave around food and body, which will be the primary focus of Part 3.

PART 2:

Embracing Self-Compassion

"Developing and showing self-compassion allows you to attract positive opportunities into your own life that also happen to promote the welfare of others and the planet"

All You Need is Love – Mostly for Yourself

When I first began to embark on a mission towards living more compassionately it shocked me to realise just how unloving towards myself I had become. Apart from having a severely negative view of my own body, it struck me to find that almost anything I did never felt good enough.

I was forever telling myself off for not trying harder, persisting longer, reaching the best grade or eating the most perfectly clean diet. Anything I experienced that was pleasurable seemed like something I was completely undeserving of – even to the point of denying myself a hot shower or cup of tea (yes, this tea addict denied herself tea!).

However, when playing these negative memories over in my mind, I can't help but laugh at the sheer silliness and uselessness of it all. Was there ever a point in being this harsh and unloving towards myself? Did the punishments make me a better and more loving person?

Definitely not. In fact, it produced the exact opposite results. Being unloving towards myself meant that I could only focus primarily on myself. If I wasn't good enough, I needed to solely focus on becoming better, even though the actual act of doing this only made me feel even worse.

Inevitably, the anxiety of trying to always live up to my unrealistic expectations was a huge distraction from finding my true purpose in life. Although it has taken many years to realise this simple fact, being able to unveil the truth that you can't make progress in the world without being self-loving was a very worthwhile and empowering discovery.

As you yourself might have experienced yourself, living in a world that constantly tells us that we should all work our bottoms off, get the best grades, and attain the most prestigious job positions in order to be happy aren't really the things in our lives that lead to happiness and health.

Instead, in our bid to strive to reach society's expectations, rather than living in line with our own values and what we truly enjoy, it is easy to follow a path of self-loathing rather than compassion.

Nothing might ever seem good enough, whether that be our own bodies, the foods we eat (or don't eat), our daily activities, or the things we are formally graded and socially judged upon. Even when some of our goals are reached, we might be tempted to set the bar even higher, so we are never genuinely satisfied with our success. Our goals become ever more unrealistic, unattainable and ultimately the demons in our lives that prevent us from moving forward and reaching our full potential.

Now armed with my own experiences, research and the philosophy of Nourishing Routes, I am here to remind you that you are good enough right now – just as you are in this very moment.

If we can really accept ourselves for who we are, as well as learn to love each and every part of ourselves, this is where authentic success, happiness and health can emanate from. By learning to love ourselves, we are setting a positive example to live by while also leaving ourselves more open to the world's many positive opportunities.

At this point, you may be quite tempted to say that I am a bit crazy. I mean, why would any sane person ask you to walk around hugging yourself and proclaiming self-love? However, this is not what I mean by self-compassion.

As we discussed at the beginning of this book, being loving towards ourselves acts at a much deeper level, where we understand and accept that we have flaws – like any other human being. However, at the same time we also appreciate and believe that each of us is unique and has the capacity to do wonderful things in the world.

Loving yourself involves viewing yourself, from the inside out, as worthy of enjoyment and the affection of others – without experiencing guilt or feeling ineffective. It also means that we don't have to strive for perfection each time we set ourselves a goal. In fact, the factors that limit our ability to be perfect are the beautiful elements of what make us human and able to empathise with others in order to be compassionate beings.

What can we do to show ourselves a bit more self-love?

As a personal example, one act of becoming more self-loving was to decide to minimise engaging in work-related tasks at home in my leisure time. This involved not reading text books or online journal articles at my computer while eating (I often used these as a distraction to stop feeling guilty during meal times). I also decided that I would use my new spare time to spend more quality time with family, saying yes to invitations to eat out, and start engaging in activities that I loved – volunteering, playing the piano again, taking up yoga and engaging in a little bit more self-pampering. That sometimes meant booking myself in for a relaxing spa-treatment, not to make me look better, but because I wanted to nurture my body.

Self-loving activities don't have to involve anything expensive or overly indulgent. For example, it might simply involve making yourself a hot bubbly bath followed by putting your feet in a foot spa while reading a favourite book or an online blog among the fresh scent of a beautifully scented candle. As long as you recognise that your actions and feelings towards yourself are born from motivations that involve wanting to nurture yourself, then self-love is possible and it sometimes doesn't even cost a penny.

Although I am still developing my own ability to be more self-compassionate, as it is part of a positive lifelong journey with no single end point, I have continued to incorporate it into my everyday life. A key example of this in relation to food is how I now choose not to read or take nutrition labels of every packet of food I buy too seriously. I now only use ingredient labels to ensure that what I eat doesn't contain any animal products or unethically sourced ingredients, rather than trying to ensure that everything I eat is as 'clean' and healthy as possible.

The Calorie content of foods no longer matters to me, which is honestly one of the most liberating things I have ever experienced in terms of letting go of an unhealthy obsession with food and my body. Despite how I initially thought that nutrition labels were helping me to develop a better relationship with food, by making sure I was eating 'enough', this habit led to me spending lots of my time thinking about perfecting numbers rather than the many other beautiful and meaningful things food has to offer to my mind and body.

So what are some of the many other practical ways that you yourself can become more self-loving in a way that aligns with the Nourishing Routes philosophy and becoming a Compassioneer?

❋ Seek out what you love

What is it that make you feel energised and fully engaged in the moment? What activities make you feel authentically you? This doesn't have to be an amazing hobby requiring a great degree of talent or money, it could even involve colouring in (even outside the lines), baking a cake, or spending time at your favourite cafe with a close friend.

Whatever it is, identify it and pop it in your diary. Make room for it at least once a week and dedicate yourself to making it happen. Enjoy each moment of the activity if you can, and don't dwell on feeling guilty for putting aside that essay or exercise routine. You totally deserve it!

❋ Pinpoint what parts of yourself you feel grateful for

As low as our self-esteem can become, these feelings are in no way a reflection of reality. Every single one of us has something positive to offer the world, and this doesn't have to come in the form of looks, what we eat, or how much exercise we do.

To find what you can appreciate about yourself, find a time in the day or night to write a list every other day or once a week. This might seem difficult at first, but beginning with a small list of three things and working your way up from there at each 'self-appreciation' occasion should do the trick.

❋

It also helps to pretend you are writing the list from the perspective of another person who knows you well. You can include anything on your list, whether that be a characteristic (e.g. being empathetic, caring or determined), body part, an activity (e.g. volunteering, making time for friends and family), or even something you think you are good at (e.g. a particular sport or having a breadth of knowledge on a certain topic).

No matter how simple or complicated, there is something beautifully unique about everyone and yourself that is fully worth your appreciation.

❋ Donate something back

When becoming more self-loving, some of the essential ingredients in this process involve being more open to helping others. Also, a large part of our wellbeing is influenced by our sense of what we have contributed to the lives of others, and not just our own.

When we give we are more likely to experience satisfaction and greater admiration for ourselves, while feeling more energised to pursue the things we were made to do. Giving can be something so simple and can do wonders when it comes from the right place (e.g. wanting to help others for its own sake without expecting something in return). However, even if you give to others without expecting anything in return, there are still so many benefits you can experience.

Giving can be in the form of something small, such as a genuine smile to a stranger, donating clothes to a charity close to your heart, or giving some of your spare time to volunteer with an organisation or cause you believe in.

If you really want to go that extra mile, giving could also come in the form of raising money for a charity when getting sponsored for a fun run or other random challenge.

As a famous supermarket brand once told me, every little helps, and so does every little we can give in whatever form that may be.

❋

✳ Be kind to your body

While embarking on a new diet or fitness regimen might seem like a great health kick, getting into a routine of being punitive to our bodies and feeling guilty about not looking like a fitness model can take a huge negative toll on our self-esteem and ability to love ourselves. However, being loving towards ourselves requires us to love and be kind to our bodies – no matter what they look like.

Our bodies are the tools to do amazing things in the world, not just objects to get looks and 'likes' from others. Unfortunately, however, body shame is possibly one of the most debilitating types of thoughts we can have.

It might seem frustrating and uncomfortable at first, but try to set out a time each day, even for just one minute, to look at yourself or think about your whole body. Think about the real function of one specific body part and the important role it plays in not only keeping you alive, but also allowing you to carry out every day or extraordinary activities while enabling you to help others.

What would happen if those legs (the ones you might have often loathed and wanted to be slimmer) could no longer allow you to walk to work or to your friend's house? What about your arms, what if they could no longer give other people a hug? Even when looking at our 'extra' fat around our thighs and hips, this can be viewed as the protectors of our organs that also helps to keep us warm.

Each and every part of you is unique, and appreciating this in all forms is one of many routes to self-love.

✳ Love what you put on the inside

Being kind to your body can also come in the form of what you put into it. This doesn't mean following a rigid meal plan lacking in enjoyment. Where is the self-love in that?

Loving what we put on the inside involves taking care of what we eat in a way where we can be flexible with our eating choices, experience enjoyment, and eat what meets our physical, emotional and social needs while knowing that what we eat is in line with our values. We will also touch upon this in much more detail alongside practical aids in Part 2.

Obsessively counting Calories, depriving ourselves of food, feeling guilty about what we eat, eating or binge eating to fill in a void that would otherwise be filled with love will not do ourselves justice in our mission of learning how to nourish ourselves, our mind and body.

For me personally, following a lifestyle that involves eating tasty food that minimises cruelty to animals, where possible, while not any viewing any foods as distinctly 'good', 'bad' or off-limits, has allowed me to appreciate the important meaning of food and all the amazing things they can do for my body, mind and even the planet.

My moods are also much more stable, as are my energy levels. I very rarely experience the excruciating anxiety that used to plague my every waking minute and food definitely does not control my life or my happiness. The way you choose to eat that feels the best for you might be completely different to mine, but that is completely OK.

This book was created to help you develop your very own unique relationship with food rather than trying to adopt the one I have or anyone else's. I am just honestly so glad to have finally found the loving relationship I was born to have with food, and it feels as though the more I love it, the more it loves me back. I know you can absolutely 100% find yours too.

A Journey from Guilt to Pleasure

From a very young age many of us begin to learn that some of the most enjoyable things in life are the very things we 'should' be doing less of. For example, a young child might sneak a biscuit from the cupboard only to be told off by their parents and made to feel guilty for having disobeyed a rule. Similarly, we might learn that experiencing pain and suffering is something good as it is a sign that we have pushed ourselves to reach a certain goal. Or perhaps pain is associated with signs that a certain medication or treatment is helping to heal a wound or recovery from illness. However, is it really necessarily that these lessons should transfer into a longstanding belief that pushing ourselves to a painful limit is what we should all aim for in order to become a better person?

As our society has created even more negative associations with pleasure, some of us might have integrated the belief that enjoyable foods are unhealthy, 'naughty', 'unclean' and something we should feel guilty about when eating them. We might have also come to view that watching lengthy amounts of TV is unproductive and a risk to health, while relaxing and taking a break from work is lazy.

Of course, simply going through life seeking out immediate forms of pleasure is unlikely to lead to long lasting fulfilment or authentic happiness. However, happiness isn't born from the denial of pleasure in all its many forms. In fact, feelings of pleasure are an inevitable and important part of learning and the overall human experience. Yet, the way many of us experience pleasure involves an added ingredient of remorse, guilt and shame – even though in most circumstances there doesn't need to be any exchange of remorse to remedy what we have supposedly done 'wrong'.

If we learn to associate pleasure with doing wrong, pleasure can quite quickly turn into feeling guilty and ashamed. These might be similar feelings that a child might experience who has disobeyed their parents. By equating pleasurable experiences with feelings of doing something wrong, we can feel like pleasure is a sin that we need to take action against in order to redeem ourselves. Many of us might additionally feel as though pleasure is still something that needs to be earned. If we haven't done enough or the right thing at a particular time, we might not feel deserving enough to nurture and look after ourselves. As you can probably imagine, regular and excessive feelings of guilt can start to significantly disrupt our ability to experience the things in life that bring us joy and fulfilment. Unfortunately, continuing to make an association between pleasure and guilt throughout childhood and adulthood can lead to an ongoing need to gain external forms of approval in ways that might not necessarily be in line with a person's best interests, happiness and health.

This is not to say that feeling guilty after a pleasurable experience is innately wrong. Guilt is an evolved human mechanism that can help to protect the welfare of others while also preventing ourselves from being isolated from a group whose values we have violated. For example, there are many circumstances where guilt can prevent us from engaging in risky activities – such as cheating on a partner, stealing, or not helping someone in need. However, we may need to question when we start to feel guilty about pleasurable experiences that aren't really 'wrong' or going to lead to any considerable harm.

We need to consider how the amount of guilt we experience doesn't always reflect reality. For example, someone may feel just as guilty about eating a high fat/sugar/ Calorie food as they do when cheating on someone or choosing not to help someone whose health is in imminent danger. Similarly, it isn't right that we should experience guilt when taking time out for ourselves to have a bubbly hot bath or meeting up with a friend to go out for a tasty snack or meal.

We need to remember that a key part of happiness, health and becoming more compassionate to yourself is about accepting pleasure as something you are worthy of experiencing – no matter what. In fact, denying yourself pleasure can actually result in the very opposite of being able to avoid engaging in pleasurable activities. To support this idea, research shows that denying ourselves pleasure, whether that be drinking a glass of wine, eating a slice of cake, or resting instead of engaging in physical activity, makes these behaviours even more desirable and rewarding. We want more of what we can't have, so the saying goes, so denying ourselves of pleasure, or making pleasure conditional on whether we feel like we have earned it, can often lead to self-destructive actions that promote poor health – especially at times when we are feeling insecure, upset, anxious, stressed, or out of control.

By learning to accept that we can experience pleasure unconditionally, without negative judgement, this is a positive way of nurturing and growing our self-compassion. Alternatively, if we shy away from pleasure, then we may learn to seek out activities that aren't necessarily going to make us feel fulfilled or authentically happy and healthy. For example, while working overtime to complete an essay, skipping meals, or burn more Calories at the gym, we may miss out on quality time with family and friends or taking ourselves for a walk that would otherwise help us to replenish our sense of social connection and connection with nature.

What we can learn to do is engage in pleasurable behaviours while enjoying the moment and seeing yourself as fully worthy of it. There is also no need to think about what you need to do to 'compensate' that pleasure. Remember, time for pleasure can be a nourishing act in itself that allows time to re-energise, become more creative and think of new solutions that can enable us to embrace and overcome certain challenges in our lives.

I am not advocating that everyone should never eat healthily, or abstain from any form of exercise again. What I am proposing is that we become more relaxed about giving ourselves the breaks and enjoyment our bodies and minds thrive upon. After all, we can't thrive to the best of our abilities if our enthusiasm for life has been zapped away by ruminating about thoughts and feelings of guilt and shame. These negative feelings only lock us into a vicious circle where self-punishment becomes our prime way of motivating ourselves – which is very unlikely to be helpful at all when it comes to investing in our happiness and health in the long-run.

Although I have previously had experiences of having a very negative perception of pleasure, I am now able to take the time to incorporate this into my life in positive ways – without feeling unnecessarily guilty or ashamed. Hopefully the following statements and advice that I have successfully applied to my own relationship with food, body and pleasurable experiences will be able to help you too. All you need to do is simply say them to yourself in your own mind or out loud:

"Food is neither good, bad, clean, unclean, naughty, or nice. The enjoyment I get from food, even if it is processed, unnatural or something I view as 'unhealthy', is something to feel worthy of, even if I don't feel that I have done anything to 'earn' it."

"Eating and enjoying more than I planned or calculated in advance does not require me to compensate by skipping meals, going on a diet, following a self-punishing regimen or obsessively engaging in physical exercises that don't make me feel happy."

"It is OK to take a break from work to engage in an activity that I perceive as being unproductive – even if this means watching TV or carrying out a task without a specific goal or a desired outcome."

"Relaxing and carrying out an activity that makes me feel happy and energised is more beneficial to my wellbeing than embarking on a rigid exercise routine or an activity that currently feels like a chore or isn't adding any real value to my life."

"I will take time to nurture a hobby that I enjoy, even if this involves sedentary activities such as drawing, colouring and writing. I know that spending time to invest in these types of activities does not make me an unproductive or lazy person, and it is in fact helping me to personally develop and expand my creative potential."

"It is not wrong to eat out for a meal or visit a cafe for a drink more than twice in one day or week. I am deserving of enjoyment and pleasure no matter how frequent opportunities to experience it arise."

"Spending money on myself (e.g. self-care products, clothes, food) is not self-indulgent. Alternatively, spending money on myself in a way that is aimed at nurturing or nourishing my body is a symbol of being more self-compassionate."

⁂

"*Taking time to make a bubbly bath, foot spa and light a scented candle are not overly indulgent. They are compassionate ways to promote my vitality and overall wellbeing.*"

You can also feel free to add any more advice of your own that you would like to say to yourself.

A key take home message here is that you ARE worthy of pleasure, without guilt, shame or feelings of being 'unworthy'. You do not have to deny yourself pleasure due to feeling as though you haven't earned it. By accepting that pleasure is a natural part of life, and crucial in our overall health and happiness, this can create even more opportunities for strengthening our self-compassion.

Loving Yourself From Within

Us human beings are often pretty amazing at seeing the positive character-istics and qualities of other people. We notice their successes and achieve-ments, as well as the times when they have shown self-confidence and determination. We might also compliment others on what they are wear-ing, their hairstyle, or the way their house is decorated.

We are usually the first to compliment others and offer our support. We are attuned to helping others and inspiring them with words of wisdom and inspiration, and we try to uplift others in ways that will allow them to take action on their goals and live their dreams. By our own default human design, we are awesome mentors and best friends. That is, however, mainly when these tendencies are applied to other people rather than ourselves.

It seems that during our own creation, and through cultural changes throughout the centuries, we have become incapable of becoming our own personal mentors. Instead, we let our inner critics thrive like a vicious enemy, while the very idea of giving ourselves praise, encouragement or kindness feels surreal and unnatural – even embarrassing or shameful. Just as upsetting is how many of us are very used to beating ourselves up, push-ing ourselves over our limits, and ultimately becoming our own worst crit-ics – the annoying person lurking in our mind who always seems to have something bad to say or comment on how nothing we do is ever good or perfect enough.

In the face of life's challenges or opportunities we can often fall into the trap of telling ourselves that we are just not good enough. We haven't got the resources to embark on that new adventure, or the talent and compe-tencies to reach our life goals. Whatever we do have is deemed insufficient, especially when comparing it to what other people have or have achieved.

Instead of appreciating the gifts each of us already has, we yearn for what we haven't got and try to obtain those things through self-punishing regimens that hinder rather than nurture our mind and body.

Have you ever said to yourself:

"I just can't cope with my life or illness anymore."

or

"There is nothing about me that is good, worthy or useful. I am utterly useless, broken and imperfect."

Depending on persona and circumstances, you might have told yourself that recovery from a challenge such as stress, trauma, a mental illness or chronic condition just isn't possible. You don't or rarely believe in yourself or inner beauty. You might see the good, strength, potential and beauty in other people. But not yourself.

By doing this, we lose sight of our own self-worth and personal values while feeling more vulnerable and inclined to fall in line with other people's and society's expectations. Likewise, we can also miss out on opportunities to embark on our Nourishing Routes, as ignoring our personal strengths and putting ourselves down can lead us to say no to activities that are filled with enjoyment and excitement and that offer a pathway for self-discovery and personal growth. By not attending to opportune moments to give ourselves praise and encouragement, we make way for negative self-talk and pessimism. This only exacerbates our dwindling sense of self-esteem and energy to take action on the things that are valuably important to us.

With all of these factors to consider, how would they change if we began to view ourselves from the outside? Not in terms of how we look, but how we are viewed from the perspective of others.

Guaranteed, the individuals who know you well, whether they be friends or family members, could write an extensive essay on all the positive things about you. Perhaps more than you could ever fully realise yourself, but enough to believe that your existence and abilities are amazing. Regardless of the material resources you have, or what you look like, who you are right now is something to feel in awe about.

Apart from the teeny weeny chances of ever being born, you were placed in this world with a purpose and mission to make a positive difference. Your life matters. Hugely.

Underlying everyone is the same brain structure that has enabled us, over hundreds of thousands of years, to be creative, caring, compassionate and inquisitive creatures. We are also hardwired to be resilient to even the most stressful and traumatic of circumstances. These are just some of the amazing things that make us who we are, but rarely do we take the time to appreciate them or notice them when they are put into action. Note for example an occasion during the last several weeks when you have done any of the following:

* Being concerned about the welfare of another person or animal

* Offered your kind words or practical support to someone else in need

* Took an interest in something new or innovative

* Overcame a stressful event

* Endured pain or distress

* Expressed your creativity

* Encountered an overwhelming positive or even negative emotion

* Successfully completed a task or assignment at work or when studying

* Effectively solved a problem

You might not realise this yet, but most of you experience one or more of the above on a daily basis. Yet we rarely notice them or, even if we do, we take them for granted. Even if all of the things on this list mentioned don't seem innately positive things, they are some of the key activities that make us beautifully human and help us to grow into individuals who become even more determined to make a positive difference in the world. If only we could view ourselves from the outside, from another's perspective about ourselves, we would probably have a whole different outlook on who we are, what we are capable of, and just how vitally important our existence is in the way our world unites together and continues to flourish.

Anyone who truly knows you would be able to comment on more than one amazing aspect of yourself that you have not yet noticed or been open to fully realise.

The question is, though, are you ready to open your eyes to this new perspective? Are you ready to notice the everyday moments that make you beautiful – not in the way that you look, but by your human nature and unique character strengths?

If you would like to learn to develop this type of self-compassionate perspective, then the possibilities are endless in terms of how effective it can be to living life to the full and making a positive difference to the lives of others. Our world needs more individuals like you who are open to realising their potential, as well as helping to identify the potential in others. Ultimately this allows more action to be taken on the creative ideas that have the potential to be hugely transformational.

The reality that we have to face sooner or later is that we all have the strength and potential right now to realise the beauty inside of us all. Instead of that negative inner voice whispering or shouting that you cannot do something, or haven't got sufficient resources, make time for yourself at one point in the day where you can reflect on what amazing things you have achieved – no matter how small. This is in no way big headed or ego-centric. As we discussed before, it is part of being self-compassionate.

Things that you might appreciate about yourself could be as simple as giving someone a hug, offering words of kindness, making a choice to optimally nourish your body, completing a task at school, university or in the workplace, facing up to a personal dilemma, or getting though a stressful day or emotional event while taking time for self-care. When I first began to take time to realise some of these things for myself, I was genuinely surprised about just how many amazing things about ourselves that we do not fully notice, and how they fade into the background when turning up the volume of our own negative thoughts.

Even if we spend just two to five minutes actively taking note of how great we really are, the benefits to ourselves and others will outweigh any costs in terms of wasting time. We, just like what we might see in another person, are worth all the time in the world.

The stronger we are with ourselves, loving ourselves from within, the stronger we can be for others. Then we can really help to inspire others, act in line with our values rather than others' expectations, and allow the world to grow to become a more compassionate and amazing place to thrive in.

Don't Strive to Quantify Your Self-Worth – It Is Immeasurable

Have you ever noticed that nagging feeling telling you that you just aren't good enough yet? If only you could be skinnier, go to the gym more, run more miles, cut out more Calories, lose more weight, get higher grades, earn more money, look more beautiful, get more followers on Facebook, attain more likes on Instagram… If only we could get all or even a few of these things, then perhaps we could view ourselves as worthy and capable enough of happiness and reaching our full potential? At least that is what we have been led to believe…

Unfortunately, we live in a time where a lot of our human kind base their own self-worth on quantified terms – we strive for goals in an individualistic and self-destructive way. If we can achieve a better number, whether that be on a scale, payslip, academic certificate, or the number of compliments we receive about how we look, we use measurable parts of our lives to (de)value ourselves in relation to others.

Our sense of achievement is often based on negative self-comparisons and striving for tangible results, yet, at the same time, more and more studies are showing that true happiness and health are rarely based on any of these things. In fact, individuals with less materialistic wealth, or who don't quantify their self-worth, tend to fare better in terms of happiness and health. Why is it then that so many of us get out of the bed in the morning eager to improve ourselves in a numerical way when frequently doing so can potentially lead to negative outcomes associated with mood disorders such as depression, anxiety, and even eating disorders – all in a bid to become the best (numerical) version of ourselves?

The truth is that numbers and quantifying our abilities and self-worth are not really the things that matter when it boils down to authentic self-worth, happiness, health and reaching our full potential. It is also not in favour of being able to lead a compassionate lifestyle.

It is important to remember that the quantities that we base our self-worth on are not very precise measurements at all. Take for example your body weight and intake of Calories. We may try to get to an ideal figure on a scale, or consume an exact quantity of nutrients per day – doing so can lead to a sense of achievement for having gone about our day in the 'right' self-controlled way. But then again, when did there ever become an ideal weight or exact number of Calories to eat? As you are probably well aware of, everyone is unique in their own body composition and Calorie needs, while a specific weight or BMI can look very different in terms of body shape from person to person.

Realistically, our ideas of what the ideal is in terms of food intake and body shape, as we will discuss in Part 3 in much more detail, are very much influenced by the world around us – by what we see as being normal and acceptable in our own communities and cultures. Still, many of us can confess to striving to seek some ideal number, as if by magic it will make us a better person. Of course I am not advocating that everyone abandon any goals to maintain a healthy weight, carry out more physical activity, strive for a good career, or earn a sufficient amount of money. What I am questioning though is the value of aiming for a figure that may not be based on any hard evidence to show that obtaining it leads to greater happiness or health.

I am advocating that it is the quality rather than the quantity of our relationships, self-perceptions, values and actions that steer our happiness and health in a positive direction. For example, it might be the quality of how well-connected and valued we feel within our own families and communities. Yet, how many times does the average individual stop per day to evaluate how much time they spared to help another person, listen to the worries of a close friend, appreciate their own body, be more self-compassionate, act in line with their values, or view themselves as worthy and beautiful individuals?

To help explain why we strive for the more quantitative measures of self-worth, one answer may be that the very nature of quantitative information allows us to feel safe. Our grades, weight, exercise, Calories, work status and money can usually be assessed in a tangible way that can help us to feel safer and more effective as individuals. However, they are not really keeping us safe at all.

Take for example a situation whereby a young girl or boy begins to cope with an ongoing anxiety problem by weighing themselves, doing more exercise, or counting Calories obsessively. None of these activities is likely to help the real problem at hand, or lead to happiness and health in the long term. However, having a focus on a few measurable aspects of that person's life may at least help them to ignore other anxiety-provoking issues while being able to feel momentarily more competent and in control of their lives. The self-destructive actions that usually go along with assessing our self-worth on quantifiable terms may only temporarily fill a void that is not being filled elsewhere. Ironically, this can breed even more anxiety, insecurity, unhappiness and poor wellbeing.

This doesn't at all mean that we should abandon our quantifiable health goals or work commitments with the click of a finger. These can, when viewed and used in a compassionate way, play a positive role in our ambitions to become happier and healthier. However, it may provide us with more benefit if we can take a step back and take a perspective where we learn to appreciate other key areas of our lives and see our self-worth as something that does not have to be based on a unit of measurable value.

As a key example, we can simply acknowledge how listening intently to or supporting someone in need is something to feel proud of. We can also appreciate that nurturing our relationships with friends and family who care for us is vital, regardless of the fact that we can't simply measure our success. We don't have to have the best grades, achieve the highest fitness score, eat the fewest Calories, or have a certain number of followers and likes on our social media channels in order to attain or improve self-worth. In fact, taking the time to compassionately develop yourself more creatively in an activity you enjoy, while breaking away from work commitments, is a positive step forward in terms of self-development – even if these steps can't be measured by a specific number, grade or societal standard.

To reinstate the most important point of this chapter, I would like you to know that are a worthy individual by just being you, without needing to gauge yourself on something that is quantifiable. If you base your self-worth on more qualitative aspects of life, such as the nature and quality of our relationships and personal values, then your sense of self-worth can become more authentic and secure. So relish in your own uniqueness and measure your self-worth on your character strengths as opposed to trying to live up to some other ideal standard that can be numerically measured. Rest assured, the world we live in is much more beautiful than these false standards and, independent of numbers, each and every one of you reading this is good enough with an immeasurable amount of potential to fulfil your purpose and dreams.

"We can't expect life to treat us fairly when we treat ourselves like our own worst enemies"

Creating Peace – Not War – With Ourselves

One of the most important lessons I have ever learnt on my own journey of living more compassionately is to firstly make peace rather than war with ourselves. In real world terms, in order to begin to effectively tackle our personal demons and begin to flourish and thrive, we must firstly become more loving and compassionate with who we are right now. This is of course a continuing theme throughout this book, but I can't emphasise enough just how vitally important it is.

Unfortunately though, many of us, time and time again, end up at war rather than creating peace with ourselves. Yet, regardless of how easy or hard a battle may seem, we cannot even contemplate winning any battles in our lives or overcoming challenging circumstances if we cannot yet fully accept, nurture and love ourselves. To win just about any battle in life, or successfully engage in any form of personal growth, this requires the essential abundant army of physical and psychological nourishment. This ultimately involves doing whatever we can, as far as practically possible, to nourish our mind and body in ways that allow us to self-compassionately acknowledge our weaknesses but, more importantly, take notice of, use and develop our personal strengths.

Whatever the life challenge, whether that be physical or mental illness, conflict with others, relationship breakdown, or a specific trauma, all of these examples require us to harness our personal strengths. Not only can this help ourselves, but also others whom we meet or even with whom we share a similar challenge.

When we learn to fully nurture our mind and body we can venture on a path that inspires even more compassion for ourselves while also inspiring others to utilise and develop their own compassion. In this way our own

✻

acts of self-compassion create a positive domino effect, and I can think of many personal examples where I have seen individuals being more compassionate to themselves during life challenges, to then feel inspired to better understand and incorporate compassion within my own life.

So what does becoming more at peace with ourselves and harnessing our inner resources actually involve in practice?

In a simple list, it could mean:

* Taking time to just sit and be with yourself for a while – away from work or other obligations.

* Making a small list of things that you genuinely appreciate about yourself. For example, this can be in relation to your character, acts of kindness, an essential function of a particular body part or a creative talent.

* Making time to unleash your creativity, even if this simply means drawing, colouring in or writing a poem.

* Setting a goal to learn something new, such as trying out a new recipe, learning how to fix something, setting up an online blog, or trying your hand at a new form of art or craft. Achieving the ambition of learning something new can create a whole new sense of confidence and appreciation for the skills you have or have further developed.

* Beginning to read a book that you would love to read, just for relaxation and pleasure rather than as a way of trying to attain more knowledge about the world or a particular academic topic.

* Trying to make yourself one of the most nourishing meals or snacks that you truly enjoy. If doing this, also take time to enjoy the whole preparation, smell, sound, taste and satisfaction of food as well as the physical and psychological benefits of treating your body with the nourishment it deserves and thrives on.

✴ Aiming to engage in at least one activity that you genuinely love each day. All too often we are bombarded with tasks that don't align with our values or come from our own motives, so taking time to do something we love is really important for being able to reconnect with and be compassionate with ourselves.

✴ Making a small list of all the things in your current life that you appreciate as well as the people who provide you with unconditional love and care.

✴ Writing a letter to yourself that is written from the perspective of your own body in terms of how it feels about how you treat it. Within the same letter, go on to describe how this is the same body that genuinely loves you for who you are, regardless of what and how much you look like, eat, weigh or exercise.

Don't worry if you can't do all of the things on this list. Completing just one or a couple each week, if you set the intention of carrying them out with an open heart, is a great accomplishment.

Ultimately, the more we take time for unconditional self-love, rather than creating an inner battle with ourselves, the more we can step into our life challenges with the confidence and strength to pursue our goals and reach our full potential.

When we take time to regularly nurture ourselves from the inside out, in body and mind, we no longer have to feel like prisoners within our own bodies. Instead, we can stand up for ourselves and become our very own mighty hero.

Accepting Ourselves Now

We have already mentioned or suggested many times that real happiness and health lies within our own minds – not our physical bodies. Yet so many of us strive to attain the perfect body, diet or fitness regimen – or some other perfectionist standard that ultimately leads to beating ourselves up when things don't go exactly to plan or we can't be perfect or 'the best'. In a way, we have all been implicitly taught that there is no such thing as self-compassion, or time to find it. But since when did we come to believe that, as well as the lie that we aren't good enough the way we already are?

* When was the point that we thought, I will only start loving myself:

* When I look better, when I have lost 'x' amount of weight

* When I am a certain body size, when I buy nicer clothes

* When I am more physically attractive

* When I am able to complete a new fitness regime or push my body to the limit

* When I can get the highest grade on a piece of work

* When I attain a higher salary

* When I can climb another several steps on the career ladder

Surely by striving for and achieving these things, this will make us much happier and more content with our lives… right?

*

Well, maybe temporarily. But, in the long run, unlikely not.

Part of the problem lies at the beginning of each question. The word when. The word we really need to focus on is now, in order to realise that there are already so many beautiful and awe-inspiring things that we have got or have achieved in our lives today.

A huge reason for a greater focus on the 'when' rather than the 'now' is because we live in a world filled with expectation and commercial businesses that thrive off our insecurities. Profit simply would not be made if we were able to realise that we are good enough as we are now. And, even when we do achieve a particular standard, the bar usually gets raised even higher, so we never really reach where we want to be as the goal posts are forever changing.

The distance from where we are now to where we want to be becomes further and further away, especially when we continue to invest in meeting the expectations of other people and much of our manipulative society.

This is a truth that may seem hard to accept for many of us, but it is a very important truth that is essential to uncover for yourself. By uncovering this truth, this is one of the keys to realising how happiness and health lies not with striving for things outside of ourselves, but instead realising and being grateful for what we already have. This doesn't mean that we need to stop striving to move forward in our lives and meet certain goals and personal aspirations. Alternatively, it simply means that time spent investing in being able to accept love and be kind to ourselves right now is a fundamental step before trying to change what we can physically do or what we look like.

Yes, this does mean that it is more effective to love our bodies whatever size or fitness level they may be, rather than waiting to reach a certain physical shape or ability before we become willing to be kind and loving towards ourselves.

As many of you already know and understand, I am firmly passionate that everyone who has a compassionate heart for others is beautiful and worthy of happiness and health just as they are – no matter what they look like or weigh, how much or what they eat, or how much physical activity they accomplish. I also strongly believe that

beauty and success does not lie in our actual image, but only in the image we hold of ourselves.

With these passions and beliefs in mind I would like you to honestly question why many of us believe that a worthy, lovable and successful person should be defined by their physical and materialistic assets. Some of these assets may symbolise good physical health, but they are by no means the defining factors for a good quality of life filled with happiness and both physical and psychological health.

Perhaps if we spent more time investing in how we think about ourselves, rather than striving for becoming physically better or more superior to others, we would feel more content and have more spare time to spend on activities that really make us happy and healthy. For myself this involves spending time with those I love, caring for others, cooking, yoga, learning new things, living for the now, and feeling grateful for what I have already.

Even individuals with very few materialistic possessions can attain the greatest happiness and healthy simply by focussing on the sentimental value of what they already have. These things usually come in the form of social rather than physical assets, such as the positive relationships individuals hold with family and friends – not what they weigh, their career progression, or level of physical activity.

If we really want to create a happy, healthy and meaningful life for ourselves, one of the first steps involves choosing our behaviours with intention and because they fit in line with our inner values – not because we want to reach others' or society's expectations. This can translate into the act of loving for ourselves without fearing how others or society might negatively judge us, as well as acknowledging and eradicating any experiences of guilt in relation to not feeling good enough or perfect.

Acting out of love for ourselves rather than striving to meet the expectations of others might involve questioning whether we really want to eat well to nourish our mind and body so we can do awesome things in life, as compared to depriving ourselves of energy and enjoyable foods so that we can fit into a pair of skinny jeans, reach the 'perfect' number on the scale, or look great at a party.

Truth be told, the real person inside of ourselves – our compassionate self – probably couldn't care less about how much we weigh, unless this started to negatively impact our physical bodily functions. But our compassionate self genuinely does care about how strong, healthy and happy we feel, as well as how much genuine love we are able to give ourselves while being able to live life to the full and reach our full potential.

If we stay in a place of fear, by acting out of wanting to please others and deprive ourselves of the things we enjoy, then regardless of how society associates such behaviours with health and prosperity, this does not count as loving ourselves – no matter how physically attractive, fit, beautiful, rich or academically successful we become.

OK, so it may all seem simple to say, but you have probably already realised that acting in ways of self-love can be quite difficult – without feeling apprehensive, lazy or guilty about it at first. This is a completely natural response as most of us are told that we are not good enough as we are, so why should we accept ourselves? Of course this book was created and designed to help tackle these irrational fears, while making a big point of the huge fact that:

YOU ARE worthy of love and self-acceptance right now, and rest assured you are even more BEAUTIFUL and AMAZING than you think.

I know I may sound like I have repeated myself nearly a thousand times already, but I am so passionate about getting this message across. Even though I rarely promise anything, I do promise that you are totally worth loving now – not tomorrow, next week or in a year's time when you have reached another fear-based goal – just right now.

So what does accepting ourselves as we are mean in practice? Does this mean that we are totally free to engage in every indulgently excessive or addictive behaviour known to mankind? Well, to the second question, of course not.

In fact, the more we act out of love for ourselves, the less likely we are to become inclined to become obsessed with that next quick emotional fix, or become lazy, weak, incompetent, or obsessed by things such as dieting, rigid fitness routines or bingeing/purging on food.

Instead, acting out of love for ourselves means that we are more likely to become more conscious and aware of what our bodies and minds really require in order to feel nourished. If this means enjoying a delicious piece of cake, a glass of wine, packet of crisps, or your favourite ice cream, then so be it! These foods are not to be avoided or obsessed about to the point where we develop an unhealthy relationship with our whole food and body. But our body will often cry out for us to nourish it with home cooked meals prepared with fresh fruits and vegetables as well as vitality-boosting snacks and drinks. For me, this often involves my body asking me to nourish it with hearty bowls of fruity muesli soaked in creamy almond milk, mid-morning and afternoon snacks of date and nut bars, one-pot dinners crammed with roasted vegetables, bowls of pasta with homemade pesto, crusty toasted breads dipped in pots of hummus, glasses of brightly coloured smoothies, endless pots of hydrating Earl Grey tea and a packet – or two – of my favourite raw dark chocolate buttons. Whatever foods your body asks you for in order to feel nourished in mind and body, listen to, respect and fulfil those requests.

When we learn to self-love, we can recognise what our body is saying, so in the end we can find an optimally loving and nourishing balance rather than a vicious cycle of deprivation, depleted energy and self-destruction. This can involve the way we exercise too. For example, rather than pounding away obsessively on a treadmill, or hitting the weights at a gym, our body might ask us to take it on a relaxing walk in the park, do a very gentle yoga routine, or even take a whole day to sit down and do something creative – even if that means colouring in, preparing a meal, or journalling about things that we have experienced or feel grateful for.

Again, the magic key is about balance, and acting out of love for ourselves is a crucial step to creating this balance. By really nourishing ourselves in a way that promotes this balance, there is no reason to feel guilty for overindulging in your favourite foods, not engaging in enough physical activity, or not working hard enough on an assignment or within your job. At the end of the day, you have done what is essentially best for you.

By becoming more self-accepting and loving, we can learn to appreciate that our behaviours are not to be acted out for other people, or made too rigid so as to restrict us from living in the moment while acting in line with our values and intuition. Importantly, these make the journey to self-compassion such an enjoyable and liberating experience, and one that I hope you will experience throughout your own life.

✷

Compassioneer Activity: Morning Self-Love Ritual

The best time to place yourself in a positive mindset and allow yourself to be open to positive and endless possibilities is usually the morning – preferably before you do anything else or even check your email and social media accounts.

It is all too easy to wake up with a sense of urgency that various things need to be done. This can be really overwhelming, and before we know it we have already started to place these tasks, and the demands or expectations of others, over and above our own personal needs.

If this happens regularly, we may start to notice that our own energy becomes depleted, as there are few resources left that can adequately take care of our own selves.

There is absolutely nothing wrong with putting ourselves first. Without making ourselves a target of the compassion we want to develop and show, then we won't be able to show as much compassion for others or the planet. Ultimately, the quality of care and love we give ourselves is what is reflected outwards onto others. If we continue to not give our own happiness and health much time of day, then this will eventually become the reality of what we can give out.

To ensure that we can place ourselves in an optimal position to do the best we can do to help others, then we must take time for ourselves – ideally first thing in the morning.

For myself, stepping into a place of self-love in the morning was not on the menu for a significant number of years. I used to wake up extra early to check my emails, prepare work, finish assignments on time, rigidly plan what I would be eating that day, and try to feel good about myself through trying to meet the expectations of work and other people. It was uncommon for me to ever wake up with a sense that I would ensure that I was optimally nourished in both mind and body before stepping out of the door.

This led to me feeling drained and lacking in enthusiasm and confidence to follow my true life passion. Instead, I was caught up in a vicious cycle that just felt like the norm – a ritualistic routine that wasn't giving me any pleasure or sense of purpose. Each day was like going on the same journey, again and again. But I knew that journey wasn't really being followed with the aim of going anywhere important.

It took a long time before I could genuinely step into a place of wanting to put myself first and value the art of being able to love myself. With it though, life quickly turned towards an empowering direction where I could genuinely feel energised, passionate and ready to pursue my dreams with a deep understanding that anything was possible. Making time for self-love in the morning also enabled me to feel more able to give that same quality of love and care to others and the work that I accomplished. So, rather than becoming lazy or unproductive (as is the common myth with the idea of self-compassion), I became more productive and able to help others in a more empowering and inspiring way too.

But what does self-love look like in the morning?

Well, first of all, let's establish what it isn't. A morning routine of self-love does not include a sense of urgency to:

❋ Check and reply to all of your emails and social media

❋ Plan out the Calories and nutrients you will aim to consume for the day

❋ Exercise to the point of exhaustion in a way that is not enjoyable or makes you feel caught up in a rigid routine rather than exercising for pleasure

❋

✻ Make other individuals' breakfast while skipping or skimping on your own breakfast

✻ Think about all the things you need to do or accomplish in order to meet the expectations of others or a particular perfectionistic standard

✻ Ensure that you will achieve perfection in everything that you do

✻ Get up extra early so you don't feel lazy or guilty

To flip this negative perspective around, self-loving mornings can involve:

✻ Greeting yourself with self-respect and kindness when you wake up

✻ Saying thank you to yourself for waking up, and offering some words of positive encouragement for the day ahead

✻ Sitting still for a few minutes with your own positive thoughts, without negative judgement, allowing any feelings and thoughts you have to just be and then pass by

✻ Spending a few minutes stretching or doing a bit of gentle yoga

✻ Taking time to prepare a nourishing and enjoyable breakfast that will be satisfying and energising

✻ Going for a walk outside and appreciating the small details in things that you pass by, whether that be the leaves on the trees, the freshness of the morning air, or the mist of a new morning

✻ Spending time pampering your body, whether that involves slowly and carefully body brushing your skin, enjoying a shower, or soothing your skin with a moisturiser that feels and smells as lovely as you want to feel

✻ Saying to yourself that you will appreciate that you can't be perfect today, but that you will try your best in whatever you do

❋ Setting an intention to be a positive example to others by living in alignment with your own beliefs and not going out of your way to violate your own beliefs or meet other people's unrealistic expectations of you

❋ Making a pledge that, no matter what happens today, you will continue to appreciate, care for and love yourself. If what you aim for doesn't happen today, then there is always tomorrow or another day

A self-love activity I have found particularly helpful is mirror work. Mirror work is my first enjoyable and empowering task of the day, as it places me in a mindset that enables me to feel uplifted, energised and ready to be the best version of myself.

Mirror work, as the name suggests, involves a mirror, and standing in front of it (with or without clothes) and positively talking to the figure that is reflected back at you.

This may sound a little odd. We aren't exactly encouraged to talk to ourselves without being considered a little crazy. But, let me assure you now, talking to yourself in a positive way, as you might do a friend or family, is in no way crazy. In reality, it is one of the smartest things you can do in terms of being the best version of yourself.

If we can be our own positive mentor, can you imagine the possibilities of what this can help us to accomplish?

Mirror work doesn't have to involve repeating philosophically deep quotes to yourself. Of course this might be useful, but may not be practical or comfortable for everyone. Sometimes, all mirror work involves, apart from a mirror, is a simple sentence that resonates with you. This might be something along the lines of:

"I think you are a beautiful person with so much to offer the world. I give you permission to care for yourself and fully enjoy your day."

❋

"Today I will allow you to place you as a number one priority and ensure that you feel nourished in both mind and body."

or even more simply:

"I love you so much, and wish you all the best for today in everything you do."

"No matter how much you achieve or don't achieve, I will not judge you and I will still love you."

You can pretty much say anything to yourself. As long as there are no harsh words of criticism, or limiting conditions that you place on yourself, such as:

"I will only love you more or treat you when you accomplish x,y and z."

Mirror work and any morning self-love ritual you can think of are activities that don't come with any conditions. They are self-compassionate activities that are carried out mindfully, in your own time, without judgement.

The key aim of mirror work is to empower you to step into a loving relationship with yourself as soon as possible, so that day you can be optimally nourished in body and mind. This ultimately means that you will set yourself up for being the best version of you, living in alignment with your beliefs, and also being able to recognise when and how you can optimally care and show compassion to others.

Being Your Authentic Self

Have you ever found yourself immersed in social occasions when you begin to realise that you are not feeling or acting the way you normally do, and perhaps taking on a personality that, well, really just isn't you?

Perhaps you come away from most social occasions, whether they be parties, meetings, or one to one conversations, feeling psychologically or even physically drained. This might be especially so if you are with lots of people you have not met before, or if you are with other people you feel like you need to please or appear good in front of. For me, feeling drained in this way was a very common yet very unnecessary feature of my life. I would enter into conversations feeling too tense to speak in case I said something I shouldn't, agree with most of what other people were saying, and laugh along with things that were not very nice or in line with my values. I would even fear contradicting my teacher's opinions in college or university, even though I knew I had a very valid alternative opinion. I would also joke around and act as though I was really happy and loved my life when I was around others, when in truth I couldn't be feeling any more of the exact opposite.

The key issue I am talking about here is inauthenticity. Not being our authentic selves when we communicate with others can be our way of using a security blanket and not wanting to reveal any of our vulnerabilities or insecurities. Like any other human being, we want to be accepted, and for many of us that means going along with everything we feel is the norm or expected of us.

In a bid to win over the approval of another person or social group, we can begin to over-think our actions and what we say to the point where our true, authentic (and often much more naturally likeable) selves gets pushed to one side. We shut down, but open ourselves up to other people impinging their beliefs on us, or even walking all over us. Similarly, we might also alter the way we eat, exercise, dress and our overall physical appearance just to fit in with and please other people.

For example, I literally spent over a decade trying to straighten the heck out my hair just to avoid being recognised as 'the girl with curly frizzy hair'. I felt like curly hair was completely unacceptable to have in comparisons to everyone's luscious straight locks. Even though I now know that this belief is completely false, and I actually now love my hair (as tangly and as frizzy as it may be), there was once a time where there would be nothing you could say or do to prevent me from straightening or styling my hair to make it look anything but curly.

But rather than making me feel more comfortable and secure, I felt that doing this was hiding the real me, and that if someone did so happen to throw water over me and unveil my tangly locks, then they would no longer like me, speak to me or accept me as part of their peer group.

Another key point I would like to highlight is the detrimental impact that not being our authentic selves can have on us, i.e. the person we really are including all of our quirks, uniqueness, strange habits. The physical and mental energy it takes to be someone we are not, while trying to be someone we feel others want us to appear like, creates a similar effect to feeling exhausted after several hours exercising or performing on stage. It creates wear and tear on both our physical and psychological systems, leading to stress, anxiety and even depression.

But such outcomes are completely unnecessary. We weren't born to spend most of our lives as actors or self-disappearing magicians. You, like me, were born to be yourself, and thankfully no one in the whole universe is better suited to that role than you are.

You may be thinking that it is OK once in a while to act in a way that you don't normally do, such as at a business meeting or formal party. You may be right there, as there are many different social and professional situations that require us to wear different hats.

However, the problems arise when we take on board the responsibility of trying to steer too far away from our authentic selves while wearing too many hats (or in my case, straight hair styles) continually and unnecessarily.

When we are not being our authentic selves we are not able to portray our natural quirks and the things we our most passionate about. In our minds we might think it is best to try and 'go along' with the rest of a groups' beliefs and social norms, rather than risk having our natural quirks and personalities exposed and becoming vulnerable to criticism.

If we do this, each social situation brings a whole new bunch of people, and a whole new set of potential threats and overwhelming challenges. Our learned defence mechanism is to shut down our real personalities in order to ensure that we fit in with the crowd and can be accepted.

From an evolutionary perspective, there may be some truth in human beings having a natural tendency to not be our authentic selves around others, which perhaps evolved from the survival benefit of being able to adapt to a diverse variety of social settings and groups so that we could be accepted and given permission to share valuable life resources. However, in a modern world where there are many opportunities to be different people in both online and offline settings, there is unlikely to be any real survival benefit in modern times if not being our authentic selves eventually begins to have a detrimental impact on our overall happiness and wellbeing. We can't be everyone, or a person who appeals to and pleases everyone, all at once.

If we can turn this situation on its head, it is alternatively much more beneficial for us to become more authentic and confident with being our own selves rather than trying to transform into multiple identities. Not only does this enhance social credibility, as individuals are more likely to sense that they can trust you, but also they feel more open and accepting of who you are as a person. Being your true self additionally attracts people to you who share the same positive energies, values or similar perspectives on life.

Placing our authentic selves out into the world says a lot about who we are as individuals. It tells others that we are confident, not afraid to have an opinion, and that we might also possess knowledge and resources that they can benefit from too. Fitting in isn't a bad thing, but being your own person who appears unique and interesting to others does have its own vast set of benefits.

Although it isn't wise to advise being the exact same in every single situation, it would be much more beneficial for us to find out who we are as individuals so that we can utilise our true characteristics and quirks according to the situation at hand.

Even if we find that you have many different personality characteristics or mood states within different situations, as long as these states are genuine to your authentic nature and make you feel energised when you personify them, then there really is nothing wrong with fully expressing them.

A final crucial point to conclude upon is with my advice to not be afraid to show your true colours in life. No one will know the unique beauty of your own inspiring rainbow like you do, unless you express it willingly and openly. Express your vibrancy in all its forms, and feel free to live through the charismatic personalities and physical characteristics you were blessed with.

Bedazzling Yourself

Why is it that sometimes we make ourselves dress or act in certain ways, even when we know that the main reason is to please or meet the expectations of another person or society in general? This question very much relates to our topic about being our authentic selves, but you may still be trying to contemplate how you can get out of a cycle of trying to meet other people's expectations rather than your own.

Perhaps you currently experience days when you are about to dress for an outing with friends, family or even a date, but turn the occasion into an activity that primarily involves assessing how others will perceive you as a result of what you wear and your actions.

In other words, you continue to place living up to certain norms or pleasing other people before pleasing yourself and living according to your own values, true personality and what you really like.

As we have recently discussed, trying to do this can be a huge physical and psychological energy drain, especially when we have to repeatedly appear like somebody we know we really aren't.

This was definitely the case for me even just a couple of years ago. I would spend hours or even days worrying about how I would be perceived by others when going out. I would try to prepare as much as I could in advance in order to reduce my overwhelming fear that I wouldn't be accepted for who I was. For years this prevented me from wearing what I wanted to, speaking about what I was passionate about, and even leaving the house. I also believe that it contributed to me venturing down a dark path where what I ate and weighed on a scale became my main obsession. My life felt completely and utterly false, and the only thing I ever gained from this way of living (if you could call it that) was ill health, feeling depressed and a sense that I was living a lie.

This is certainly not the case anymore, as living more compassionately has helped me to become more fully open to living as my authentic self. I would also like you to know that you too can do this while placing yourself back in alignment with being able to become and live according to who you really are. The phrase I use for being able to live more compassionately in a way that allows you to become your authentic self, while not always striving to meet the expectations of others, is called 'be-dazzling yourself'.

But what does the phrase 'be-dazzling yourself' even mean? Perhaps it sounds like a made up word, right?

Well, perhaps the made up part is true, but I think that 'be-dazzling yourself' sounds quite fitting for a term that, for me, means being able to dress, act and live in ways that allow you to take pride in your authentic self.

'Be-dazzling yourself' places YOU back in alignment with YOU.

'Be-dazzling yourself' might involve standing in front of a mirror and noticing that you are happy for just being you, or the natural joy and excitement of being able to wake up and wear what you want to wear – not because it is what might please others, but because you genuinely love it or it suits your mood and personality.

Unlike what some people may initially think, 'be-dazzling yourself' is not selfish or indulgent in any way (not that there is anything wrong with indulgence anyway). 'Be-dazzling yourself' is an essential element of self-compassion, as it places your health and happiness back on the priority list – exactly to a position where it belongs and deserves to be.

When you 'be-dazzle yourself', you are more likely to 'be' yourself – living in alignment with your authentic self. When you are also more accepting of your ability and need to 'be-dazzle yourself', it can also boost your confidence and even make you more attractive to others who pick up on your radiating positive energy.

What I have learnt from being able to 'be-dazzle' myself is that my physical and psychological energy levels grow more and more throughout the day, rather than depleted. I genuinely think that this has made me more positive to be around, without me acting like someone I am not, while also attracting other more positively minded individuals into my life. 'Be-dazzling' myself has created a perfect recipe for great conversation, meeting new people and sustaining positive relationships. In other words, I believe that 'be-dazzling beings' attract other 'be-dazzling beings', and so the positive cycle continues.

The key message in this chapter is to not be afraid of 'be-dazzling yourself' by being more open to becoming the real you. That person is within you somewhere, just ready and waiting to be beautifully expressed in a way that fills you with joy and radiating energy.

Just like you were born to live compassionately, you were born with the ability to 'be-dazzle yourself'. Investing time in making that a reality is not just a potential opportunity or a short lived goal – it is a necessity.

In line with the whole concept of Nourishing Routes, leading a more compassionate lifestyle, especially when this involves being more self-compassionate, can allow you to 'be-dazzle yourself' in ways that can only lead you to greater happiness and health. I therefore challenge you, the next morning you wake up, to think of three ways that you can 'be-dazzle yourself' that day. Whether that be dressing in the way you want, telling someone about something you are passionate about despite your fear of their judgement, or showing your true personality to others who you might not normally. Who knows, you might even inspire others to try the same, as well as eventually become the full-time 'be-dazzling being' you were born to be.

"When you go through life tuning your own strings and creating your own rhythm, you will end up dancing to a unique beat and soulful song that can only be described as a genuine masterpiece"

Unleashing Your Creative Potential

Part of what makes us beautifully human is our ability to be creative. Our minds just haven't evolved to think rigidly or work in ways that involve carrying out repetitive tasks – especially when they are demanded by others rather than instigated from within ourselves. Yet, very few of us actually spend time on ourselves to enable our creative potential to flourish and thrive.

Just like the many positive outcomes and innovations that arise from being creative, the actual definition of creativity can be described in various ways. However, there is actually no concrete definition of creativity. What most experts agree on, though, is that creativity involves being able to express ourselves, 'think outside the box', solve problems with new solutions, or develop ideas that lead to novel ways of thinking and feeling.

Think back to a time when you felt free to express your true creativity. Perhaps you were feeling lustful at all the amazing paints, colouring pencils, beautiful pens or inspiring journals in your favourite stationery or art shop. Sometimes you might have even found that your most creative time points occur in the shower, or when you go out for a walk on a sunny day while coming up with a new innovative idea. Without a pen and paper to hand, you may feel that this is a bit of an inopportune time to think of an innovative idea, but such moments go to show how creativity is best instilled when we have some quiet moments to ourselves – away from our most prominent worries and the obligations that others or society places over us. The freedom of being alone, often when engaging in some form of self-nurturing activity, allows the sparks of creativity to burst into full flame.

You might have been feeling in the moment with expressing your creativity while colouring in a picture, writing about your personal thoughts, getting lost in the touchy feely world of play-dough, or really just about anything that made you feel that you could unleash your inner thoughts, emotions and creative urges.

But how long ago was it though when you felt creatively free, without wondering whether there were better or more productive activities for you to be spending your limited time on? No matter how short or long ago that time was, the point I want to help you realise is that it is absolutely essential for us to create opportunities for creativity and self-expression.

Creativity is one of our biggest gifts, and to not allow our creative selves to flourish and thrive would be like not going to the toilet for a whole week – can you imagine the discomfort? However, we have been taught to think and act in a way that has allowed us to ignore and bypass our creative urges. Profit making societies don't seem to think that expressing creativity without a financially beneficial end goal is a worthy investment. But we really need to turn that unhealthy norm on its head for the sake of our happiness and health as well as the future wellbeing of our whole planet.

We are, by nature, novelty and inspiration seekers, with our thoughts and emotions to express in many creative shapes and forms.

Being creative has allowed us to expand our intelligence and develop new technologies over thousands of years. But, perhaps most crucially of all, creativity is one of the number one elements of our lifestyle that allows us to experience optimal health and happiness.

To contradict the typical stereotype, creativity doesn't have to involve becoming an eccentric artist, a prolific writer, an emotive poet, a professional dancer, or a famous musician. Creativity involves all sorts of different activities, no matter what type of hat you are wearing – so don't go out and buy a French beret just yet...

When we take time to be creative, we often enter a state of 'flow', which simply involves being fully engaged and feeling 'at one' during a particular task. Time might seem to float by, and the creative task itself might have the effect of alleviating any negative thoughts, feelings and emotions.

Creativity can also lead to mindfulness, where we feel connected to the present moment rather than worrying and ruminating about the past or the future. Similar to creativity, individuals who are more mindful have been repeatedly shown to experience significant benefits to their happiness and health, especially in terms of their sense of self-compassion, gratitude and life fulfilment. They are also at a significantly reduced risk of anxiety and depression.

Interestingly, both mindful and creative individuals tend to be more compassionate. This is possibly due to how creative and mindful individuals are more likely to invest time into themselves, reflect on the impact of their behaviour and give themselves permission to be creative and make time to look after their own and others' welfare.

What the above information really means is that unleashing your creative potential can have unlimited benefits, and can arise in multiple forms, whether that be colouring in a picture, completing a puzzle, writing a blog, drawing a picture, taking up a new hobby, playing an instrument, or just about anything! You also don't need to be an expert in anything, as even complete novices at a particular activity have a key to unlock their creative potential. The key thing that matters is enjoyment, and that the activity you do feels satisfying and in line with your own values rather than other people's expectations or an unrealistic goal of being perfect.

Even if you don't feel completely overjoyed when engaged in a creative activity, the real satisfaction can come afterwards, where the resulting piece of work leads to feelings of accomplishment and positive self-esteem. Also, expressing our emotions and thoughts through things we create can be a powerful tool that unburdens us and allows our mind to become free to think about our stresses and anxieties from a whole new positive perspective.

As any psychologist will tell you, activities that enable us to experience a sense of achievement and purpose, while also helping to become more resilient to stress and anxiety, can be alike to a wonder-drug in terms of our long-term health and happiness. Countless studies are now showing that it really does matter about how much quality time we can spend being creative. Creative expression can also help individuals to overcome trauma or

✳
155

poor mental health, as it can help to retrain the brain and reframe their perspective to view challenges as opportunities for personal growth. Perhaps even more interestingly, unlike any miraculous drug or superfood, most creative activities won't cost you the Earth...

But how can we actually unleash our creativity?

The first important thing is about providing permission for yourself. Many of us feel guilty for spending time on things that we think won't lead to a particular outcome, especially if it is not related to their work, financial profit or something they need to do to please another person. For some reason, taking time out for ourselves can seem foreign, especially when we are so used to being constantly on the go and trying to complete a routine set of tasks.

However, let me reinstate that you DO deserve to take time for creativity, no matter how hectic your schedule might feel or appear. In fact, creativity is essential to your everyday functioning, and those who spend more time being creative also tend to spend more time being productive both within and outside of work. I can guarantee you that unlocking your creative potential is not a waste of your or anyone else's time. It is a worthy investment with a wealth of positive outcomes.

Compassioneer Activity: Compassionate Creative Expression

The next key step is to think about a creative activity that you would genuinely enjoy engaging in. Remember, you don't have to be an expert or even good to start – simply willing to learn and see what happens. There are so many creativity activities you could choose from to suit your own mood, lifestyle and budget, so even the act of choosing something might be creative in itself. This endless list could involve:

* Colouring in a picture

* Writing your thoughts and feelings in a journal

* Playing a game you enjoy, even if it involves setting up your computer or a Playstation

* Writing a poem, story or a letter to someone you care about

* Arranging plants in the garden

* Designing a vision board of how you would like your room, website or even future life to look like

* Paint a collage using your favourite colours and anything that makes you feel positively energised

* Invest in a pretty journal and write your thoughts in it each morning or evening

* Think about and create new recipes of your own that will allow you to enjoy food and nourish your mind and body

❈ When sitting down to eat a meal, arrange the food on your plate so that it looks vibrant, colourful and aesthetically pleasing

❈ Start reorganising or redesigning your bedroom

❈ Clear out your wardrobes and cupboards to help clear clutter and revitalise your mind

❈ Buy some pre-made craft projects to make something such as a cross stitch pattern

❈ Go to the library or a book store and pick a new form of craft for you to take time to learn

The list could go on, but ideally just pick one to focus on at first.

Now that you have chosen an activity, arrange a date and time at least once a week where you can spend at least an hour or couple of hours engaging in your activity of choice. It might be early in the morning, mid-morning, afternoon or even at night. The time doesn't necessarily matter, but what does is that the time you choose is a time you can schedule into your diary so that you can completely dedicate to yourself to your creative task. If you can, try to ensure that the place where you will carry out this activity is somewhere calm where you feel that you can relax and let your mind wander freely away from distractions.

Some everyday activities can even be tailored to have their own creative twist. For example, instead of reading a story from a book to your children, you could try making one up of your own to tell. Preparing food could also involve writing a list of your favourite ingredients, or what is currently in the fridge/store cupboard, and then trying to make a meal out of it without a pre-made recipe. The way that you arrange food on your plate or set the table in the way you like can also be a very creative activity, as well as allowing you to be mindful and appreciative of how your food looks, smells and tastes.

❈

Another step I have found helpful when aiming to express creativity is to make a log of your progress and feelings. For example, after a creative task, making a note of how you felt before, during and after can help you to notice how useful the activity is in terms of your happiness and wellbeing, as well as deciding whether it is worth continuing or choosing a different creative activity to try.

Taking pictures of what you have created and sharing them, or writing about what you have created, can additionally help you to gain a sense of achievement, fulfilment and positive feedback from your work. From doing this it is likely that your perspective and creative direction will change as time goes on and you become ever more competent and aware of your unique creative style and personal preferences.

The key take-home message here comes back to enjoyment and the compassion needed to know that you deserve to take time out for creative expression. Not only is it in our genetic makeup to do this, but it is an essential element of your Nourishing Routes to leading a more compassionate lifestyle.

Time to Date Yourself?

When we enter into any relationship we also enter into a relationship with ourselves. Whether that relationship be with a friend or a loving partner, getting to know someone will usually mean getting to know more about ourselves.

But what if we started by taking time to date and develop a better relationship with ourselves before entering into one with another person?

For many of us, entering into a relationship can be quite a scary prospect, as it involves revealing part of our authentic selves. The parts of us we are sometimes used to hiding away through fear of being negatively judged.

Even though some individuals might appear confident in a relationship, the real truth lies in how underlying this confidence are insecurities being masked by a false smile, thick makeup, or an overly bubbly and outgoing persona.

Unfortunately we still live in a world where not everyone feels happy or secure in who they currently are, and hides their authentic selves even in their relationships with others through fear that they will be negatively judged – just for being natural.

But when individuals do this, potential friends or partners can usually sense that you are not yet ready to enter into a relationship with them. In order for relationships to flourish and thrive, individuals need to firstly love themselves in mind and body.

If you are not ready to accept yourself and love who you are right now, relationships can quickly enter a place of fear and insecurity.

❖

If we step into any relationship with a motive of not wanting to reveal our true selves this can inevitably lead to feeling uncomfortable, anxious, and emotionally drained. As we discussed in the chapter about being our authentic selves, it is definitely not an easy activity to continue acting like someone we know we are not.

Such ways of acting can also leave our current or potential friends and partners feeling as though they do not have a strong connection with us, as they can't seem to break through our hard-core barriers no matter how they try. Instead, they might go along with your act, but only for so long until cracks in the relationship begin to show – before they rapidly crumble and leave us feeling even worse about ourselves.

Strong relationships are based on trust, mutual connection and, at times, being honest about and sharing our deepest fears and insecurities. Although we might view doing this as a sign of weakness, they are more likely to be a sign of self-love and openness to accept and talk about our natural flaws that simply make us all human.

To restate the obvious, to really experience the true beauty of a compassionate relationship we must firstly start to work on the one we already have, or don't have, with ourselves.

It might sound a little 'cheesy', but love really does originate and emanate from the inside, and there is little point in trying to gain validation and love from another person if you cannot already provide it to yourself.

It's true that being in a relationship can help us to develop that all important sense of self-compassion, but to find it out by ourselves makes for an even stronger outcome.

These concepts can apply whether you are single, dating or already in a relationship, as there is unlikely to be a time when it is not a useful activity to work on our own ability to show self-compassion. The benefits will almost always show on the outside too, and signal to others that we are ready to enter into a new or even deeper relationship with them. Not only that, but we are also more likely to attract more compatible individuals to us who share our deeper values.

So how can we begin to work on our own self-love in an action-focussed way? Well, this is where the idea of dating yourself comes into play.

Don't worry, I am not advocating that you try to hug or hold hands with yourself. Instead, I am strongly suggesting the benefits of embracing the idea of taking time out to nurture, trust and love yourself in more ways than you can currently imagine. When we date ourselves, this simply involves spending time just for us, so we can learn more about who we really are, while becoming more confident about expressing our authentic selves to others.

Dating yourself can come in all sorts of forms, and can include:

❋ Buying yourself your favourite flowers, snack or chocolates

❋ Taking time out to go on a nature or woodland walk

❋ Treating yourself to your favourite home-cooked nourishing meal

❋ Going out for dinner or a tea/coffee by yourself

❋ Watching a movie on your own at the cinema you have been wanting to see

❋ Going to an activity class that you genuinely enjoy, such as yoga, crafts, or a meditation class

❋ Clearing out your bedroom/home and making a loving atmosphere (e.g. using softly lit candles and soft pillows)

❋ Relaxing in a hot bath with some relaxing music or a good book

❋ Lounging in a cafe all afternoon and buying your favourite tea, cake or coffee

❋ Taking some annual leave from work to visit a place of interest

❋ Booking a mini break to explore a city you love or have never been to before

There are many, many more that I could list and you could think of, but the most important thing in all of these activities is that you do them alone and with an acceptance that you FULLY DESERVE to take time out for them.

I can assure you there is no better time wasted than to take time looking after yourself.

There is absolutely no need to feel guilty for indulging in self-love activities, as the many benefits are certainly much greater than any negatives, including reduced time spent tied up with other work or family obligations.

In fact, your work and family will probably benefit too from you becoming a person who is better able to love themselves in a way that makes them more energised, productive, kind and fun to be with.

Ultimately, dating ourselves can accomplish absolute wonders in terms of our relationships in all areas of our lives, whether that be with other people or even our own food, body and the planet.

As well as being able to live in love and peace with ourselves, we open a universe of opportunities to step into authentic relationships with others that are no longer filled with anxiety, insecurity and fear.

Instead of feeling lost in an emotionless dark hole, dating ourselves can allow relationships to become a playground of exploration, adventure and sharing emotional experiences, while bringing harmony and wonder into our own and others' lives.

If you create loving time for you, by dating yourself, then you really do have all the time in the world to give love and be loved.

Compassioneer Activity: Embracing Compliments

All too often we go about our lives giving other people compliments. Yet many of us still feel uncomfortable about accepting other people's kind or supportive words about us. By doing this we end up reinforcing the distorted idea that we are not worthy individuals – not worthy of our own love and kindness, let along anybody else's. In order to fully embrace the idea of being more self-compassionate, though, we need to learn to fully accept, appreciate and harness other people's kind words and compliments about ourselves.

The following activity has been designed for you to do exactly that. All it simply requires is:

❀ Making a mental or physical note of everything that has been positively said about us or given to us on a given day. This can even include seemingly very insignificant or small things, such as someone appreciating what you are wearing, or even saying thank you for something that you have done for them.

❀ If someone does give you a compliment or says something that recognises something positive you have done for them, don't brush it off or follow it with your own negative words. This not only devalues what they have said, but it also reinforced the false idea that you aren't worth others' or your own appreciation.

❀ At times where you are given a compliment, make a note of what was said about and how it made you feel. Did it feel uncomfortable, embarrassing, exciting? Even if you didn't experience anything positive from a compliment, take time to ask yourself why that might be and how you can be open to accepting a compliment next time.

❀

❋ At the end of each day, reflect on what you experienced – even if you only gained one compliment. This can again involve noting what was said and how it made you feel, without dwelling on any negatives.

❋ For each compliment that you take note of and remember, say to yourself: *"I deserve this appreciation. Even if I don't realise my own beauty and worth just yet, I will take this compliment or signal of appreciation with gratitude and my full acceptance."*

I can guarantee that you will be able to take note of and remember at least one occasion where someone said something nice to you or about you – unless you did not venture outside and stayed away from all forms of social media and contact...

The above activity really helped me to reframe my negative mindset into a positive one, while realising that there were many great things about myself that I often didn't notice or deliberately chose to ignore due to feeling unworthy of receiving them. It was also a fundamental step in realising that it was OK to acknowledge and accept the positive attributes about myself without feeling self-centred, as well as enabling me to integrate these positive attributes into my own compassionate self-awareness about who I am rather than who I 'should' be. Ultimately, this activity can act as a firm stepping stone on your own Nourishing Routes to living more compassionately and becoming a Compassioneer.

Living Life in the Flow Lane

When we create structure and routine in our lives, whether that be a certain work activity, creative hobby, fitness regimen, or food plan, it can help us to reach our goals and gain a sense of effectiveness in what we do. It can also feel like a safe haven when we regularly pursue activities where we feel in control and can keep track of our progress. However, when our lives become so revolved around ensuring that we stick at these routines, it can distract us from being able to engage with our intuition or being able to enjoy life and seek out new opportunities.

Many of us, including myself, have had experiences of constantly striving to find more and more things to add to our daily routines. Spare time soon becomes extra time spent at the gym, looking after someone, starting another piece of work or assignment, tidying up, or focussing on what we eat. Even a hobby we once loved can soon become a chore, or at least something we go about in a mindless way, because we are on auto pilot and feel an urge to simply tick it off our 'to do' list. For example, even a relaxing hot bath may come to seem like a necessary activity that needs to be 'ticked off' in order for you to feel accomplished for the day. The idea of following a routine doesn't initially sound like a bad thing, but many of us will start to notice problems if we begin to fear what will happen if we don't meet the high standards we have set ourselves in our everyday routines.

Take another example, that of exercise. We might have successfully added a number of work or family-related activities into our week, but when realising that we can't make the morning walk, yoga routine, or lunch time meal time we always do, this can bring a sense of unknowing, fear and anxiety. This is a natural experience since our brain is very good at making us feel at ease with familiar activities, but quite distressed at the idea of change and encountering something new. However, unlike many thousands of years ago, sticking by our routines is no longer necessary for survival in a modern age. Also, is sticking to our rigid routines really the best way to foster more self-compassion if we excessively worry, negatively judge ourselves or feel guilty and incompetent if we are unable to successfully pursue our usual routines?

By choosing to stick with our routines, whatever the weather, we tune out from our intuition, instead feeling safe to savour the familiar. We might choose to pursue the routine activity over the opportunity to meet a friend, or engage in a completely different activity, which could have otherwise led to new opportunities that allowed you to feel happier and more fulfilled.

I can count many, many times where I have turned down social opportunities just so that I could feel 'safe' by getting up extra early to prepare breakfast, eating a snack at a certain time, taking a shower, completing assignments and research outside of work or going out for a walk for a set amount of time on the same route. They might have helped me to feel safe, but they didn't help me feel free to be me, or spontaneous.

Regardless of the positive feelings that come when we can 'tick off' our completed routine activities, I can't help but think what other people and activities would now be in my life if I hadn't turned down those opportunities to deviate from my pre-planned everyday structure.

But why do we continue to stay in our safe routines without stepping into a flow lane where we can appreciate the natural spontaneity and excitement of life? To partly answer this question, many of us live in a society that promotes constant striving to make ourselves a better person, usually in a way that involves asking people to add more and more into their day. However, what we rarely get asked, or have a chance to think about doing, is to take away something from our daily routine. It may sound counterintuitive to your level of productivity, but asking yourself what you could do without today isn't something to feel incompetent, guilty or lazy about. In reality, it is something to feel proud of, since it can take great courage to break free from the safety of norms and structures in order to live life in the flow lane.

To live life more in the flow and become more mindful of the spontaneous opportunities that come our way, a first step towards this goal can involve taking something away from your daily routine rather than adding something in. This change doesn't have to be forever, but allowing yourself to not have to go for that run, or eat a certain type of meal for a day, not answer emails away from the workplace isn't going to do any great deal of harm in the long term. Alternatively, it can give us the essential time and space to think, reflect and be compassionate to ourselves. We can then 'go with the flow' and be led to engage in something different that might give us that 'jump start' out of our usual auto pilot mode. Because the brain is no longer expecting the expected, we can better engage with what is going on around us, and feel even more switched on to the positive opportunities that may head our way.

Living life in the flow is not necessarily the complete opposite of having structure and routine un your life. Living life in the flow is about being more mindful and open to the world around us, rather than falling into the trap of overly structured, rigid and ordered thinking that usually happens on auto pilot. Living life in the flow lane is also about learning to love and trust yourself while placing confidence in the idea that the world won't fall to pieces when you take one or even a few structured activities out of your usual routine.

The world comprises thousands upon thousands of opportunities that are just waiting for you to mindfully observe and take action on them. Ultimately, by choosing to start living life in the flow lane, rather than saying no to unexpected opportunities, we can develop a more enriched life that allows us to trust ourselves, develop new skills, help others, live life to the full and ultimately reach our full potential so we can flourish and thrive.

"If you feel like you are a mis-shaped jigsaw piece that sits uncomfortably in a foreign puzzle, break free by finding or creating your very own jigsaw puzzle where you fit into perfectly"

Applying Compassion to Our Work and Relationships

As I mentioned in the beginning of this book, becoming more self-compassionate allows us to release more self-compassion to others and into the world. It is also important to recognise that showing compassion is not only vital in relation to how we develop personally, but also in other areas of life such as our careers and the loving relationships we wish to develop. This isn't just my opinion, but something that I have avidly researched and experienced in my own life.

Despite what we may currently think or believe, pushing ourselves excessively, trying to live up to others' expectations or putting other people's needs before our own in either our work, physical activity or the relationships we experience isn't a positive route to happiness or health – for any party involved...

The key message in this chapter involves exploring how being able to develop compassion for ourselves and others allows us to become more successful at flourishing in our careers, engaging in pleasurable movement and developing long-lasting positive relationships with those we love and care about.

Applying compassion to workplaces

Being part of a culture where there are so many organisations and individuals who spend overtime at work, and experience many competing demands in their life that lead to work-related stress, anxiety and other mental health problems, it can be difficult to apply the ethos of living more compassionately. This can be especially so if we are trying to practically apply the concept of compassionate living within the workplace, and that includes studying at school, college and university too.

Take for example an employee who has a job that frequently involves taking their work home with them (physically or psychologically), or a student who works late into the night and also at weekends as well as balancing a part time job. Social outings and spending time with family and friends, including preparing and eating meals together or weekend outings, may have become a rare occasion. Time spent relaxing or pursuing non-work related activities may also feel foreign or like something they don't deserve.

In our fast-paced and competitively driven culture, we are bombarded with messages that we should always have a work or career-related goal in mind in order to be a successful person – pursuing it at all costs regardless of the health consequences.

For a student this might mean hours spent studying in isolation, and for an employee it may mean placing most of their energies in climbing the career ladder.

Of course attaining good grades at school, college and university are important if an individual wants to step into their dream career, as is moving up the career ladder and earning a higher salary if this will enable a family to remain more financially stable and enjoy more time together. However, problems arise when work begins to interfere too much with our innate drive and capacity to be compassionate individuals. Sometimes work itself can interrupt the very goals that are related to why we want to work so hard in the first place, such as being able to have more resources in order to self-develop and enjoy more time and fun experiences with family and friends.

Spending excessive amounts of time studying or working, regardless of any long or short term benefits to your career, can lead to having little energy or time to spend enjoying the company of friends and family. Overworking can also leave little time for taking pleasure in preparing nourishing meals, finding out new things about ourselves, and developing into the beautiful people we were born to be. I can guarantee right now that the person you were born to be is not a work-a-holic who is unable to enjoy natural plea-sures, engage in fun leisure pursuits and take opportunities to socially con-nect with friends and family.

Alternatively, placing all of our physical and psychological energies into work can leave us feeling exhausted, with very little energy left for being a compassionate individual, whether that be with others or ourselves. Instead, we can beat ourselves up for not being good enough, not getting the best grade, not getting that promotion and not being praised enough by our employers or teachers. We dig ourselves deeper and deeper into a tur-moil of guilt and self-punishment, where the bar for being 'good enough' gets higher and higher as we try to meet the expectations of others. But, no matter how hard you work, or what grades you have, real happiness and life fulfilment will not solely result from the grade you achieve or what rung of the career ladder you are able to climb to.

For myself, my own five-year stint of being a 'work-a-holic', as both a student and employee, meant very little or no time to express my creativity. Time spent relaxing just felt like sometime I was unworthy of, unless I had 'earned' it in some way. Despite studying health and nutrition, my own health and nutrition was severely neglected. I didn't have any time for self-care, or so I believed, in a bid to escape the anxiety and stress that would arise from feel-ing out of control at college, university and within the workplace.

This brings me to another point – control. When we over-work ourselves, or get caught up in a work culture where we exhaust our energies through trying to please others, we can very much feel out of control and not living in alignment with our own values. This loss of control, as you may already realise, can be very anxiety provoking, stressful, and trigger the brain into panic mode. By triggering this panic mode, we go in search of ways that will help us feel more in control. Unfortunately, many of the ways we do find are not very adaptive or compassionate. For example, some individuals (myself included) plough themselves into working even harder, longer and more brutally, usually as a form of distraction, and to feel at ease that they won't meet their own unrealistic standards of self-worth.

Some individuals might alternatively pursue control in the form of their appearance, food or fitness by becoming ever more rigid in what they push themselves to accomplish or restrict. This not only adds to a vicious cycle of overworking and feeling absolutely exhausted, but such controlling activities pull us further and further away from being Compassioneers. I am also guilty of trying to place my control in restricting my diet and weight as a distraction from feeling very much out of control in many areas of life.

To the outside it might look to others that we are doing quite well – good grades, a well-paid job, a healthy diet, a slim figure, an outstanding fitness regimen. By society's standards of wellbeing, we would probably be given a big thumbs up, even though in reality our psychological fitness and body cells would be under a constant state of toxic stress. In effect, we would be depleting our physical and psychological resources, including those that we require to become our more compassionate selves.

A huge part of following a compassionate lifestyle involves taking time to nurture ourselves, connect with others, express your creativity, be more mindful, and take time to be grateful of what we have already. These are just a few of the Nourishing Routes elements that are pursued by Compassioneers, but they would remain very much unfulfilled if we pushed ourselves too hard in the workplace or studying environments.

Unfortunately there may be many individuals (and even whole workplaces, universities and large corporations) who disagree with this view. In their eyes, a more productive and talented employee or student is the one who over-works and applies perfectionistic standards to their goals and activities. However, their argument would not displace the startling figures of just how many employees and students suffer from chronic stress, mental ill health and work-related injury as a result of them over-working and believing in the false notions of being the best or perfection.

Not only is having non-compassionate employees financially costly for employers, but it also sends a bad impression to potential employees and investors. Not many people would want to work for or invest in an organisation that prides itself on slowly (but surely) helping to kill off its employees! It might be legal if it goes unnoticed by Human Resources, but definitely not attractive or cost-effective! However, a compassionately driven employee or organisation definitely is.

If you can identify with this message, or if you feel like you too have experienced the stresses of working yourself into the ground in the pursuit of being a 'better' or a more successful employee or student, you might be wondering what you can do to take back some control and invest your spare energy (the energy you deserve) into becoming a more compassionate individual in light of your work and/or studies.

Well, a large part of the responsibility can be placed on yourself, and also your employer.

First of all, it is your employer's duty to ensure that you are not chronically stressed or in danger of overworking yourself to the point of ill health. For this reason, many organisations do invest in employee wellbeing programmes, but getting all employees to attend and take action on what is learned about health and wellbeing in the workplace is another story – especially if employers don't provide the facilities and time to act on advice (a common yet sad case).

Employers can also promote ways of being compassionate in the workplace, whether that be regular breaks, friendly staff meetings at a nearby cafe, team building activities, policies on not checking emails outside of working hours and providing opportunities to provide and receive support from other colleagues.

Most importantly, though, promoting compassion in and outside the workplace involves acting on your own behalf – even if this means going against the 'work-a-holic' norm of your fellow colleagues or students. This could mean ensuring that you spend at least a couple of days per week, or ideally every day, making time for activities that you enjoy. Pursuing hobbies, expressing creativity, engaging in enjoyable physical activities, spending more time outdoors or in green space, making yourself a lovely hot bath, taking up a volunteering for a charity you really believe in, reading your favourite genre of book and making time for close friends and family are just as important as work or trying to achieve a certain grade, career goal or financial security.

We might be able to achieve amazing things in the workplace, but it is unlikely that work or study will fulfil our innate human needs to love ourselves and others. Without prioritising compassion for ourselves at work, then we also won't be able to re-energise ourselves or be as productive both within and outside of work, which isn't exactly a positive outcome for anyone.

Learning to be more compassionate at work doesn't necessarily have to involve paid employment. It could also involve learning to be more compassionate to yourself when volunteering, helping someone else or campaigning for a group or a cause that you believe in. While these activities are likely to be compassionate at their core while also giving us a sense of meaning and purpose, they can also involve a great deal of anxiety, negative emotions and stress. For example, volunteering to assist individuals going through rough times in their life, or campaigning in groups linked to animal rights or human justice for instance, can be emotionally burdensome if we place all of our physical and psychological energies into helping without looking after our own needs. This might take the form of ruminating about a particular vulnerable person or a cause where there is much that needs to be done in terms of ensuring that justice is eventually achieved. However, because we sometimes can't take action on our concerns, this leaves us in a state of ongoing stress. This not only depletes us of our own physical energy and psychological resources, but it also prevents us from being able to achieve our volunteer-related goals and help others as best we can.

We can't possibly hope to help someone else or a particular cause if we ourselves are lacking in the energy or resources to do it. An example of this can be highlighted when acting on behalf on animal welfare. All too often individuals who stand up for the rights of animals continually think about the trauma other animals go through when being exploited. This can cause individuals a considerable amount of stress when they realise that animals are literally being harmed unnecessarily every single second of every single day – and there is nothing they can directly do to eradicate it as matters often lie out of their own control. Eventually, this type of stress can lead to showing anger and hostility towards others, acting impulsively without considering any negative consequences. It can additionally lead to a lack of self-care, with some individuals no longer being able to act in the best way possible in order to make real positive changes happen for the cause they believe in.

A way around becoming stressed and 'burnt out' when volunteering or acting on behalf of others' welfare involves, perhaps unsurprisingly, taking time for self-care. This can mean allowing yourself to 'cut off' from others' problems when you are not in direct contact with them, while also allowing time solely for you to relax and enjoy yourself. Sometimes we might feel guilty for enjoying ourselves when others are suffering or in pain, but part of being compassionate beings means that we must realise that there will be even more pain for more people if we can't learn to detach ourselves from a situation where we can no longer be of aid.

Alternatively, self-compassion in the examples we have discussed involves learning the art of acceptance and self-care. In this context, acceptance means being 'OK' with the fact that horrible things will happen in the world and that sometimes we will have no power or control over that. Secondly, self-care means allowing ourselves to detach ourselves from such situations while making time to nurture our own selves in a way that aids our energy levels and psychological resources. Only then can we go out onto the battle field and help others in a way that is most beneficial for everyone.

The key points made in this chapter are fundamentally about compassion in relation to the workplace, or volunteering and defending the welfare of others. A vital message that you can integrate is that overworking and not spending time in activities that allow us to enjoy life and thrive as human beings can be detrimental to our own and others' wellbeing. Also, if we really want to make a long-lasting positive difference in the world while being able to lead a happier, healthier and fulfilling life, then we need to place compassion for ourselves as a high priority. As Compassioneers, we can realise that no amount of success at work or a form of study can make us truly happy or healthy, but making time to develop our ability to appreciate and enjoy life, while being able to better love ourselves and others, definitely can. With that in mind, where would you place your investment?

❖

Applying compassion in loving relationships

We enter relationships looking for love.

Perhaps I am stating the obvious here; what are relationships for, after all? But what I really mean is that many of us are willing to do whatever it costs to experience a loving relationship with another person. For some of us, this strong urge to feel loved grows from a sense that there is something in our lives that is missing, or a feeling that we aren't yet a whole person. However, in reality, rather than these feelings being a sign that you need to enter into a loving relationship with someone else, they could be a sign that the real person you should be loving more of is yourself.

I believe feeling as though something is missing, or that we aren't yet a whole person, stems from the fact that many of us are not self-compassionate enough to realise that we are already complete and whole. In others words, when there is a lack of love for ourselves, we seek it elsewhere. Yet, because society expects almost everyone to always be in search for a happy and loving relationship, it is hard to interpret the signs that signal to us that living more self-compassionately is the key to feeling complete and whole – not another person.

If our own self-compassion and general view of ourselves is less than satisfactory, and we don't work to change our self-destructive perspectives, it becomes ever so easy to fall into the trap of trying to gain others' approval or acceptance in the form of seeking out a relationship. At other times it might involve buying into the latest beauty product, getting on board with the latest diet or fitness trend, or just trying out anything that might make you feel a more worthy person according to someone else's standards.

This isn't to say that loving relationships can't help you to learn how to love yourself more. Loving relationships in my own experience have greatly helped me to realise that I am worth so much more than the very little I used to think, and that I am also deserving of love no matter what or how much I eat, weigh, exercise or look like.

Loving relationships with another person really have helped me to transform my perspective into a more self-compassionate one. However, entering a loving relationship from a place of self-love, rather than a lack of it, have made for the best relationships.

Seeking out a relationship for the main reason that we can't yet love ourselves is probably not the best direction to venture in. The thing is, relationships can rarely become fully loving and reach their own potential if we are not yet ready to accept, love and be compassionate with ourselves. In this way, self-compassion is not only a key to healthier and happier lives, but also relationships.

Even if our self-esteem is high, lacking in an ability to self-love can have hugely detrimental impacts to a relationship, as well as the wellbeing of both partners involved. Take for example an individual who goes on a date who is not very loving towards themselves, and regularly appears to others as someone they are not through fear of negative judgement. Perhaps they may be too scared to show their real selves on that date, act differently or wear something they wouldn't ordinarily for fear they might not be accepted by the other person. Sooner or later though, trying to make another person believe you are someone you are not won't last very long. Not only is it physically and emotionally exhausting to keep pretending to be someone you are not, but this type of behaviour doesn't exactly promote trust or being able to be completely open and honest within a relationship.

Within a loving relationship, an individual with a poor sense of self-compassion can become very defensive, jealous, untrusting and impulsively aggressive in situations where there is a threat to their self-esteem. Arguments can escalate much more quickly than they would if they were able to consider a broader perspective other than their own, which most individuals would be much more able to do if they were authentically self-compassionate.

A lack of self-compassion can actively pay out in the way we treat our partners when we are having a self-hate moment, day or even week. This can allow a vicious cycle to occur, where a lack of self-compassion, arguments and self-hate go on continuously – further perpetuating how we have learned to devalue ourselves. Similarly, a lack of self-compassion can allow some vulnerable individuals to enter relationships that are emotionally or even physically abusive. Just like they haven't learned to allow room to love themselves, they may not have learned the value in being with someone who can treat them with the love and respect they really deserve. The disrespect they have for themselves in effect takes the form of a disrespectful, abusive and ultimately unhappy and emotionally unhealthy relationship.

But don't take my word for it. If you haven't experienced less than satisfying relationships for yourself when not being self-compassionate, there is a growing amount of research that shows just how important being self-compassionate in relationships is. This is not only for our own happiness and health, but also that of our partners' and the overall longevity of our relationships.

Some more recent research by pioneers in the field of positive psychology and compassion has shown that self-compassion is predictive of:

❋ Greater relationship wellbeing (e.g. feelings of trust, self-worth, positive emotions, and ability to express emotions)

❋ Greater resilience to traumatic events and arguments

❋ Increased positive actions, such as being more caring, intimate, trusting, accepting and supportive of partner's own needs and interests

❋ Reduced controlling behaviours

❋ Reduced verbal and physical aggression

❋ Increased overall relationship satisfaction and longevity

Alternatively, individuals who are described by their partners as being self-critical and unloving towards themselves are often seen to be hostile, controlling, aggressive and emotionally abusive – with such relationships frequently suffering without adequate resolution of any conflict.

In simple terms, the kindness and love we are able to show to ourselves is very likely to manifest during the formation and development of a

❋

romantic relationship – ultimately dictating its quality and how long it lasts. Considering that the impaired quality of our romantic relationships, and how they eventually end, can have a huge negative impact on our wellbeing, then it makes sense to consider self-compassion as very important to understand and develop. This is even more so if we also want to experience the benefits of being in a relationship fuelled and nourished by self-compassion from both partners, so a relationship can truly flourish and thrive.

This above perspective on being self-compassionate in loving relationships means that it is a good idea when searching for a partner to look for someone who is already or willing to be more self-compassionate. This way, two individuals who realise that they are already two amazingly complete wholes can come together to create something even more beautiful. You might therefore want to ring the alarm bells if you frequently fall into relationships that involve self-destructive behaviours or conversations where each partner speaks about not feeling good enough, failing at things, or trying to meet some form of ideal standard as a way of gaining more self-esteem. For myself, I know the alarm bells start ringing if one partner starts obsessively exercising, dieting or buying into expensive grooming or beauty products.

The following idea might not come as a surprise to many of us, but I do believe that love breeds more love, and that the same goes for self-love. In other words, the more we are self-compassionate, the more feelings and behaviours we apply to our own relationships. This will likely enable both partners to experience how amazing, happy and fulfilling a relationship can be, without pressing any self-destruction button. Showing self-love also shows to our partner that we expect the same from them, including in terms of how they treat us and how they treat themselves, so in effect our self-compassion can flourish and thrive with the person we love.

Ultimately, if we want to love someone else, rather than looking at what we need to do to fix ourselves, look better, or appear like someone we aren't, the real tool involves taking steps towards loving ourselves first. This might initially feel like a journey backwards, but in truth any relationship fuelled by self-compassion is the one true route and exciting adventure to being able to develop a loving partnership that has so much potential to improve each partner's health and happiness.

The Outlook for Part 3 and 4 of This Book

The third part of this book will allow us to further explore our relationship with food and body, including what, how and why we eat, as well as how we view our physical appearance and the way we exercise. We will also overturn the idea that we need to lose weight in order to experience optimal health – throwing any faddy regimens out of the window in exchange for true food and body love in all their unique forms and sizes. Throughout our eye opening discussions, we will relate our ideas to compassion and its integral links to the 10 key elements of Nourishing Routes as well as becoming a Compassioneer.

A crucial topic of discussion will involve critiquing the diet and fitness industry that viciously preys on and profits from individuals' insecurities and vulnerabilities. This critical viewpoint comes at a time when vast numbers of individuals in our society are obsessed with embarking on the next faddy diet or fitness regimen, which are ultimately useless solutions to improving happiness and health while avoiding an 'obesity crisis'. In fact, as scare mongering around an 'obesity crisis', eating 'clean' and poor physical fitness has increased, so too has the number of individuals of all ages suffering from eating disorders and disordered body image.

In the UK alone there are around 800,000 sufferers of eating disorders, such as anorexia nervosa, bulimia, binge eating disorder, orthorexia (an unhealthy obsession with healthy eating) and a wide variety of other disordered eating patterns that negatively – and often severely – impact individuals' quality of life.

Quite shockingly, a Global Beauty and Confidence Report, which involved interviewing 10,500 women from 13 different countries, found that 85 percent of all women and 79 percent of young girls openly admitted that they

✤

181

dismiss taking part in important or enjoyable life activities when they don't feel great about their food intake, body weight or appearance. It is also concerning that, in the same report, 9 out of 10 women stated that they deliberately stop themselves from eating or engage in other behaviours that place their own health at risk when they experience negative thoughts and feelings about their body image.

Body dysmorphic disorder and experiencing any form of negative body image is significantly on the rise, not only in terms of feeling too 'fat', but also too 'thin' or lacking in muscle. These experiences are completely unnecessary and counterproductive, as we were all born to live in a loving relationship with food, body, others and the planet. Yet the very opposite seems to be happening as our diet and fitness obsessed culture infuses every nook and cranny of our lives.

This bleak situation is completely unacceptable and action must be taken now. Yet, any societal focus on tackling eating disorders or disordered body image lags significantly behind the focus placed on exacerbating fears around obesity and creating a market for various faddy diet and fitness regimens. As a consequence, eating disorders and issues related to poor body image go relatively unnoticed – simply shoved under the carpet as though they aren't worth our time preventing or resolving. But this is inevitably what happens when our society makes a profit by preying on individuals' insecurities, usually by endorsing costly self-improvement products as a route to happiness and wellbeing.

In spite of this challenging situation, the fact of the matter is that we can't let disordered forms of thinking or behaviours around food and body to continue along the slippery slope it currently is. I have therefore made it part of my own mission with Nourishing Routes to empower individuals like yourself to realise that you don't need to buy into any self-improvement products in order to be authentically happy or healthy, and that these experiences involve a change of perspective rather than alterations to what we eat, weigh, exercise or look like. Are you with me in this mission?

Although Part 3 does not specifically discuss eating disorders or body dysmorphic disorder in relation to the psychological and physical predictors and consequences of these, I have written it in a way that will empower anyone who believes that they have a less than positive or loving relationship with food and their own body – whether they have a diagnosed eating disorder or not. For some of you reading this, Part 3 will enable you to locate a more self-compassionate pathway towards loving and living in harmony with food and your own body. Alternatively, depending on your personal circumstances, it may help you to recover from disordered eating and body dysmorphic disorder.

Ultimately, Part 3 is an essential component of Nourishing Routes that will be the fuel to applying the confidence to make your own personal pledge to become a Compassioneer. In this context, being a Compassioneer involves becoming empowered to practically apply your understanding of compassion, especially self-compassion, in a way that enables you to develop lifelong positive relationships with food and body, as well as diminish any forms of disordered eating and body image. Together we will journey towards a destination that involves loving and nourishing yourself from the inside out.

PART 3:

Compassion-Eating

"*Make life more of a piece of cake, by finally making peace, rather than war, with cake*"

A Lifelong Relationship with Food

From the moment we arrive on the planet, all if not most of us enter into a relationship with food. And, like all relationships, we need to lovingly nurture and have trust in them so that they can flourish and thrive.

From receiving nutrients from our mother's placenta, to then finding comfort from being breast or bottle fed as a newborn, we immediately learn that consuming energy and nutrients is essential for our growth and survival – even if this at first only happens at a subconscious level to begin with. Even at this subconscious level, though, we have entered into a lifelong relationship with food.

It is very important to realise that food not only serves to nourish us physically in terms of nutrition, but that the way we view and eat food creates social bonds with who we eat with, significant memories and a deeper understanding of the cultural rituals we use to create our own sense of identity. Whether that be eating a spaghetti bolognese every Friday night with your family, ice cream along the beach, or popcorn with your friends when watching a film – food is associated with people, times and places. Not just Calories and nutrients.

As we go throughout life, food can take on multiple meanings and become a way to identify how 'good' or a self-controlled a person we are. Unfortunately, this association between food and self is not always a positive one. Instead of being linked with positive memories or becoming part of our cultural sense of belonging and identity, food can become a way of negatively self-judging and comparing ourselves with others. In other words, we enter into a toxic relationship with food, similar to the way you might enter a toxic relationship with another person.

Most of us have at some time in our lives experienced an abusive relationship – whether that be physical or psychological – with another person. But
is this the type of relationship you really want for yourself in order to truly
nourish and flourish? More specifically, is this the type of relationship you
would want with food, which is the relationship we will inevitably have for
life?

Ask yourself: would you rather enter into a relationship with food defined
by authentic trust, support and love? Or, do you want to continue feeling
physically and emotionally abused?

Unlike a loving relationship with food, a toxic or abusive one usually
involves vicious cycles of dieting and feeling as though life's problems can
be solved simply by following the latest faddy eating routine. We can use
food as a form of control or as a way to mask feelings of emptiness, loneliness or low self-worth. This leads many individuals to fall into the trap of
believing that they can overcome our life issues and negative emotions if
they could just:

✤ Eat less and lose weight, but eat more frequently to lose weight even
   quicker

✤ Cut out sugar

✤ Cut out fat – but then eat more fat because we need a bit of fat

✤ Use more healthy oils in cooking – but not too much because we don't
   want to eat too much fat

✤ Cut out bread and gluten – but then eat bread as a source of wholegrain

✤ Cut out any other food group you can think of

✤ Cut out caffeine – or drink more to boost your metabolism...

✤ Embark on a detox programme or juicing plan

❄ Go on a Paleo diet and eat more animal products to increase muscle mass – but then go vegan and cut out all animal products to extend your lifespan

❄ Drink more green juices and smoothies – but then don't, as they contain sugar

❄ Count Calories more accurately

❄ Log every single food and drink item we consume

❄ Increase protein content of all foods consumed

❄ Add more 'superfood' powders to cereals and smoothies

As you read this long list of ludicrous messages you might notice just how confusing and often contradictory they are. Yet these are the very types of messages we are bombarded with each and every day in relation to what we should and should not eat. Even if some of the behaviours that are suggested in the above list are backed up with some evidence that they improve our physical or psychological wellbeing, they still don't consider the wider picture of health – such as the quality of our relationships, experiences of stress, body image, feeling as though we are acting in line with our goals and values, our sense of purpose in the world and how many good quality social connections we have. As far as these messages are concerned with promoting long term happiness and health for everyone, who each has their own unique needs, they are quite a few miles off track.

Is it really a good thing that our society endorses the concept that having a more nutritious diet will allow us to solve almost any of life problems – by literally slimming and 'nutrifying' them away? Also, is it right that our society continues to view food as a gauge of how healthy and 'good' a person someone is, as well as how able they are to meet someone else's expectations?

Regardless of your answers to the above questions, the reality remains that our relationship with food is a much better gauge to assess how happy and healthy someone is or will become. This means that the way we

❄

psychologically relate to food, including how we use it to alter our emotions, says a heck of a lot about the bigger picture of our lives. But instead of high-lighting the wider role that food plays in our lives, our society continues to view the perfect nutrient and Calorie intake as being the key to happiness and health rather than the lifelong positive relationships we have the potential to form with food. By doing this, many of us are lured into a life-long battle with food, where nothing we eat feels good or healthy enough. What we really need to be doing, though, is promoting lifelong peace and love with food.

The Many Meanings of Food

A scientist of nutrition would be able to tell you that certain foods contain certain nutrients and different energy contents. However, without undermining their knowledgeable expertise, what they wouldn't be able to tell you, or measure, is what each individual experiences psychologically before, during or after eating. This part of eating is completely subjective, and it is influenced by our memories, cultural norms, emotions and the social context eating takes place in.

Take for example the act of eating a cake or biscuit where each one has the exact same nutrient and energy content. For one individual eating this cake or biscuit might be symbolic of sharing time with family and friends and stimulate positive emotions such as joy. However, for another person it might symbolise deviating from a particular way of eating, such as a weight loss diet or a plan where all processed foods are to be strictly avoided. As a result, negative emotions and feelings arise, such as fear, guilt and shame. The food, energy and nutrients eaten in each scenario would be the same or at least very similar, but the meaning given to it is completely different.

As another example, a person might sense the pleasant taste of sugar and fat, while also feeling a pang of guilt as the act of eating that cake conflicts with another goal – e.g. losing weight or eating 'clean'. Similarly, eating foods that are not typically classified as 'healthy' may conflict with the expectation of avoiding foods that are viewed as nutrient deficient, toxic, 'unclean' and indulgent. These negative connotations we associate with food not only apply to that moment, but also the long lasting feeling we have towards ourselves after eating it.

Instead of experiencing food as part of a balanced diet that allows us to connect to other people and create memories, food in our body-obsessed society can quite easily becomes a symbol of what we haven't got – i.e. the ideal diet, capacity for self-regulation, or reaching a 'perfect' weight.

You can probably see from these examples that food can become a source of pleasure as well as hate; all the while, a vulnerable person buying into the lies about what food 'should' symbolise and how it 'should' be consumed falls deeper into the trap of believing that what and how much they eat defines their self-worth. Eating food may become tied up with negative thoughts about how they just aren't good enough, and how they dislike their physical appearance. At times it might even feel as though they will never be able to experience joy with food or love themselves for who they really are. However, while we might believe that these types of thoughts will lead to increased motivation to eat 'better', they can lead to the very opposite. Viewing ourselves negatively in relation to what we do or do not eat can make individuals feel incapable of being able to 'control' what they eat, either leading to an urge to eat even more or a drive to place even more restriction over food. For example, it could lead individuals to engage in disordered behaviour that involves going to any means to eliminate the effects of the food they have eaten, such as over-exercising, skipping meals, or being sick. Of course these may seem like extreme examples, but they are unfortunately quite common in a society where our relationship with food is linked to self-comparison and judgement.

Our capacity to apply meaning to food can be harnessed in a negative way, as suggested in the above examples. However, it can also be utilised in a positive way.

When eating becomes a source of showing kindness to yourself, and even as a way of acting in line with your values, this can bring a positive sense of wellbeing. By viewing food as having greater meaning than its nutrients, energy or value in terms of our health and weight, we can develop a lifelong positive relationship with it.

Even if a food/meal you eat is not specifically 'healthy' or 'low' in Calories, seeing the food as an opportunity to create a new memory, break away from rigid rules, or appreciate someone's time and effort to prepare that food can feel liberating and enjoyable. Also, by developing lifestyle choices that allow you to consume foods that have no/little exploitation of humans or animals involved, this can feel quite empowering when realising that your eating behaviours contribute to creating a better world to live in. If we alternatively continue to have a relationship with food where we beat ourselves up about what we have or have not eaten, this can turn into an untrusting and abusive relationship with food and ourselves, which isn't good for anyone or the planet.

We could ask ourselves, can self-compassion ever grow when we continue to have a negative relationship with food and view its meaning in terms of nutrients, energy, body weight and physical appearance?

If the answer is no, then what can we do about it? Should we just accept that food will always be associated with certain positive or negative connotations that involve judging ourselves by what and how much we eat? Or, can we develop a way of thinking and feeling where food becomes an empowering tool to reconnect with ourselves, others and the world around us?

If we go for the last option, which I would definitely recommend we do, this would likely mean learning to view food as being more than a means to reach a certain standard set by society. You can also begin to become more critical of these standards. For example, you might begin to question the ingrained idea that you are a bad gluttonous person if you eat a certain type or amount of food. Similarly, you might question the concept of how eating a certain food means we need to be punished or forced to take action in order to burn off and eliminate that food using any means.

Asking these questions may not lead to any specific actions to stand up against them at first. But critical awareness of how we are encouraged to simply view food as fuel and a source of negative self-judgement is an empowering step to living more compassionately. If we can realise that, as human beings, we have much, much more than what and how much we eat to define ourselves by and offer others, then we can finally begin to develop a positively healthy relationship with food.

But what does this positively healthy
relationship with food look like?

Over many years of learning to become more self-compassionate with what and how much I eat, I feel that there are several components that are crucial in order to develop a positively healthy relationship with food. We will discuss these in more depth when we soon talk about the concept of compassion-eating, but for now the following points are important to integrate into our understanding:

❋ Not viewing food solely as a mixture of nutrients (e.g. fats, carbohydrates and protein) or Calories

❋ Not relating to food in a way that symbolises your weight or self-worth

❋ Eating when and how much you like, while not feeling like you have to abide by certain rules or rituals

❋ Saying yes to opportunities to try different foods, and not fearing how you might feel about yourself after eating them

❋ Seeing food as part of your most important memories and relationships with others

❋ Appreciating the smell, sight, taste and touch of foods – being mindful when eating and not rushing to eat due to lack of time or not wanting to face any negative thoughts about yourself while eating.

❋ Engaging in positive talk to others about food – i.e. not referring to food as a way of moulding the body into a certain shape or negatively judging others based on what and how much they eat

❋ Acknowledging that food brings us all together, rather than using food to gauge how you compare with others

❋

✳ Eating in a way that connects you to your deeper values of nourishing yourself (in mind and body), while being compassionate to yourself and others.

By placing an emphasis on these key points we can begin to view food as something we can enjoy in many forms and contexts without a need for control, guilt, compensatory behaviours or self-punishment. We can also become more nourished, happy and free to focus on other significant parts of our lives that contribute to our ability to live more compassionately so that we can flourish and thrive.

Compassioneer Activity: Viewing food as More Than Just Nutrients and Fuel

As we have just discussed, food is not just about nutrition or fuel for the body. As important as it is to nourish our bodies with energy and certain nutrients, it is also vital to recognise and appreciate the many other functions of food. Food by nature brings us joy, connects us with other people, rekindles memories, and joins us to a culture while establishing our sense of identity.

In this next activity, I invite you to reconnect with some of the ways that food plays a meaningful role in your life. This activity also prompts you to think of which specific foods have different roles and functions within your life, as well as challenging you to alter the perception that food is just about nutrition and fuel.

Hopefully by the end of the activity you will be able to identify the deeper role food plays in our lives and that enjoying food without guilt or needing to eliminate and restrict certain foods is essential when developing a compassionate relationship with ourselves and how we eat.

Ask yourself and note down:

* What foods do you have strong memories about? List these and then describe how the foods listed remind you of certain memories. Try to be as specific as you can and notice the different sensory experiences you can recollect – taste, emotions, smell, sights, sounds, touch.

* What foods do you eat or not eat when you are upset, sad or angry, stressed or anxious? Is this different to how you would eat usually, and if so how is it different?

❋ Is food something that you use to comfort yourself or feel more in control, regardless if this involves eating more or less?

❋ What type of foods connect you to your identity and culture?

❋ What type of foods bring you pleasure and enjoyment?

❋ What type of foods do you eat when celebrating (e.g. at a birthday, Christmas, festivals)?

❋ How does your eating behaviour change when you are with other people (e.g. with friends, family, a partner, new person or a public space)?

Finally, write a few sentences or a paragraph to yourself explaining why you think that food is not just nutrients or fuel for the body. In these sentences you might wish to describe your thoughts on how food is really important to your current social life and relationships, or how you are motivated to value food in a way where eating is also about enjoyment as well as physical nourishment.

Nourishment – Not Numbers

A key element of Nourishing Routes as you may remember is based on the concept of Nourishment and Not Numbers. I strongly believe that this key element deserves a special mention of its own – especially in the context of the relationship we develop with our food and body. It also strongly interlinks with what we have just spoken about in terms of how we need to appreciate that each of us has entered into a lifelong relationship with food and how food has a greater meaning than simply energy and nutrients.

For most individuals reading this book, you probably have experience of growing up in a society that places a lot of value on food in terms of what, how much and even when and how we eat – and not necessarily in a positive way.

Instead of food symbolising culture, enjoyment and socialising, much of the way food is presented to us is with a word of warning or some form of negative judgement. You might be very familiar with the following messages we are presented on regular basis:

❋ Don't eat too much of this or that

❋ That has too many Calories

❋ Don't eat anything with added sugar

❋ That food will make you fat

❋ That food is associated with 'x', 'y' and 'z' disease

❋ Eating that food is naughty

❋ Clean eating is the way to reach optimal health

❋ Undertaking a diet, detox or healthy eating plan will help me get back on track after eating something unhealthy

Messages about counting Calories, as we will discuss in much more detail later, is a prime example. Calories are quite literally everywhere. On the backs of food packets, on the fronts of packets, on restaurant menus, on online supermarket food lists, in recipe books and blogs. They are also countlessly mentioned in health programmes, magazines and nutrition-related research. According to health organisations and the government, our nation, and most of the globe, are eating just 'too many' Calories, which is contributing to why we are becoming more and more 'overweight'. Apparently, eating a specific number of Calories will make us an ideal 'healthy weight', and we will no longer have to put up with the stigma of being branded as 'bad' or lacking in willpower for eating the foods that (we have been made to believe) will lead us to be overweight and place increasing costs on the health care system.

Not only is the above information false, as there are many other aspects of our lifestyle that contribute more greatly to our overall wellbeing than our energy intake, it belittles the fact that Calorie counting is a VERY inaccurate way of gauging the energy content in food or how it contributes to our weight and overall health.

Everyone will naturally digest and metabolise foods differently than others, and even the climate that certain food is grown in or how they are mixed together during the manufacturing process, creates great variation in the Calorie content of certain foods and meals. However, the Calorie numbers on the packet tend to stay the same. More importantly though, Calorie counting distracts us from thinking about the bigger role, meaning and significance that food has in our lives and our overall wellbeing. With Calorie counting, food is simply fuel. Eat too much and you will gain weight, and eat too little and you will lose weight.

A similar story can be said for counting macro and micronutrients such as proteins, carbohydrates and fats. At one point in time fat is bad, then good,

❋

then bad again. The same story happens with carbohydrates, protein and more or less anything contained within or added to foods that you can think of. Then there is the worry about getting the right number of vitamins and minerals we need. Of course, getting enough energy and the nutrients we need to thrive is very important. But viewing food as fuel ignores the many other nourishing components and functions that food places in our lives.

Well, I am here to remind us that food is so much more than fuel and numbers. Food and the way we eat offers so much more nourishment in the way we think and feel about it. I am also here to challenge the idea that eating a certain number of Calories, macronutrients, or vitamins and minerals is the main route to health, while questioning whether we should ever place moral judgements on food.

To place societal views about food in relation to the philosophy of Nourishing Routes, below is a list of myths around food that we are almost forced to buy into – often at the expense rather than gain of our own happiness and wellbeing:

❋   We should always aim to control exactly what, when and how much we eat, with the best methods being Calorie counting, weighing food and calculating the micro and macro nutrient content in everything we eat

❋   By counting Calories we can maintain a 'healthy weight'

❋   Everyone should only ever eat as much food as their body physically requires to function

❋   Some foods are 'clean' and 'good' to eat while others are 'dirty' and 'bad'

❋   We should aim to consume the perfect ratio of carbohydrates, proteins and fats in our diet

❋   Our main aim when choosing a food or meal to eat is ensuring that it meets our energy and nutritional requirements.

Nourishing Routes philosophy is quite the opposite of these myths. It involves viewing food as more than something we should control, count or place a moral judgement on. Alternatively, it involves appreciating the many vital functions of food as well as our psychological and social relationships we have with it – including our memories, emotions and the way we eat when we are with other people or during certain occasions.

As I have recently discussed, we are complex social beings and eating is rarely an activity that simply involves a pure motivation to refuel the body. Of course, we do eat to survive and satisfy physical urges of hunger, but the way we eat is very much shaped by our social and cultural contexts. Food and eating are absolutely central to the concept of our sense of self and identity. When we quantify it into a measurement of Calories or anything along these lines, we aren't really seeing food for what it truly is.

What we eat additionally symbolises the 'type' of person we want to be or how we would like others to view ourselves, such as a certain social group, or whether we label ourselves as unhealthy, healthy, a dieter or non-dieter for example. For many of us meal times represent a period of socialisation, and are looked forward to for a number of reasons other than satisfying physical hunger. Eating is also an opportunity to experience pleasure, reduce stress, alleviate boredom, feeling accomplished after preparing a meal, being reunited with family or friends, relishing comforting memories, or carrying our traditional cultural practices in the form of food. For example, eating habits can function as a way to mark boundaries between different cultures and religions, such as when carrying out certain rituals, traditions and festivals in a particular way.

Although many countries still view food with an appreciation of the many pleasurable aspects it involves, such as its sensory experiences, in western societies such as the UK and USA food has taken on a more negative and moral meaning. More specifically, what, where, how much and when we eat has come to symbolise how 'good' or 'bad' we are at living up to societal health standards. For example, in addition to the sensory appeal of certain foods, customers purchasing or preparing food now want additional information about the nutritional properties and health value of food.

In recent years, we have come to label food as healthy, unhealthy, good, bad, clean, super, junk and everything in between. This is partly due to living in a world where medical advancements have involved placing an increasing value on knowing more about our wellbeing and risk of ill-being, and the goals that have been set to achieve optimal health in order to be a 'good' citizen who is living in line with societal expectations. Such expectations advocate living a life that does not involve 'selfishly' overindulging on food, being overweight, and experiencing costly food-related health problems such as obesity, type 2 diabetes and heart disease.

With the above information in mind it becomes a bit clearer as to why food is increasingly becoming a moral issue, and how living 'out of line' with societal expectations around food can leave individuals feeling guilty, ashamed, disgusted or an unworthy person. Eating an 'unhealthy' food or 'giving in' to temptation by eating a forbidden food is now a symbol of committing some form of sin. But we know that food is not just about numbers – it is about nourishment in all its many forms too.

By nourishment I don't just mean the vitamins, minerals, antioxidants or phytonutrients in certain foods. I also mean nourishment in terms of the many different roles that food fulfils in our ever changing lives. This form of nourishment is what nutritional science CAN'T measure. Nutritional science may be able to help us calculate our specific nutritional requirements in terms of Calories or various nutrients, but when it comes to how food fits in with our relationships, culture, memories and identity, it usually fails – massively.

Over the last few years I have come to view nourishment with food as being just as much a social and psychological need as it is a physiological one. Nourishment with food occurs when we eat with several of our human needs in mind, such as the way food can be used to connect us with other people, experience pleasure, remind us of pleasant memories, inspire us, allow us to feel psychologically revitalised, be creative in what we choose and prepare, as well as even allowing us to alleviate stress, anxiety and negative emotions.

It would be a bit of a shame if we were to ignore all of these functions of food by solely focussing on nutrition and numbers, or whether we should eat or not eat based on the physiological experiences of hunger and fullness. Yet, this is what we are told to do on a daily basis. It is also hard to escape Calorie content labels and news about the latest superfood or 'bad' food, or the type of diet we should jump on the band wagon with in order to attain a longer lifespan and a reduced risk of various illnesses.

Food does play a key role in health at a nutrition level, but I really do question the amount of time and energy we waste by thinking with such a limited perspective. Take for example the situation of sitting on your own over lunch time, at your work desk, feeling stressed while munching a 'superfood' salad (one that doesn't taste particularly nice) and contemplating how this is something you have carefully Calorie counted in order to lose weight, even though you would much prefer a more filling and satisfying meal. The body may be getting nourished by essential nutrients from this meal, but is that really enough to promote wellbeing? Also, is it healthy enough to counteract the toxicity of stress-related chemicals pumping around the body from feeling isolated or in a mindset of restriction?

We know from vast amounts of research that loneliness and placing necessary restrictions on our lives is one of the biggest predictors of mortality and poor physical as well as mental health – much more so than being overweight or an 'unhealthy' weight. Yet, more and more people are spending excessive quantities of time alone, not making human contact, in order to ensure that they eat 'correctly'. Somewhere along the lines here the balance has been lost, and there are even cases where individuals make themselves excessively stressed and ill because of worrying about food and exercise in the first place.

As another example to help you understand that food is much more than just numbers, you may see a person eating a huge slice of cake topped with all sorts of sugar filled goodies at their favourite cafe catching up with a friend. Some might call this gluttony and adding to a crisis of type 2 diabetes and obesity. However, we can't give such a black and white judgement to a complex activity where an individual is not necessarily enacting a dysfunctional form of eating. Instead, that person is likely engaging in positive social interaction that has a cultural meaning (e.g. friendship and celebration) while feeling able to relax in a safe, familiar space with someone they care about. In this way, we really can't define whether eating that cake is 'good' or 'bad', although I would argue that the situation appears more along the positive rather than negative spectrum of health.

In simple terms, the wellbeing of society is not solely suffering because of not eating a 'healthy' Calorie controlled diet. There is a much bigger role to consider in terms of the social and psychological relationships we have with food – beyond nutrition and numbers.

But what can we do to restore this essential balance and develop a positive relationship with food that is not just based on nutrition and numbers? Well, a simple first step involves acknowledging what your current relationship with food, body and exercise looks and feels like. In which case, asking yourself the following questions can be helpful.

Is what you eat based on:

✳ Calculating every Calorie you consume or expend?

✳ Ensuring that you eat no refined sugar, carbs or 'empty Calories'?

✳ Feeling guilty or ashamed for consuming things that are 'off limits'

✳ Sticking to a rigid preplanned meal regimen

✳ Trying to burn up so much energy within a given workout?

✳ Valuing your body on how it looks and how well it fits with a certain standard of slimness or within an ideal BMI range?

If you can answer yes to any of these questions, and can be honest with yourself and realise that you deserve to be so MUCH more than what you eat, weigh or look like, then that in itself is an amazing leap forward already.

Secondly, it is important to remember that experiencing happiness and health entails embarking on a journey to being a Compassioneer, which initially involves learning to accept and love yourself as you are now, while viewing food with all the amazing social and psychological functions it is able to nourish us with – both outside and within.

When we look past numbers and nutrients, food becomes more joyfully about nourishment of the mind, as well as our social and physical needs. You might also choose to look a bit further to see how what we eat can be compassionate in the way that you view how what you eat has an impact on others, such as the wellbeing of animals and the planet.

Whatever you do, try to ensure that why or what you eat is not just based on a bundle of nutrients, Calories or an ideal body weight that you 'need' to attain. Remember, you don't just have to fulfil a certain Calorie of nutrient target to achieve health, and trying to do so might you lead further and further away from this goal...

Ultimately, looking at food as nourishment and not just numbers allows us to appreciate that food has so much more to offer than Calories and energy if we want to nourish flourish and thrive.

Myths Around Dieting and Weight loss

Before going on any further with our mission to develop a more compassionate lifestyle and relationship with our food and body, it is crucial to become critical of how weight loss or any form of body weight manipulation is currently promoted.

You have probably already integrated the idea that health and happiness do not simply arise out of embarking on a diet or losing weight. But, the fact remains that we are bombarded with messages day after day to do exactly that. The number of individuals, of all ages and nationalities, who continue to pursue the next latest diet are literally in the hundreds of thousands and even millions nationwide.

Quite a depressing piece of information is the statistic that the average person spends over £1000 per year on diet-related products and memberships, with most individuals in our western culture being expected to be on a diet for about 17 years of their life. Could the time and energy spent used during these years worrying about weight and food be spent much more wisely elsewhere? Of course it could! Yet, the weight loss market continues to thrive (including magazines, books, gym memberships, supplements and 'superfoods'), and is estimated to be worth around £60 billion globally. Wow. That's a lot of money being gained through preying on individuals' insecurities.

In the UK, diet products alone are worth around £2 billion, which is around the same amount as we spend in the NHS on A & E services. This might not be as shocking if it wasn't for the even more notable fact that the large majority of individuals who buy into the dieting industry don't need to lose weight, and most don't achieve the results they hoped for. Perhaps even worse, many individuals end up feeling in a poorer state of physical and psychological wellbeing than they were prior to investing in the diet industry. To give you a clearer perspective, in the UK:

✤ Over 1/3 of individuals who regard themselves as occasional or chronic dieters eventually develop disordered forms of eating, and up to 1/4 develop a pathological eating disorder such as anorexia nervosa, bulimia, orthorexia or binge eating disorder

✤ Around half of young girls and boys have a fear of becoming fat, and have engaged in either dieting or binge eating

✤ Around 700,000 individuals suffer from an eating disorder (with over 50% of cases lasting more than 6 years)

✤ 60% of adults report feeling ashamed of how they look and that over two thirds suffer from poor body image

✤ One third of men would sacrifice a year of their life to achieve their 'ideal' body

✤ 80% of individuals, including males and females, are unhappy with their body

We also need to remember that:

✤ There are hundreds and thousands of businesses that make multimillion and even multibillion pound profits by investing in, creating and marketing products related to dieting, losing weight, eating 'clean' or more 'superfoods', eating foods low in sugar, fat, etc.

✤ Most dieting industries and related products do not have their target customers' physical and psychological wellbeing as a priority. However, there is a great priority placed on making money, even if there are negative consequences for customers.

✤ Campaigns about an 'obesity crisis' and decisions to lower the weight or BMI that is deemed to promote optimal health are often driven by an underlying motive to pave a way for a thriving diet industry – whose customer base and product range can grow as a result.

A critical awareness of the above issues in more depth is crucial in our quest to becoming empowered enough to develop our own Nourishing Routes and Compassioneer lifestyle in relation to our food and body.

So, without much further ado, let's get our hands dirty by tackling, using some of the latest scientific and most rigorous evidence, the most common myths that still persist about dieting and the need for weight loss.

✳ Diets enable individuals to lose weight in the long term

Everywhere we look there seems to be yet another diet being promoted in order to 'help' individuals lose weight. But at what gain and at what cost?

On average, more than two thirds of individuals who go on a diet and lose weight will regain all the weight they lost, and usually more, within the first year. Perhaps even more shockingly, almost 100% will regain the weight and even more in five years. There is also evidence, in research with identical twins, that siblings who have been on one or more diets are significantly more likely to be overweight than their non-dieting counterparts.

But why is this?

Well firstly, the psychological effort involved in losing weight and sustaining it is quite large, and often not sustainable. This is especially so in times of stress or when other life priorities apart from food take over. Also, weight loss is primarily driven by complex metabolic systems and behavioural patterns that go against how we evolved to survive – as well as social systems, food industries and environments that encourage us to eat more and exercise less (despite this opposing society's negatively moral judgement in relation to these behaviours). Eventually, the way our body is naturally designed allows it to reprogram itself so that the energy from the food we do eat is more likely to be stored. In other words, the way our bodies have been designed does not promote losing or maintaining weight loss.

Another reason why diets don't enable individuals to lose weight in the long term is that they usually involve eating in a way that goes against social norms while placing us in a mindset of restriction. This tends to result in 'forbidden' foods becoming much more tempting and irresistible, and whether we act upon these urges or not, it can create an untrusting mindset where food and eating is concerned. Inevitably, dieting with the main aim of weight loss comes with a whole host of psychological changes, which not only hinder our relationship with food, but also lead to increased disorderly eating patterns such as bingeing on food or restricting food. There are many individuals who are on a diet who can confirm that their way of life and restrictions placed over their eating makes them think about food obsessively. Unfortunately this leaves them very little time to invest their energies in enjoyable activities, social opportunities or hobbies that would likely have a much greater impact on their overall happiness and health.

Another key point to mention is that feeling as though you have 'failed' at a diet, or have not lost as much weight as expected, often leads individuals to view themselves as even more ineffective and worthless than before they started dieting. One way of alleviating the negative emotions associated with this can sometimes involve turning to food for comfort – quickly followed by feelings of guilt, shame and the urge to start again by embarking on yet another diet. And so the vicious cycle continues...

❋ You can't be overweight and healthy

There is so much of a black and white focus on being an 'ideal' weight or BMI that it can feel quite foreign to colourfully think outside these lines when it comes to achieving happiness and health.

What most magazine headlines and news stories don't tell us is that there is no clear point at which a person's weight makes them healthy or unhealthy. In reality, there is a bit of a 'U-shaped' curve when it comes to weight and mortality – just one key indicator of an individual's health status. By this I mean that at a very low weight there is a high risk of mortality, and that there is also a high risk of mortality at a very high weight. But such outcomes are just speculations based on averages of evidence, and are not set in stone.

In truth, weight or BMI alone don't really give a realistic picture of the many lifestyle factors or state of psychological wellbeing that an individual experiences or will experience in the future. Also, there is the not-very-well-promoted fact that there is a greater risk of mortality at a lower weight compared to a higher weight.

In terms of overall health, an 'unhealthy' weight from a Nourishing Routes perspective is a weight that restricts you from being able to live life in the way you would want to and can experience optimal psychological and social – not just physical – wellbeing. This means that an individual who does happen to fit into the slim ideal category of weight may still be unhealthy if the way they view their body and ability to function is being impaired. Similarly, someone who is 'overweight' by BMI standards might be perfectly content with their body, have a positive relationship with food and also engage in activities that allow them to connect with others, express their creativity and lead a fulfilling, meaningful life. In each scenario a person's weight, when judged by society, would state the opposite of their more authentic state of happiness and health.

✴ Individuals who are not a healthy weight have no willpower

This is a widespread myth that is not only false, but it also perpetuates the stigma experienced by individuals who are not an 'ideal weight'. Willpower or self-discipline, which is defined as the capacity to exert self-regulation and conscious control over your own behaviour, accounts for hardly anything in relation to being 'overweight' or even 'underweight'. Most behaviours are actually driven by subconscious habits or as a consequence of the body trying to fulfil its needs rather than sabotage its wellbeing.

Many individuals who attribute their 'non-ideal weight' or unhealthy eating to a lack of willpower or self-discipline are actually behaving in ways that, to the body, are driven by the goal of promoting rather than diminishing wellness. This might seem a bit contradictory, but the actual act of going on a diet or any form of controlled meal plan goes against the body's needs to stay in control by disallowing it to act and eat intuitively. For example, the more rules and regulations placed on how an individual eats makes them feel more restricted, out of touch with their own body and as though their true physical and psychological needs aren't being met.

Just to be clear, we human beings are complex emotional and social beings who are not designed to make ourselves out of control. To be out of control feels dangerous, unsafe, terrifying and even death-defying. So, although eating 'forbidden' types or quantities of food might initially feel like a form of self-sabotage in terms of a person's goals to lose weight or eat healthy, it can actually symbolise an underlying desire to place yourself back in the driving seat of your own life. For some individuals this takes the form of binge eating or excessively eating quantities of food that have previously been denied. For others it may involve feeling 'safer' by restricting food more and more as feeling in control seems to become harder and harder. As a prime example there are many individuals whose response to feeling out of control when dieting leads them to exert even more and more control over what they eat – which is where many eating disorders begin or become perpetuated. So, depending on the individual, dieting can either lead to episodes of excessive eating, extreme starvation or both.

As you may have experienced in terms of eating 'forbidden' foods, many of us have learnt to associate these actions with terms such as bad, naughty, fat, worthless and shame. At the same time, we may feel a compulsive urge that we should embark on yet another diet or pursue some similar extreme method to erase our 'sins'. We tell ourselves that, this time, the outcome will be different and, sure enough, another faddy way of eating begins by the time the weekend is over.

✳ **Being overweight or obese is mainly caused by a lack of physical activity and unhealthy dietary habits:**

Regardless of the fact that weight is not the most significant contributor to health and happiness, most individuals, including health professionals, attribute obesity to too much eating and too little physical activity. This line of thought follows a simplistic 'input equals output' model. However, much more evidence to date suggests that some of the biggest factors that contribute to weight gain and obesity include poor psychological wellbeing, insufficient sleep, stress, genetics, medication, metabolic disruptions

✳

(independent of how a person eats and exercises) and, ironically, episodes of dieting. These factors are often outside of an individuals' personal control, yet remain key detriments of energy expenditure, eating behaviour and metabolic disruptions that lead to increased weight gain and/or difficulty maintaining a certain weight.

✳ Weight loss does not have any adverse effects

This is one of the many myths around dieting that bemuses me the most. How can any health professional truly believe that a lifestyle filled with negative self-judgement and ritualistic routines that frequently cut us off from our friends, family, culture and hobbies has no negative impacts – especially to a person's psychological wellbeing? The fact is that weight loss, to a much greater degree than weight gain, is significantly associated with early mortality.

Interestingly, there is a growing amount of research to suggest that weight loss (even as little as 5% of a person's original weight) can have longstanding negative impacts to individuals' physical and psychological wellbeing. Loss of fat and muscle tissue from the body when losing weight also increases the urge to eat while reducing the amount of energy we burn each day. In terms of psychological health, weight loss is additionally associated with increased stress, anxiety, disordered eating, depression, as well as increased levels of hormone and metabolic complications in the brain and body.

Most weight loss plans and diets don't consider how they impact individuals' body image, self-esteem, relationship with food and the unhealthy behavioural extremes that some individuals pursue in order to lose weight. For example, there is an expanding body of evidence to suggest that focussing on weight loss as a goal of dieting or healthy eating has very negative impacts on health by contributing to a preoccupation with the body in a negatively judgemental way. A focus on weight loss is also linked with experiencing repeated cycles of weight loss and weight gain, obsessing about healthy eating and an increased risk of eating disorders. Even the fact that diets and controlling food intake are widely promoted contributes to a culture where weight stigma is widespread, while many individuals are made to believe that their self-worth and self-esteem should rest on what and how much they eat, weigh and exercise.

✤ **Not being on a diet or rigidly controlling what I eat will lead to gaining weight and not optimally nourishing the body**

This myth relates to our need to feel in control with food and body, which is exactly what the diet industry thrives on. However, feeling in control does not start – or end – with working out the exact amounts or types of food we should or should not eat. There is also a common worry that, without dieting or rules in place concerning our food intake, we will lose all sense of control of our food and body. The reality is, though, that the less control we try to forcefully place over food, while aiming to develop a positive relationship with our whole selves, we will naturally want to nourish the body in an optimal way. Not being on a diet also means less time obsessing about what we should and shouldn't eat, which allows us to get back in tune with what our bodies and minds really desire and thrive on.

What our bodies really crave is often not a whole cake, packet of biscuits or pizza. However, I believe that in most cases it is completely OK to eat these types of foods in such quantities if it occurs as part of a social occasion, celebration or even by yourself just because you really feel like it. As long as eating occurs without negative judgement, compensatory behaviours or with the aim of trying to numb psychological pain and block out negative emotions and issues in your life that you are not yet ready to face, just about anything is OK to eat.

More likely than not, when our real selves are placed back in the driving seat, without the annoying passenger of another diet or rule system, we begin to ask ourselves what food will really make us satisfied, happy and nourished. Of course this might sometimes mean eating foods that would normally be forbidden on a typical diet, but most of the time you will be driven to choose wholesome foods because this is what you have naturally been designed to do. It is also part of nurturing your body and mind in ways that makes you feel the most energised and able to flourish – without punishing yourself.

✤

By following a rigid routine that involves following a specific diet, individuals become less able to eat intuitively. In other words, eating becomes dictated by preplanning and set rules, rather than gut feelings about what will be satisfying and nourishing for the mind and body.

There is also the whole controversial issue with referring to some foods as 'good' 'bad' 'naughty', 'points' and 'sins' – suggesting that eating is in some way a morally offensive crime that should be punished! Consequently, individuals can begin to associate snack and meal times with deprivation, guilt and other forms of negative self-judgement, while their real need to feel nourished and loved (whether than be physical hunger or psychological satisfaction) remains unfulfilled. Soon enough, the mind becomes untrusting of food – not knowing whether meal times will bring safety and allow the body's physical needs to be met, or whether negative self-judgement and guilt will occur soon after eating.

It makes sense then that a preoccupation with food becomes extremely common when embarking on a diet, as does the urge to binge on food as soon as dieting rules have been broken in a bid to fulfil needs that might not be fulfilled at a later date. Sooner or later, though, the same person may be ready to place their hope and faith in yet another diet, miracle food, or faddy eating regimen. This vicious cycle is what allows the dieting industry to continue making masses of profit, because we are made to believe that 'falling off the wagon' means that we immediately need to jump back on it in order to get back in the driving seat of our own lives. But now is the time to place these false claims out into the open for your own judgement. Now is the time for you to become empowered by muting the myths.

Time to Mute the Myths

If you are currently thinking that there are quite a lot of unnecessary myths that are still swarming around regarding dieting and weight loss, then you wouldn't be alone.

To stand up against these myths we need to find a way to ditch the diet and weight loss strategies for good. The same mission can be applied for any restrictive mindsets regarding food, so that we can step into a much more compassionate, loving and nourishing relationship with food and our own bodies. Unfortunately, for the time being, many individuals do not give their bodies the credit or appreciation they deserve – even though our bodies are much wiser than we have been led to believe – mostly by the ludicrous diet industry, of course. However, millions of years of evolutionary adaptation bamboozles any diet mentality.

The truth is that when we lean to listen to our body by stepping into a more compassionate relationship with it, we will be able to hear, much more clearly, our authentic voice. This is the voice that mainly craves nourishment from nutrient rich foods, as well as the occasional less nutrient rich foods too, which is largely because our bodies intuitively 'know', unlike the dieting industry, that food has many more vital functions and meanings in our lives other than just energy and nutrition. This ultimately means that taking dieting and weight loss off our menu, hopefully for good, will make it completely normal and acceptable to sometimes crave a bowlful of delicious roasted veggies or a fruit packed smoothie, and at other times chocolate, cakes, biscuits or just about anything that is enjoyable to eat too. It also means that even though many of us have unnecessarily adopted the identity of someone addicted to sugar, chocolate, cake, crisps or just food in general, for most of us the likelihood of these negative food identities being true is very slim. Rest assured there is a beautiful balance and harmony to

*

be uncovered with our food and body, and trusting the wisdom of our own body rather than the ludicrous diet industry holds the magic key.

A question you may be asking now though is how we can go about muting myths around dieting and weight loss, and finally put a stop to them for good? Well firstly, muting the myths involves being willing to step out of your comfort zone and break free from them by developing a more compassionate relationship with food and body. Thankfully, it just so happens that the rest of this book is dedicated to exactly that, and we will begin by discussing one of the most fundamental concepts: compassion-eating.

"Food is never distinctly bad, dirty or unclean. But, thinking that it is will likely be more toxic to your mind and body than eating any 'unhealthy' food ever will be"

Compassion-Eating

In a battle to attain a healthy positive relationship with food and body you may have come across the term 'normal' eating. But what on earth is normal eating if anything at all? And is there a better term we could use that would help us to understand what a positive relationship with food?

You might question whether anyone can really be a 'normal' eater, as normality, by definition, is actually a standard that constantly changes depending on a particular social or cultural norm – in this case in relation to food and how we eat.

In my personal opinion, I don't believe that a static sense of normality around food is possible. For one, how we perceive food and the types of food we eat are constantly changing, depending on our own life experiences, cultural development and the latest trends and norms of society and even local communities. Also, if we were to become a 'normal' eater, based on what we define as normal, that would mean that 'normal' eating would most likely be a disordered way of eating. This is because the majority of individuals in western societies have a self-sabotaging approach to the way they perceive and eat food. Such an approach also often involves dieting, which in the long run doesn't really do anyone any good.

To avoid leading you down a path where food impacts negatively on your life, I think it is more suitable – essential even – to view an optimal way of developing a positive relationship with food as 'compassion-eating' rather than normal eating.

But what do we mean by compassion-eating?

Compassion-eating is a form of self-care, not a diet, and involves viewing food as something that will nourish your mind and body rather than just being something to rigidly control, meet nutritional requirements, obsess about or see as a means to be perfect in order to manipulate your weight and self-worth. Compassion-eating comes from an authentic place of wanting to be kind to yourself while understanding your physical, psychological and social needs.

Compassion-eating additionally allows you to get back in tune with what your body and mind really want, so you can eat more intuitively – rather than rigidly – while being able to optimally nourish yourself without set routines, guilt or negative self-judgement. These characteristics make compassion-eating very distinctive from dieting, which is often based on self-criticism in order to mould yourself into something you are not – usually with methods that involve punishment or dismissing other essential elements of happiness and health. Individuals who embark on a diet also tend to experience times where they feel like 'cheating' or being 'naughty'. These terms simply do not exist in the realm of compassion-eating. Instead, compassion-eating is a way of viewing eating occasions as an opportunity be as nurturing and kind to yourself as possible, rather than self-sabotaging. With compassion-eating, you are never at war with food or your body, and it is yet another key way to living more compassionately.

When I refer to compassion-eating I think of someone who is not preoccupied by the next dieting fad, or who has an all or nothing approach to food. With compassion-eating, food is something to enjoy and cherish in the moment, whether that be to suit a particular mood, social occasion or cultural tradition, as well as nutritional needs. Also, the concept of good, bad, dirty or naughty foods do not exist, and neither does an 'all or nothing' mentality where eating one forbidden biscuit almost immediately leads to an empty biscuit tin – closely followed by guilt and self-loathing.

Put into more simple terms, compassion-eating is the Nourishing Routes way of viewing food and eating occasions as an opportunity to nourish the body and mind while also experiencing enjoyment – not deprivation, guilt, shame or punishment. The aim of compassion-eating is not to follow a rigid meal plan or routine with the aim of losing weight or meeting your exact nutritional requirements with anxiety provoking precision. By stark contrast, the real aim of compassion-eating is to feel nourished from the inside out because you genuinely love your whole mind and body and want to nurture them as much as possible.

It may be true that eating or preoccupying ourselves with food can sometimes be used to fill a void or sense of emptiness in our lives that might be best fulfilled or addressed through engaging in another activity (e.g. gaining support from friends and family, gaining a sense of belonging, or resolving a conflict). But the fact remains that food should be a compassionate activity rather than one to meet a nutritional standard we think will lead to optimal health. In relation to this, compassion-eating allows us to get back in tune with our whole needs and be aware of why we might be eating certain foods at certain times. We can then become more mindfully aware about when food (eating or even just thoughts about it) might be filling a void that could be better addressed through other thoughts and behaviours – without necessarily using food.

But how does compassion-eating feel?

Compassion-eating is driven by wanting to feel really satisfied – without guilt, shame or negative judgement. After eating, it feels as though you have just stepped out a refreshing hot shower or a relaxing bath. You feel warm, revitalised, clean and re-energised from having taken the time to pamper and nurture your real needs. There is also no negative judgement when stepping out of that shower or bath (i.e. after eating), because you know that regardless of the type of water or products you used to wash yourself (i.e. types of or how much food you have eaten), you were able to deservingly take care of yourself and enjoy the process. Unlike how many individuals view food, I very much doubt that many people step out of a shower or bath and say to themselves that they need to compensate for their recent pleasurable experience by denying themselves a wash for the next several days or using considerably less water next time (as a person may do in the context of skipping a meal or skimping on Calories and denying pleasurable foods).

If that example is still a bit to abstract to understand, perhaps the following lists of what compassion-eating is and is not might help to clarify the term even better.

What Compassion-Eating IS NOT:

❀ Setting rigid rules about what you should and should not eat, and taking extreme precaution to avoid eating these forbidden foods

❀ Feeling fearful, guilty or low in self-esteem before or after eating a certain type of food

❀ Feeling preoccupied with making the 'best' decision you can around the 'healthiest' food to eat

❀ Saying no to going out with friends or family because there is a high chance there will be food around that is 'off limits'

❀ Viewing the food you eat as something that needs to be burned off as soon as possible

❀ Using thoughts about food or eating food as a way to mask a personal conflict or fulfil needs in your life that could be better addressed and/or met using a different approach or activity

❀ Only eating at specific times, or ensuring that there is a rigidly set time interval between different meals

❀ Feeling anxious if you can't weigh food or calculate how many Calories it has in it

❀ Referring to what you eat as 'bad', 'naughty', or 'sinful'

❀ Creating rules around the types of foods you can eat, how and when – even though they don't relate to a necessary dietary requirement such as an allergy, intolerance or genuine ethical decision (e.g. following a vegetarian or vegan lifestyle)

❀

❋ Spending large amounts of time calculating Calories, logging the food you eat and pre-planning exactly what you will 'allow' yourself to eat

❋ Saying to yourself that eating certain foods or deviating from a diet you are on will make you fat, ugly, dirty, naughty or an unlovable person

❋ Cutting food up into small pieces, using extra small cutlery, or chewing for very long periods of time in order to make it last longer – you may want to feel fuller for longer or possibly don't know when you might allow yourself to eat this type of food again

❋ Eating a food you would normally not freely let yourself, and then feeling compelled to eat lots more of it or ensure that you compensate the next day – perhaps by skipping meals, starving yourself or excessively exercising

What Compassion-Eating IS:

❋ Feeling free and lovingly accepting of yourself to choose the foods that suit how you feel – whether that be something sweet, salty, or comforting to your emotions without worrying about the consequences

❋ Throwing out your own or any other rule book when it comes to setting necessary boundaries around foods you wouldn't normally allow yourself to eat

❋ Wanting to eat in ways that makes your body and mind feel energised and nourished

❋ Realising that food has so many more functions than just fuel – it creates opportunities to connect with others, rekindle memories, create new memories and complement our feelings and emotions

❋ Believing that rarely can any food be distinctly good or bad, and that there are many ways that food contributes to nourishment of our mind and body other than nutrition alone

❋

❋ Taking another biscuit, eating a slice of cake or any other form of food normally classified as 'unhealthy' or non-nutrient dense and fully enjoying it without equating this with being 'naughty', being a 'bad' person or feeling like you now need to compensate for what you have eaten by restricting food, going on a detox or 'burning it off' by engaging in more exercise.

❋ Being able to prepare and cook food while allowing yourself to taste test your recipe and tasty creations as you go along (yes that includes eating cake mixture off your fingers...)

❋ Finding ways to be more adventurous and playful with food in your own kitchen or when going out for meals and snacks, where trying new foods and recipes becomes fun and exciting rather than something to fear or get stuck in a rut with.

❋ Adding more nourishing and enjoyable foods into your diet that make you feel happy, satisfied and energised, as compared to trying to find more foods to cut out or jump on the next dieting trend

❋ Noticing when negative thoughts about food, or certain eating patterns, are related to fulfilling a need that could be better addressed in ways other than using food as a coping mechanism.

❋ Living a life where food is something you take time to prepare and enjoy because you love and want to nourish your body and mind, while not obsessing about it to the point where other important activities or creative pursuits in your life are neglected

❋ Being trusting of yourself around food, in whatever form or quantity, with the reassurance that your body is an amazing self-regulating system that will enable you to eat as much as you need – without depriving yourself or bingeing on food.

With the above lists in mind, you might think that throwing out the 'rule' book around what you eat is a very daunting, anxiety provoking or even scary task.

❋

I can completely resonate with the ingrained fear that we will lose control around food, regardless of whether an individual has experience of an eating disorder or disordered eating. It is almost as though throwing out our rule book or meal plan around food might result in us becoming completely out of control around food in a self-sabotaging way, even though the exact opposite is more likely to happen. This is because by really loving ourselves, appreciating our body and listening to its innate wisdom (rather than a rule book) we will realise that what our body is really asking for isn't ever going to be a shed load of biscuits, mounds of unlimited cakes, or bottomless bags of crisps.

Of course, we will want to eat these types of foods occasionally – we are all human and they can add to the quality of our emotional and social lives. However, our bodies weren't designed to crave these types of food in order to feel nourished, and energised in order to function optimally. When we begin to trust that fact, we will naturally find a beautiful balance – a balance where rigid rules and planning do not exist, but eating enjoyably and flexibly does and takes centre stage. This balance is also part of what enables us to live more compassionately while feeling nourished and able to flourish and thrive.

Personally I like to think of compassionate eating as a positive cycle, which initially begins by learning to accept ourselves as we are now (a key aspect of self-compassion). Growing out of this acceptance comes an authentic openness and willingness to be compassionate to ourselves. The way that we view food and nourish ourselves becomes flexible rather than rigid – without feelings of shame, disgust or low self-worth around food.

The positive cycle looks a bit like this when applied to ourselves:

1) "I am willing to accept myself as I am – including how I look, what I weigh, or the way I eat"

2) "I respect myself enough to want to take care of and nurture myself from this moment onwards"

3) "I want to step into a place where I can listen to my physical, psychological and social needs, so that I can eat in a way that nourishes my mind, body and social relationships"

4) "I am ready to let go of any unnecessary rules or rigid control that I have placed over my eating, while taking steps to feel more flexible around food without negative judgement"

5) "I will allow myself to eat because food isn't just fuel – it is also about enjoyment, self-nurturing and also reconnecting with my values, memories, culture and the world around me"

6) "As I eat in a more flexible, nourishing and compassionate way, I will be willing to step into a place of body confidence"

7) "The more I trust my food and body, the more I can trust myself and finally let go of the rigid control and unrealistic expectants that I have placed on myself/have been placed on me"

8) "I can become empowered to step into a positive relationship with my whole self, while being able to eat and live more compassionately"

This might all sound well and good, but what about the actual actions you can take to become more positively aware of your own capacity for compassion-eating and actually taking steps to regularise taking part in compassion-eating yourself?

Firstly, to identify your own current take on compassion-eating, go back to the lists we recently described about what compassion-eating is and is not. Go through each point and ask yourself how much that statement relates to your own life and relationship with food in a positive or negative way.

At the end of these lists, ask yourself whether you feel as though your current way of eating is more aligned with what compassion-eating is or is not. A key thing to remember is that it is not necessary to judge yourself on whether you currently engage in compassion-eating or not. The main point is to accept yourself in the present moment without negative judgement, and be willing to address on which side of the compassion-eating spectrum you would like to be. Do you want to remain in your current position, or take targeted action in a way that allows you to step into a life filled with more compassion-eating?

Of course this is your own decision. For myself, compassion-eating was the only way that truly aligned with my goal of recovery, living more compassionately and eventually being able to help others too. Without it, or being able to learn to love myself, I quite literally wouldn't be in the place I am now. Loving food and experiencing a life that has a deeper meaning and purpose that doesn't solely revolve around what I eat or do not eat has been the key to finding freedom and finally listening to my own natural instinct – my compassionate inner compass.

Before we look at any more specific steps we can take in order to integrate more compassion-eating in to our lives, it is useful to first have a little look at some of the reasons why compassion-eating is quite a foreign concept for many of us. To begin with, we will look at, in a bit more detail than previously, how the concept of 'healthy' eating in our society might be leading us to develop a more negative relationship with food rather than actually leading to wellbeing.

Is 'Healthy' Eating Consuming You?

Can healthy eating ever become an unhealthy obsession, or even a form of disordered eating? Surely putting healthy nourishing foods inside of our bodies can't be doing any harm, as that is what we are all told to do on a daily basis, right?

Many of us do happen to live in a society where we are constantly bombarded with talk and images about the need to eat as cleanly, healthily and nutritiously as possible. Along with these expectations comes the 'reward' of appearing pure, superior and competent at self-regulating our behaviours.

Some individuals feel that these expectations mean that we can no longer tuck into our favourite meal or snack without feeling a pang of guilt or a need to compensate their behaviour in some punishing way. But at what expense might some individuals pay to avoid feeling like this? All you are doing is trying to be as healthy as possible, and that's what everyone wants, right? No one would ever recommend eating whatever you like and enjoying it too.

Healthy eating isn't bad in itself – at least on a physical level as long as you are getting enough of the energy and nutrients your body requires. But it is additionally and very crucially important to consider the types of thoughts and feelings you have about the food you eat – not just what and how much you eat. To do this we can ask ourselves, is healthy eating a positive part of our life and something we do almost subconsciously, without negatively intruding on our social life and everyday functioning? Or does our whole day revolve around meticulously planning and preparing every single morsel of food that we think we should be eating for optimal health or trying to attain or maintain a 'healthy weight'?

Does the thought of eating something 'unhealthy', unplanned, processed, or pre-prepared out of your control fill you with dread? Perhaps treat foods, such as anything that includes refined sugar, flavourings or artificial ingredients – whether that be chocolate, sweets, cakes, or pretty much anything in a packet – have become forbidden, feared or avoided at all costs. Similarly, eating late at night, on the go, or outside of your usual healthy eating schedule has become a huge no go.

What about the way you feel after you have eaten something you view as 'clean', or 'healthy'? Some individuals may feel quite positive and revitalised before getting on with other fulfilling activities throughout the rest of their day. However, you may feel as though the snack or meal you prepared was not good, clean or healthy enough. As a consequence, you sense a growing urge to make your diet even healthier by cutting out more high Calorie, processed or unnatural ingredients.

Alternatively, perhaps the way you meticulously plan and eat your meals with precision might allow you to gain some temporary sense of control in your life and superiority over other individuals. For example, individuals who eat 'unhealthy' food may appear inferior, simply based on how they eat a minimally nutritious diet. You might even question how some individuals can do this without feeling guilty or having a desire to 'burn off' what they have just eaten.

For yourself, eating certain health-orientated foods might help you to reduce negative feelings, such as stress, anger and anxiety, by helping you to feel more in control and able to cope with uncertain or difficult life circumstances. Similarly, you might think that the result of not eating 'clean' or as 'healthy' as possible involves feeling incredibly guilty, dirty and maybe even a gluttonous unworthy person – which you avoid by ensuring you eat nutrient dense foods at all times, even if this involves excessively spending your hard earned money on expensive superfood powders and unnecessary nutritional supplements.

Perhaps your social media pages are filled with perfectly choreographed images of 'clean' food recipes, while you are often on the lookout for a new health guru, or blogger' tips on how to prepare and eat more nutrient rich organic foods that are as pure and unprocessed as physically possible. Your own time spent creating social media content might also involve taking and editing your own food photographs at every opportunity – ensuring that, to the outside world, you appear to have one of the most nutrient rich diets known to mankind. Your healthy eating is almost a status symbol or a mask to hide your deeper insecurities of how others might judge you if they thought you didn't eat healthy food.

With such an importance placed on what, when and how much you eat, much of your day might be spent thinking about food. The following questions might frequently dominate your thoughts:

❋ What should I eat?

❋ What can't I eat?

❋ When will I be able to eat my precisely prepared meal?

❋ What activities will I have to postpone or cancel in order to fit in time to plan, prepare and eat my 'clean' food?

❋ How can I avoid eating out with friends?

❋ How will my family be able to cater for my lengthy dietary requirements?

❋ What is the latest superfood to invest in?

❋ What even more 'unhealthy' foods can I cut out my diet?

❋ How can I begin to eat even cleaner and source my food more organically and ethically as possible?

If you notice that some of these situations are sometimes true to your own life on a regular basis, or impede your ability to be compassionate to yourself, feel connected to others, or engage in creative and enjoyable activities in your life, then it might be worth asking yourself whether your 'healthy' or

❋

'clean' eating regimen is actually doing you more harm than good – at least for your psychological and social wellbeing.

From my own experiences of being obsessed with healthy 'clean' eating, while also being in a very disordered mindset regarding food and body, I noticed that my whole identity and view of myself completely revolved around what I did and did not eat. It became so much a part of me that to think of myself as anything other than a 'healthy' eater was scary. Also, not being fully aware or in control of what and how much I ate seemed a very foreign and anxiety provoking concept. If you took my obsession with food away, I thought there would be nothing worthy left of me.

Food had completely consumed me, but in the process I had neglected a relationship with food that was worth nurturing and learning love. Of course my ideas about not being a worthy person or deserving of enjoyable food were false ones, and the reality remained that there were many other parts of me – other than what I ate – that made up my identity and purpose on the planet. However, it was only by learning to love myself, pursue creatively enjoyable interests, incorporate lots of diverse foods (non-Calorie counted) into my meals and become more flexible with the idea of 'healthy' eating that other parts of my identity and sense of purpose became clearer in my own eyes. Soon the prospect of letting go of the 'food as my whole and only identity' label became a possibility that I couldn't afford to ignore any longer.

While it may be helpful to question or improve some of our less nourishing food choices, if our obsessive thoughts about healthy eating are having a negative impact on our wellbeing it is important to ask ourselves whether we are becoming consumed by the pursuit of the perfect diet.

Is it really realistic to try and obtain a diet of purity and perfection?

Why should we even attach negative feelings such as guilt and self-hate to what we eat or don't eat?

These are just some of the questions that experts in the field of eating behaviour and eating disorders are currently asking. So, could eating healthy to an obsessive extent actually be a form of disordered eating? Current research findings and anecdotal evidence along with insightful case studies seem to suggest that this might be the case.

More specifically, research studies refer to the term 'orthorexia', with 'ortho' being derived from the Greek term true or correct. Orthorexia is a term used to describe an individual who becomes obsessively preoccupied by a need to obtain purity through perfecting what they eat.

These days it might seem as though we have a word to label everything, including how we medicalise every negative behaviour, but perhaps the term orthorexia might at least shed some light on how we can address obsessive healthy eating when this begins to have a detrimental impact on individuals' lives. But first let's paint a picture of what orthorexia looks like in terms of its impact on individuals' lives.

As I am all too familiar with, orthorexia usually manifests in aiming to eat foods that are deemed as being as nutritious, healthy, unprocessed and 'clean' as possible. What an individual views as good and bad foods to eat is influenced by their personal experiences, which inevitably involves the negative messages we are told by the health, fitness and dieting industries.

A consistent preoccupation with healthy eating, without doubt, can lead to worries, fear and guilt about eating impure or unhealthy foods, which for some individuals might include foods containing preservatives, saturated fat, animal products or synthetic ingredients.

Individuals who develop 'orthorexic' thoughts feeling and behaviours (if we wish to refer to them in this way) may spend large or excessive amounts of time reading about and preparing healthy food, assessing the quality of what they have eaten, and sacrificing family, friends and loving relationships over their need to prioritise what and how much they can eat and when. They may also restrict their consumption of various food items, or eliminate more and more from their diet completely until they feel safe with just eating a limited few foods that they feel are 'safe' and can be consumed without experiencing guilt, negative emotions or wanting to compensate in some self-destructive way.

Although a person's weight might stay stable while fulfilling their healthy eating obsessions, many individuals with orthorexia will experience nutrient deficiency, metabolic dysfunction and unhealthy weight loss – ironically despite them trying to attain the best health via the diet they consume. If we are to consider orthorexia as a disorder though, a key factor to consider is how individuals with orthorexia often neglect their social life and other psychological needs over what they eat. As a consequence, many individuals become socially isolated and unable to engage in meaningful activities, feel connected to others, find a sense of meaning, or lead a compassionate lifestyle.

In other words,'orthorexic' eating behaviours can lead individuals to experience poor rather than optimal wellbeing, even to an extent which prevents them from reaching their full potential. Orthorexia, in some cases, might be additionally accompanied by other mental health disorders, such as obsessive compulsive disorder, depression, anxiety, or additional eating disorders (e.g. anorexia nervosa or bulimia), so the distinction between orthorexia and other forms of mental illness may be quite blurry. However, orthorexia can be distinguished from other forms of disordered eating, such as anorexia nervosa or bulimia, since the obsession with healthy eating does not necessarily include experiencing poor body image or being obsessed by a need to become slimmer or avoid eating too much and gaining weight.

Orthorexia might seem like an extreme form of healthy eating that only a small minority of individuals experience, but an emerging body of research suggests otherwise. For example, some studies have shown that cases of orthorexia may be above 50% in some vulnerable populations, such as athletes, dancers and employees in the nutrition and fitness field of work.

Although better assessment tools are needed to accurately identify orthorexia and outline it as being distinct from a slight preoccupation or interest in healthy eating, it is worth pointing out that many populations in Europe are becoming ever more critical about what they put into their bodies and what this symbolically means in terms of their social status and chances of being accepted by others. So why is this the case?

Instead of simply striving for a healthy balance through food, many of us are sent messages that encourage us to strive for perfection, and this includes what we 'should' and 'should not' eat. Food now symbolises to others how good we are at adhering to social norms and self-regulating our behaviours, and can even signify our social status if eating makes us appear more affluent or superior in terms of the behaviours we carry out. While this might benefit companies who sell nutritious products at a more expensive price, it is not of benefit to the many individuals who are left feeling guilty and unworthy as a result of not buying into them or failing to eat healthy and clean 100% of the time...

A key message to note here is that becoming obsessed about healthy eating is not a route to follow if you would like to become more self-compassionate. In fact, orthorexia, and the high hopes individuals have for seeking perfection and purity through their eating, may alternatively lead to negative self-comparison, feelings of inadequacy, and poor self-esteem. Is this really a recipe for happiness and wellbeing?

So what can we do to tackle this problem and what can you do if you feel your own thoughts, feelings and behaviours around eating are becoming obsessive or even orthorexic?

Firstly, part of the solution involves being critical of the messages we regularly come into contact with about healthy eating. Having the 'perfect' diet is by no means the only avenue to a long and happy life (if a perfect diet is even possible), and striving for it obsessively can lead us down a dark path of feeling miserable rather than revitalised and optimally nourished in both mind and body. For example, magazines, blog posts, and news articles that claim to have found the next best superfood or diet regimen need to be taken with a pinch of salt.

Secondly, we need to raise awareness about the negative impacts some messages about healthy eating can have. Apart from many of these health messages not being evidence based as well as promoted by organisations on the look out to make money, some advice is simply not practical for the majority of individuals – such as living off juice drinks, protein powders, or eliminating all sugar from your diet and living off a 100% organic food diet that only consists of raw vegetables.

Perhaps some individuals might thrive on these type of diets (although I very much doubt it), but for most individuals I do question the practicality and motivations behind pursuing them – especially if they involve more appearance related goals rather than values or genuinely wanting to sustainably achieve authentic happiness and health. Such lifestyles might sound like a great idea if you are looking for a quick fix, but in reality that is all they are. As another dark undertone, they might even lead to developing disordered relationships with food, mind and body.

To nip cases of orthorexia or any form of disordered eating in the bud, ideally before the roots begin to grow or deepen, we need to look at ways that we can prevent food obsession from occurring. This might involve devising methods of identifying vulnerable individuals, including ourselves, who might be at risk, and enabling them to access supportive resources and positive message about food and body as early as possible. Enabling our society to become more critical of the bombardment of health-obsessive messages we receive on a daily basis through various forms of media outlets is also essential.

Perhaps even more crucially is the act of helping individuals, perhaps even our own selves, who are currently struggling with food obsession or orthorexia to identify and accept that they may need help. Such individuals can be provided with opportunities to access effective support systems, such as one to one coaching or counselling to enable them to rekindle a positive relationship with food, body and their whole self. During coaching or counselling, for example, it is important to help individuals develop a deeper and clearer understanding about food, such as the importance of where it comes from, enjoying it to the full, and how they can make compassionate food choices in ways that allow them to feel energised and nourished in both body and mind without succumbing to society's obsession with healthy or 'clean' eating.

A key part of this mission will ideally involve helping others and ourselves to realise that we are already pretty awesome human beings without having to be defined by the quality or quantity of food we do or do not eat. Self-acceptance and love comes from within – not from seeking external validation or approval through eating in a way that is perceived by ourselves or others as healthy.

Dieting + Weight Loss = Health + Happiness?

Have you ever noticed how near enough every lifestyle magazine, news article or advertisement involving a diet or weight loss plan is portrayed with someone looking happy or at least very content next to it?

There are also those (often annoying) before and after pictures, with the before image being of a person who looks notably unhappier that the after version? And then there are the masses of publications that speak about the joys of losing weight, and how it helped someone to finally be themselves again and lead a much happier and more successful life.

Although losing weight might benefit a minority of individuals (mainly those involved in the organisations that thrive off selling weight loss gimmicks), what we are regularly told about losing weight is part of the mythical assumption that doing this will instantaneously result in happiness and optimal health. In actuality, as we recently discussed, there is very little evidence to suggest that losing weight, or intentionally going on a diet, leads to any sustained health benefits or happiness.

Even when weight is not the main issue that is stopping someone from being healthy, happy or leading a fulfilling life, the clear association between losing weight and happiness portrayed by the media makes it hard to ignore such a method as being one of the best ways to wellbeing. Regardless of the fact that this assumption is a false one.

Add this to the frequent victimisation and stigmatisation of individuals who are deemed to be 'overweight' or 'too fat', and we have a disastrous recipe that involves many individuals striving to lose weight – perhaps even at the expense rather than the gain of their wellbeing.

✣

What might be concerning is that intentionally aiming to lose weight, or even succeeding at this goal, may increase the risk of poorer health as opposed to leading to any health benefits at all.

For example, as we briefly mentioned earlier, most outcomes from research on dieting suggests that not only do dieters regain the weight they originally lost (and sometimes even more due to changes in metabolism and the way individuals view food), many go on to experience even poorer self-esteem as well as diminished happiness and overall life satisfaction.

More recent research also found that out of 2000 individuals who were instructed to lose weight to improve their health:

✤ 14 % lost 5% or more of their body weight

✤ 15% gained more weight

✤ 71% stayed the same weight

✤ Ratings of overall happiness and wellbeing decreased

✤ Dieters compared to non-dieters were twice as likely to be depressed

The research outcomes of another large study led the author to make the bold statement that:

"One third to two thirds of dieters regain more weight than they lost on their diets, and these studies likely underestimate the extent to which dieting is counterproductive because of several methodological problems, all of which bias the studies toward showing successful weight loss maintenance.

In addition, the studies do not provide consistent evidence that dieting results in significant health improvements, regardless of weight change... The benefits of dieting are simply too small and the potential harms of dieting are too large for it to be recommended as a safe and effective treatment for obesity."

This is quite a bold statement, yet what we read and listen to in terms of promoting health and combatting a so-called obesity crisis involves the exact opposite – going on a diet and intentionally aiming for weight loss. Also, regardless of whether individuals embark on a diet or not, there is quite a large body of evidence that shows how being overweight, according to the standards of BMI, does not have a direct relationship with health, happiness or longevity. However, we additionally mentioned a bit earlier on that we do know that there is a notably significant relationship between being underweight and the risk of premature mortality.

So if weight really isn't that important, what is?

In relation to a person's diet and weight there is a much more damaging impact to health other than being overweight or eating unhealthy food. Much bigger forces that impact our happiness and health involve feeling socially isolated and stigmatised (especially in relation to weight), as well as not showing self-compassion, experiencing a sense of purpose or being classified as an individual who has a low social status (e.g. living in an area of deprivation or where there is an inequitable distribution of resources in society).

The simple message from findings in diet-related research translates into the fact that dieting and weight loss cannot be viewed as the main route to wellbeing and happiness, and that in some cases it could even lead to psychological and physical harm. Also, despite how goals around dieting and weight may lead to some physical health benefits (e.g. when an individual's weight is placing pressure on their joints in a way that limits their physical activity), there is no guarantee. The prominent fact also remains that there are many other more evidence based psychological and social factors to consider when it comes to predicting happiness, health and wellbeing.

Take for example some of the psychological and social changes that are likely to happen when someone embarks on a diet:

❋ Increased time spent thinking and worrying about food

❋ Placing more restrictions on what foods are deemed as 'good' or 'bad'

❋

* Avoiding social occasions or times that involve celebrating with 'off limits' food

* Increasing risk of social isolation the more individuals opt out of social occasions that involve eating with others

* Rigidly counting Calories

* Experiencing mood swings and negative mood states

* Negatively judging self-worth based on how much weight they have gained or lost as well as their appearance

* Developing rigid rituals around food that increase the likelihood of developing a disordered relationship with food and body

* Time spent on methods of losing weight limits time spent on activities where happiness and wellbeing are more likely to evolve, such as spending time with family and engaging in enjoyable or relaxing hobbies.

* Not eating enough nutrients to fuel metabolic activities of the whole body

* Increased likelihood of becoming a 'restrained' eater and developing a tendency to binge on foods by viewing eating occasions as an 'all or nothing' activity

* Losing weight and not getting enough nutrients can have a detrimental impact on brain function, as well as increasing the likelihood of mental illness such as eating disorders, anxiety and depression.

* Becoming more hostile towards others due to changes in our mood and social habits, which means that dieting behaviour could technically impact the welfare of others too.

❋ Engaging in behaviour that encourages other people to believe that dieting is the key route to wellbeing, and even encouraging them to gradually develop their own negative relationship with food and body.

As you might be able to tell already, there is definitely no linear process between dieting, weight loss and happiness. A key concern of mine is that the many ways we promote dieting or altering our food intake in modern times are actually encouraging individuals to move away from health rather than towards it.

We have to remember that our bodies were not designed and did not evolve to lose weight in order to gain a survival advantage. The opposite is true, and when the body experiences a phase where starvation is interpreted as being an issue (e.g. when embarking on a diet or restricting food intake), there are so many subconscious processes going on that encourage the body to alter its metabolism or behaviour in a way that promotes weight gain – even long after a phase of restriction has ended.

By turning the concept of dieting + weight loss = happiness + wellbeing on its head, I would like to help you become more aware of this fact, and that there are many other more compassionate routes to wellbeing.

Don't wait for your weight

It is often the case that individuals – my previous self included – think that they can only pursue or achieve certain things once they have lost or even gained a certain amount of weight, or reached their 'ideal' weight. This perception is completely false, and one of the main reasons why many of us never pursue or achieve our ambitions, most likely because we don't think they are worth our time until our weight goals have been met. If there was a prize for the best lie that we ever tell ourselves, being at an 'ideal' weight to accomplish our goals or be the person we want to be would be right up there in the rankings.

I can confidently say that we no longer need to wait for our weight to be 'perfect' in order to reach our potential. Only when we start to make time for the activities and goals we want to pursue, regardless of what we weigh, will we really be making steps forward. Even if you did wait for your weight to be 'ideal', this would unlikely lead you to feel able to journey towards the life that you really want. This journey has to start now – today even.

What I really mean to say is that living the life you truly want can happen at any weight, and it is our minds that are the main barrier to taking action and moving forward. Removing this barrier involves placing ourselves in a place of self-love and acceptance, while realising that the time is now to get creative, plan and take action on our ambitions. For example, if you can imagine your ideal future self going out there and starting your own business, engaging in a new form of physical activity, spending more time being creative, or dressing in clothes you would like to wear, do it now.

If you are honest with yourself, do you really need to be at a lower or higher weight to begin living? In some cases, there may be a yes answer to that question. For example, some individuals suffering from an eating disorder may need to gain weight or remain at a stable weight before engaging in a certain type of physical activity. Similarly, if someone wants to increase their chances of having a child, they may have to either increase or reduce their weight. However, this doesn't mean that there will be other goals in your life that you can't place your creative energies into right now. If weight is a real issue, the likelihood is that this will resolve itself only once you start living – not after you have focussed on 'fixing' your weight.

Our bodies are highly intelligent beings, and the more we nourish our minds and take action on becoming the best versions of ourselves, the physical side will sort itself out. I found this was true for myself too. Once I started connecting socially again and engaging in creative activities and volunteering, my food intake naturally began to increase (without me judging myself negatively), as did my weight up until the point where I could then engage in the more vigorously physical activities I wanted to enjoy too – such as yoga and going on longer countryside walks with my dog. It was the act of starting with my mind, taking action on my life ambitions and gaining a sense of purpose – not my weight – that allowed me to become the person I thoroughly enjoy being today. The overall key message here is that we really shouldn't wait for our weight. If you have dreams you want to pursue, and a future version of yourself you would like to become and experience with life fulfilment, the time is now to take your first steps forward.

So, instead of aiming to lose or gain a certain amount of weight, I would like you to know that what you eat and your body is worth loving right now. We know from evidence and multiple personal experiences that our health and happiness can be pursued in so many more exciting and enjoyable ways that will really benefit us in both the short and the long term.

Another key step in the right direction of forming this loving relationship with food and your body involves challenging the concept that there really are 'good' and 'bad' foods, which is the next intriguing topic we are going to delve into.

"You can't experience body confidence by striving to a achieve a body you don't currently have. The key is in finding a compassionate way to authentically love the one you already possess"

Good and Bad Times with Food

How many of us have ever viewed or referred to certain foods as being good or bad? This might just be in terms of the food itself, such as a green kale smoothie is 'good' and a sugar-filled cake is 'bad', but it can also apply to different time periods, such as how we might refer to having 'good' or 'bad' days in relation to what we have eaten. Similarly, during new year, 'treat' foods are off limits, while at birthdays, Christmas and celebrations with family and friends they are 'good' again – stimulating us to let ourselves loose on the all you can eat buffet before we have to be 'good' again.

We can also falsely believe that eating certain foods suddenly makes the whole day either a good one or a bad one, when in truth there can never be a distinctly good or bad day. Every person's day is most likely filled with lots of positive opportunities and experiences to feel grateful for, while the exact nutrients and amount of energy in what we eat has a very minimal impact on the grand scheme of our day and even our overall lives.

Viewing food in these black and white terms of good and bad doesn't really set a good foundation for developing a compassionate relationship with food or our own bodies. Instead, it disconnects us further from our natural ability to eat intuitively while perpetuating a negative cycle of basing our food intake on how many 'bad' or 'good' foods we have recently eaten. Perhaps this might involve using 'bad' food as a treat when we have been 'good' or accomplished something. It could likewise involve eating 'good' foods or even depriving ourselves of food when we feel we have recently eaten something 'bad' or haven't achieved something in the best way that we would have hoped for.

By continuing to view food in good or bad terms, we would be relying on what and how much we eat as a very inaccurate way of gauging how worthy we are as individuals, as well as a marker for how much control we have over our lives. Also, by classifying food as good or bad, we fall into the trap of believing that one particular food is distinctly health promoting while another is definitively toxic. All of these assumptions of course would be false, yet would lead us further down a negative path that allows us to remain detached from what our real needs are.

It is important to mention here that it is very rare to place anything in life into distinct categories, or what I like to call black and white boxes. We live in a world where there are lots of grey areas in between different ends of multiple spectrums. It is only complex social beings like ourselves who like to bracket things off into their own little compartments so that we can think about them in a more simple way.

If we do eat a food that we have classified as bad, I think of this as triggering the part of our brain that makes us feel unnecessarily restricted and guilty about a 'wrongdoing' we can't undo without going to some extreme self-sabotaging measure.

We therefore really need to stop thinking about food and our self-worth in black and white terms if we are going to become a true Compassioneer, especially where self-compassion and developing a positive relationship with our food and body is concerned.

The mythical boundaries between good and bad foods

In the context of food you may classify something you eat as 'bad' just because it is not rich in nutrients, high in Calories, filled with unnatural ingredients or simply not healthy enough. But apart from the unlikelihood that what you are eating is toxic to the body, eating foods we might normally categorise as bad might actually allow you to meet some of your basic needs – even if this isn't physical hunger.

For example, that extra large slice of cake and cappuccino in your favourite cafe may not be particularly rich in nutrients, or low in Calories, but perhaps eating that cake and cappuccino allows you to enjoy time catching up with

✷

245

a friend or finally relax after a busy day at work. In other words, consuming foods that you might normally classify as 'bad' are actually nourishing your social and emotional needs, which is an essential element of Nourishing Routes. Perhaps to say that food is distinctly bad ignorantly ignores the many other roles that food inevitably plays in our complex social and emotional lives.

Thinking or saying that a food is bad suggests that every element of it will be having a damaging effect on the body and mind, which is very unlikely to be the case in one instance of eating it. Of course there is a different perspective to take when food involves placing someone at risk of food poisoning, coming into contact with a particular allergen, or eating a food that does not involve the exploitation of other animals. This is because our choice to label something as a 'bad' food in these scenarios likely stems from a need to remain safe or continue to act in line with a person's personal beliefs and values.

If we are to look at food in a bad way, then the most appropriate way to do this would be to realistically look at your diet and lifestyle as a whole. For example, does what you eat mainly function as an emotional coping tool or as a way of feeling in control when other parts of your life appear very out of control? Similarly, you could ask does food reflect the relationship you have with yourself, where what you eat is rarely viewed as good enough unless it meets some ideal standard or you have worked hard enough to earn it?

What we ideally need to do is view the much wider picture and diverse roles that food has in our overall lives and how we feel about ourselves. As we recently discussed when looking at the deeper relationship we were all born to have with our food, what we eat should not be regarded as a moral issue for us to critique ourselves on. Viewing it in such a way only adds a form of negative judgement, veering us further and further away from a life filled with nourishing compassion.

Out of many of the individuals and clients I have worked with over the years, those who describe a negative relationship with food usually have a likewise negative and non-compassionate relationship with themselves. They too have been caught in the trap of viewing food as good and bad, while simultaneously perceiving themselves as either good or bad depending on what they have just eaten. This negative judgement inevitably causes havoc when trying to obtain a stable sense of self-esteem.

But what can we do about this? Should we simply accept that whatever society we live in, we will be forever confined to thinking of food in morally judgemental black and white terms of good and bad?

If you are not ready to say yes to any of these questions then I will strongly commend you for already making a very positive step forward in being able to develop a more compassionate lifestyle.

By leaving the false belief in 'good' and 'bad' foods behind we can gradually learn to understand that food doesn't have to be a reflection of how we should morally judge ourselves, or whether we should or shouldn't feel good enough or guilty after having consumed a certain amount or type of food. Alternatively, we can learn to accept that there are no good and bad foods, just more or less positive relationships that we have with our food and our whole selves.

Instead of questioning whether a food is good for you in terms of the nutrients or Calories it contains it is much more empowering to ask yourself whether that food will nourish any other of your essential human needs – or any of the 10 elements of Nourishing Routes. For example, you could ask yourself is this food part of a positive social occasion, event or way of experiencing pleasure and enjoyment? Or, is this food a way of punishing myself for eating another bad food or not achieving one of my goals? Is eating that food nourishing for my mind and social life, or is it acting to fill in a gap where my needs to feel loved, in control and accepted are not being met?

As you might have been able to grasp from this discussion about good and bad foods, I believe that it is fully possible to finally realise that food has many vital functions in our lives, which can be more optimally be used if we discard those inaccurate labels.

So, regardless of what, how much, where, or when you eat, rest assured that this does not create a moral dilemma that needs to be solved by eating something 'good' or punishing yourself. You are good enough right now, and viewing food as a vital form of nourishment in more ways than what it symbolises in terms of its health value and nutrients will help you get off on to the right foot towards developing a more compassionate relationship with not only what you eat, but also yourself. To enable you to become even more empowered to understand this and further develop your very own positive relationship with food, we can now look at how we can move away from unnecessarily fearing foods.

Food for Fearing?

Have you heard the latest news? There is a new diet on the scene that you just have to be on – lose 20 pounds in 20 days! Or, have you been told the latest culinary secret? The new superfood that can make you look younger, cure cancer, become more beautiful and live beyond your years?

No? Well, surely you must know to avoid the certain 'evils' of food then – refined sugar, gluten, saturated fat, eating too late and just too many Calories? Failing to do so would most definitely be extremely toxic to the body, place you at risk of Alzheimer's disease, diabetes, heart failure, obesity and surely an early grave…

Hopefully I have not encouraged any one of you to truly believe in any of these mythical statements. But the truth of the matter is, that is just what these statements are – myths – and I can guarantee that there are plenty of them flying around from one discussion or dinner plate to the next each and every minute of the day. Apart from that, rather than promoting a positive relationship with food, they instil fear and anxiety.

Our planet is filled to the brim with news articles, magazines, blogs, TV shows, self-help books and health and fitness programmes that claim to hold the long lost key to happiness and wellbeing. Apparently, as long as we learn to control what we eat, avoid 'toxic' foods and nourish ourselves with the best nutrients possible, then we will all live a happy and healthy life. But of course, we know by now that this is very limited and even a detrimental perspective to take.

Although there is a fair amount of evidence to show that some types of food we eat do help us attain a more positive sense of wellbeing, such foods are by no means the only ingredients when it comes to promoting optimal health and happiness. In theory, it becomes more concerning that we have created a culture that avidly spends much of its time obsessing about what we 'should' and 'should' not eat, with many of us falling into the trap of believing that a certain diet will be the best answer to all of our problems. By following the 'best' diet or eating the 'best' food, we feel that we will lead a longer life while potentially becoming invincible – no longer at risk of any disease or illness, whether they be psychological or physical.

Even if this was the truth, how healthy would we really be if our lives got taken over by making sure that we could rigidly follow all of the rules on a particular diet – or spend lots of time and money investing in the latest superfood, juice subscription, or weight management classes?

There is also the concern about spending a significant proportion of our precious lives fearing and worrying about food, ironically with a mission to try and extend it. Here I would argue that time spent fearing and worrying about food places us out of touch with the true beauty of our current lives in the present moment. If we are not really 'here' when fearing and worrying about food, this means that we may unknowingly be erasing minutes, days, weeks or even years away from our lives. Time spent fearing, worrying about or rigidly planning food isn't really quality time at all, and I do wonder whether the length of time we engage in it exceeds any extra length we gain in terms of lifespan from 'healthy eating'.

I am not saying that any way of healthy living or eating is bad in itself, but placing all of your money on it being the way to cure and eliminate all of your problems is perhaps a recipe for disappointment – or even self-sabotage.

The key thing is, with most food-related trends or 'plans' that label themselves as a diet, they require us to believe that certain foods have healing or awe inspiring properties, while others should be feared and avoided at all costs. As we delve deeper and deeper into the regimen, what was once a 'normal' food to be eaten as an occasional treat soon becomes an anxiety provoking threat that undermines our self-esteem.

If we so much as look at it or touch one of our forbidden foods, we can feel toxic, guilty, stressed and out of control. Slipping up might seems alike to falling off the end of the world, while we can fall into the trap of defining ourselves as failures simply for not being able to live up to the standards that a certain diet, lifestyle plan or societal expectation set for us.

Instead of being left with a new lease of life or vitality, we can be left feeling fearful of certain foods, as well as psychologically and physically drained, low in self-worth, guilty and ashamed. These feelings aren't exactly a recipe for enabling us to live more compassionately or become happier and healthier. In fact, the very opposite of these things are likely to result.

Even if we do succeed in our mission to avoid feared foods we can still engage in obsessive and negative thoughts about how our own eating behaviour compares with other people's. For example, with so much weight placed on what we do or do not eat, it becomes ever more normal to judge other people's eating behaviour as well as our own. For example, you might consider that because you saw someone eating a nutritious salad this lunchtime, you are a relatively uncontrolled person because you actually ate a biscuit or a chocolate bar. Alternatively, you may think of yourself as more superior to someone who you saw eating a cake while in a cafe, while you simply ordered a black coffee or sugar-free drink. If you notice that you are having any thoughts that are related to these scenarios, this could be a sign that your self-esteem is largely based on what you eat and comparing yourself with others. This also possibly means that you might be ignoring many other aspects of your overall health and happiness, as well as neglecting your own unique strengths and ability to live more self-compassionately.

Of course, there are many individuals who can honestly claim that following a certain lifestyle or eating in a specific way has helped them to cure their illnesses or lead a happier, healthier and more fulfilled life. But, for the large majority of individuals, many continue to experiencing problems such as poor skin, digestive issues, feeling fat, or negatively judging themselves. In these cases there are still many other important physical and psychological issues to address, which I would argue take much more of a priority than food.

The point I am trying to emphasise here is that no amount of fearing food or eating healthy is a guaranteed way to nourish, flourish and reach your full potential. There is a much more complicated puzzle to be solved, with many more puzzle pieces to find. However, we can be reassured that the journey to solving this puzzle code is much more worthwhile than the journey you might go on in order to control what you do or do not eat. This is because journeying towards a positive relationship with food involves an adventure of self-discovery while finding ways to authentically enjoy life and love yourself, which is absolutely fundamental when it comes to happiness and health.

We need to realise that real joy in our lives involves viewing food through a lens of abundance – not deprivation. By doing this, we can live in positive anticipation of life, whatever form of eating that might involve, rather than fearing food.

I can empathise with the dilemma though when your eyes or ears acknowledge a new diet or food trend. I used to experience it regularly, thinking that my life's problems would be resolved if only I could eat perfectly. Sometimes there is something inside that screams at you to try a new diet. Maybe it will work this time, and you will feel better with a positive view about yourself. Or, perhaps it will at least act as a distraction during other stressful times in your life. Being completely honest though, and speaking from personal experience, this inner voice is a lie and it doesn't have the strength or sense to realise that there are better adventures for you to embark upon.

One such adventure you can alternatively choose involves asking yourself if there are any ways you can go about developing a different aspect of your identity – apart from an identity that revolves around food. Sometimes, our underlying issues with food come from not being able to express and identify our character strengths, so activities that will help you to unleash these can be hugely beneficial. Also, finding a sense of creativity and enjoyment in new activities can indirectly impact what we eat and the relationship we have with food. For example, once we find that we can appreciate and feel proud of ourselves when engaging in certain activities or using our character strengths, such as being kind to others, we do not need to mask our poor self-worth with trying to use food to make us look better or be better in comparison with others. Instead, we gain more clarity and security in who we are – not who we should be or what we should eat. By doing this, food will eventually become something to love rather than fear, while also not being the defining element of your identity.

If I could pass on only a few words of wisdom within this chapter, I would reassure you that food is not for fearing, and that you really aren't just what you eat. No one food or lifestyle will kill you, heal you, or make you the healthiest or best person alive, despite the many claims out there that try to catch out attention – as well as empty our purses and wallets.

To find your real Nourishing Routes to happiness and health, this comes from fully accepting yourself and what you eat. In terms of food, this means saying goodbye to fearing food, but saying hello to a more self-compassion-ate way of eating. This is absolutely a key part of your own self-discovery and journey towards being able to flourish and thrive. And, if this involves eating chocolate, biscuits, cakes and crisps along the way, then welcome them with open arms rather than a battle sword. We were made to create peace and joy with food – not fear and war.

Compassioneer Activity: Overcoming Food Fear

Choose a food that you enjoy but have also restricted yourself from consuming.

Perhaps it is something you associate with feeling guilty or ashamed of. Perhaps it is something you perceive is too high in Calories or contains forbidden or seemingly toxic ingredients. Alternatively, you may have experience of binging on this type of food, not allowing yourself permission to eat it due to worrying that it might lead to over eating.

Some examples (from my own original list) might include a particular brand or bar of chocolate, a cake from a cafe or restaurant, jelly sweets, white bread, anything with added sugar or E-numbers.

Of course there is nothing innately wrong with the above foods when eaten as part of a diet that is filled with other nourishing foods. It is because we have learned to identify some foods as being distinctly good or bad that leads us to feel guilty or ashamed about eating them.

When choosing your fear food, set out one occasion each week where you will challenge yourself to eat it. This can be at any time of day, but preferably in a location where there aren't too many distractions, and also somewhere you feel safe.

If it would help you can also ask a friend or a family member to be there with you for support and encouragement. From my own experience, no one will think that you are crazy for asking for support to eat a particular type of food. Most close friends and family members are more than happy to lend a hand and provide positive encouragement and praise. We all have a compassionate side, and just as we need to learn to show it towards others, it also makes sense to being open to receive compassion too.

✤

When the time is ready for you to eat your snack, prepare the space where you will be eating it so that it is comfortable. Perhaps some comfy cushions, setting the table, or making your favourite hot drink can help place you into a positive mindset too. Alternatively, if you are eating out, pick a spot to sit that allows you to feel safe and not distracted or fearful about being watched by other people. Eventually though, you might feel comfortable sitting anywhere, and you will probably realise that it is completely OK to eat in front of other people – most individuals are concerned about their own food rather than watching someone else!

Before you eat your chosen food, say to yourself that:

❈ *"I am completely worthy to eat this food. This food will cause me no harm, and I completely deserve to enjoy it to the full."*

❈ *"Regardless of how many Calories or macronutrients this food contains, or what ingredients have been used to make it, my body and mind will be nourished after eating it."*

❈ *"I refuse to feel guilty or ashamed after eating this food, no matter how much I enjoy it or how much I eat. I give myself permission to eat as much of this food as I would like."*

❈ *"This food will nourish all aspects of myself, while helping me to develop a positive relationship with food, mind, body and others."*

When you begin to eat your food, do this in a way where you can really appreciate the full sensory experience – without negatively judging yourself.

Remember that Calories do not matter on this occasion, and neither does the idea of clean eating or that certain foods are good and bad.

Embrace the food and eat it with your full permission. You are compassionately allowing yourself this food, and in no way will eating it, in whatever way or however fast that may be, define your value as a human being.

❈

To focus away from any negative thoughts, ask yourself:

❋ *"What does this food taste and smell like?"*

❋ *"Does it bring back any memories for me?"*

Also remind yourself that:

❋ *"This food, regardless of what ingredients or Calories it contains, is nourishing my mind and body, while allowing me to develop the compassion I deserve to give to myself."*

At the end of eating, find a comfortable seat or space and say to yourself:

❋ *"Thank you for nourishing me. I am glad that you trust me. I am happy that you allowed me to gain nourishment from that food regardless of what it was and what ingredients or Calories it contained."*

❋ *"I am grateful that I can eat food in a way that allows me to enjoy it and feel satisfied, without negative judgement of myself or the food itself."*

❋ *"I would like to have more experiences where I can step into a compassionate and positive relationship with food, where I can love food and food can love me without the need to restrict myself, binge on foods or view food as something evil and something to be fearful of."*

Now simply sit for a couple of minutes with some of your answers to the above questions in your mind. Try not to judge them for being there, even if you are still finding it difficult to accept them or the possibility that developing a positive relationship with food can become a reality.

Finally, say to yourself:

❋ *"From this moment on, I will be open to the idea of allowing myself to develop a positive relationship with food, where I will allow myself to eat without judging myself negatively."*

❋

❉   *"I will also consume food when I am physically hungry, and sometimes even just because of social occasions and my emotional needs. The key thing for me is that I can fully enjoy food in a flexible way while learning that I fully deserve to nourish both my body and mind."*

❉

The Joy in Emotional Eating

Emotional eating. Most of us have heard about it, most of us have experienced it and most of us are probably clued up enough to have noticed that emotional eating gets a bit of a bad press.

Apparently, it is quite 'wrong' and unnecessary to eat when we are happy, sad, lonely, or because our mood drives us to eat in a particular way.

It is also apparently wrong to eat when we are prompted to do so by external cues, such as social situations, advertisements, or the way products are placed on shelves or even online. Instead, we should all ideally be so in tune with our internal hunger signals that we should eat exactly when our body cells cry out for some fuel.

But if you aren't critical of these suggestions just yet, it is very useful to know that most of them are completely unrealistic expectations of any human being, unless you happen to have an additional functionality as a robot.

In this chapter my main aim isn't to make you become a non-emotional eater. Instead, it is to highlight that in some cases emotional eating is a symbol that we need to be observant of what is really going on in our lives and take action in order to help ourselves. My other key aim is to acknowledge that emotional eating can occur in positive contexts, as well as just how unrealistic it would be if humans were non-emotional eaters.

By default of being human, eating may result from sadness, happiness and several other emotions or internal cues – whether we are conscious about it or not. This is inevitable due to the simple fact that all human beings are complex emotional creatures – not finely tuned machines. We can't simply make eating a non-emotional affair, and even if that were possible, what a shame that would be.

This isn't to say that our biological body signals, such as appetite regulating hormones, don't play a role in our level of hunger and eating behaviour. It also doesn't mean that some forms of emotional eating aren't detrimental to our wellbeing. For example, you may have experienced over-eating or under-eating in response to stress, feeling unloved or even when feeling guilty after eating a 'forbidden' or restricted type of food. When eating this way, whether that be overeating or under-eating, it usually means that we are using food to dull the emotions, feelings or situations in life we are not yet ready to face.

Eating in this context can also suggest that there is something we don't like about ourselves, or we are using food to meet needs that aren't being met elsewhere in our lives.

In all of the above cases, though, emotional eating is not necessarily a sign of self-sabotage – it can be a sign of self-care. This may seem like a controversial speculation, but eating is often the action we take in order to help ourselves feel free from negative emotions, stress or difficult issues in our lives. So, instead of beating ourselves up for emotional eating, it is much better for us to recognise when emotional eating occurs while becoming an intrigued observer as to why that might be. Doing this is key to becoming more mindful around food in a compassionate way.

By beginning to mindfully become aware of and question why we eat emotionally, without negatively judgement, we can see that emotional eating is sometimes a behaviour that allows us to hide our deepest feelings and life issues. In other words, it is a signal that we need to take action in a way that will benefit our happiness and health. Such actions can often involve being more compassionate to ourselves and gaining the confidence to tackle certain issues in our lives head on rather than hiding away from them. It also means realising that our behaviour around food isn't the primary problem in our lives. The way we think, feel and act around food can merely be a symptom of something much deeper that we feel unready to face.

In western societies like the ones we currently live in or venture to, we are told that any form of emotional eating is 'wrong' and that we should do whatever we can to eat 'intuitively' at all times. In other words, we have been told that we must place a strong leash on our emotional eating drives, otherwise we might suffer a disastrous fate. But what use is this advice if intuitive eating means not eating emotionally? Believe it or not, emotional eating can be positive as in many cases it allows food to symbolise life events, relationships and even our identity as individuals.

This doesn't mean that food should dominate your whole identity and every thought and emotion you feel, or even be used as the main way to cope with negative experience in life. However, it does mean that emotional eating can help rather than hinder our personal development. For example, when emotions are paired with food, we can learn to associate certain foods with the comfort and love we have received from other people, whether that be family, friends or a partner.

As long as food isn't being used to solely fill in the void in our lives, I would argue that eating in response to emotion, or while feeling certain emotions, is not distinctly bad. In fact, it is very natural and can even be beneficial for us when food is associated with positive and sometimes even negative emotions.

Eating (thankfully) is rarely an emotionally neutral situation. For example, the negative emotion experienced when tasting a disliked food, or being ill after eating, can inform us to avoid a certain type of food in the future – perhaps in a way that benefits wellbeing and survival. You probably wouldn't want to eat a certain type of food again if you knew that it triggered an allergic reaction or an episode of being sick.

It is also important to mention here that there are many benefits from being able to experience joy and encounter emotional memories from eating, as it can enable us to develop stronger bonds with our current and potential friends, partners, work colleagues and family members. Also, by enjoying the process of preparing food, this can help us to establish and develop new creative hobbies that benefit our happiness, health and even our creativity.

Pairing some foods with negative emotions can also lift our mood or help us to feel better when unwell. For example, eating your favourite sweets when feeling sad may allow you to reminisce about positive memories and, consequently, help you to feel in a more positive mood while any distress or anxiety is diminished.

Our emotions might relate to memories we have once had with a particular food/meal, such as the way a drink of tea, a couple of biscuits, a particular meal, or a favourite restaurant or well-known food brand symbolises experiencing comfort, reassurance, affection and social support. Alternatively, we might have been rewarded with particular types of food for certain achievements, or deprived of it for having not met a certain goal, such as finishing a meal your parents wanted you to complete.

Ultimately, being the complex beings we are with a highly evolved brain, food choices rarely boil down to eating 100% intuitively with what our body physiologically requires to function. As well as responding to appetite stimulating or suppressing hormones, there is a dynamic interplay between our memories, emotions and social lives that influence what, when and where we eat.

To again restate the importance of emotional eating, rarely does food simply signify energy and nutrients alone. The memories we inevitably tie with it, as well as the emotions we felt before, during or after eating, will have an impact on what we eat both now and in the future.

So is it OK to eat emotionally?

At this point you may still be questioning whether it is OK to eat emotionally, despite much of the information we have been provided with that tell us otherwise.

At one end of the spectrum, it can be argued that some individuals have an emotionally unstable or even abusive relationship with food. For example, we recently mentioned that food for some individuals can function as a way of coping with negative emotions, poor self-worth as well as a distraction from distressing circumstances. This doesn't just have to involve overeating, but also skipping meals and under-eating. Each of us is unique, and many of us dissimilarly use food to cope in relation to our own specific situations.

In some situations, eating might become something that is recurrently restricted in times of stress, or binged on. As we recently mentioned, eating emotionally in these ways might be a temporary form of distraction or alleviator of negative feelings and personal problems. However, if used too frequently as the only coping tool, rather than directly dealing with our emotions and life issues in a more practical and self-compassionate way (with support from friends and family for instance), this is when emotional eating can become a problem that negatively impacts our overall happiness and health. In such situations, emotional eating can become a primary feature in an individuals' lives, whereby in order to feel back in control they continue to obsess about food, rigidly control food or negatively judge themselves in relation to food. As food and emotional eating begin to hold more and more power over a person's life, the less time and energy they have left to pursue other activities that are more beneficial to wellbeing and reaching their full potential.

As you can probably see from the above examples, this type of emotional eating can lead to a cycle of feeling incompetent, unworthy, and in need of an easily accessible coping tool. However, these examples look at one extreme end of the spectrum without fully appreciating that eating tends to happen in everyday circumstances for a variety of emotional and non-emotional reasons for the majority of the population. Thankfully, not everyone uses food as their main lifejacket to hold their head above water. Also, most individuals have several effective coping strategies they can employ in life other than food, such as focussing their energies on creativity, positive relationships, helping others, or other forms of self-development that involve leading a more compassionate lifestyle. They just need to feel empowered to use them.

But what advice can we take from all of this information in the grand context of emotional eating?

To answer this question, I need to again restate that emotional eating is an inevitable part of being a socially and emotionally complex human being.

Just because we eat in response to a certain emotion or social situation, rather than our biological state of hunger, does not mean that we are 'bad' individuals with a poor ability to self-regulate our behaviour. It also doesn't necessarily mean that we have an eating disorder or need to go on another form of 'self-improvement' program.

Secondly, there are many situations in our lives where we use food to help us cope with or alleviate negative emotions and experiences that we are not yet ready to face head on. However, this is not inevitably 'bad', but actually beneficial to our future wellbeing when we view this form of emotional eating as a sign that there is something else we need to resolve in our lives other than what we eat.

With the above ideas in mind I hope to help you embrace the idea that it is OK – in fact essential – to eat emotionally. As long as food does not dictate your emotions, or control the way you live your life, eating emotionally can be a very joyful and fulfilling element of being a beautifully complex human being.

So yes, enjoying a couple of biscuits or a slice of cake with your tea with friends, or celebrating with a hearty meal when feeling happy or reflecting on sad times, is not necessarily something to be avoided. It is definitely not something to feel ashamed of either. But if you do happen to notice that emotional eating frequently occurs in the context of trying to block out negative feelings and avoid tackling certain life issues, it is vital to realise that there is probably something much deeper in your life other than how you eat that needs to be resolved in a more practical and compassionate way.

On a final note, I would like you to know, whoever you may be, we need to start embracing ourselves as natural emotional eaters. As I have also learnt throughout my own recovery, pairing our emotions with food can be part of a harmonious and balanced form of living without feelings of guilt, shame or any other forms of negative self-judgement.

From Mindful to 'Kindful' Eating

Tell me if I'm wrong but there is a lot of hype around mindfulness at the moment.

Although the concept of being mindful and living more mindfully has been around for centuries, only recently has it popped up to become a bit of a buzz word – especially in the ever-expanding field of happiness, health and wellness. Being more mindful is also one of the 10 elements of Nourishing Route and has been popularly applied across the globe to almost every aspect of the way we live our lives. Some of these applications involve the way we take notice of everything we eat, our deeper thoughts and sensory experiences, as well as how we deal with stress and overcome trauma. Overall, this is a great thing, as being mindful and attending to the present moment without negative judgement and ruminating about the past or future can authentically enrich our lives. It can also help us get back in tune with our own values, alleviate stress and anxiety, as well as become more able to act in ways that enable us to reach our full potential.

However, if you have heard about mindfulness, then the likelihood is that you've also heard of mindful eating. More specifically, mindful eating is defined as paying attention to, and the sensory experience of, everything you eat as well as how hungry or full you feel before and afterwards. Applying the concept of mindfulness to eating has often been portrayed as a way of paying attention to everything we eat, which apparently leads to being in better control of our food and more able to lose weight – as is similar with many other dieting strategies that are preached to us on a daily basis.

There are many evidence-based benefits of eating in a more mindful way. For example, taking notice of the sensory aspects of your food and taking time to enjoy it, without rushing mindlessly from one task to the next, allows us to feel more satisfied and less likely to want to temporarily fulfil our emotional needs (e.g. for comfort or reducing stress) with food rather than other, more practical and compassionately effective methods. By being more mindful, we can also take note of whether we are making choices that will nourish our bodies and minds in a way that allows us to gain a sense of vitality and act in line with our values. This also includes ensuring that we eat more rather than less of something if we really need it.

However, there is also a common focus on the apparent necessity of basing what we eat on how hungry or full we feel, taking a longer time to plan and prepare food, as well as taking notice of each and every sensory aspect of food before we are 'allowed' to engage in the act of eating it. Unfortunately for some individuals, however, becoming overly concerned about the need to eat more mindfully can become an anxiety provoking obsession that needs to be accomplished perfectly. Consequently, although being mindful of what and how we eat can have multiple benefits, there is a line to be crossed when mindful eating becomes yet another way to feel like inadequate and unworthy individuals. In certain contexts, goals for mindful eating can become alike to a restrictive routine or diet, as it can be used as a method to gain more control over our lives in a maladaptive way. With this in mind, I would like to question:

* Is mindful eating really necessary 100% of the time?

* Is food something we should completely control based on how hungry or full we feel?

My personal answer to these questions is no. Definitely not. But I ask you, what are your own thoughts and experiences in relation to these questions as well as the concept of mindfulness more generally?

Should I give up on pursuing mindful eating or being more mindful in general?

To not dismiss the over-arching concept mindfulness altogether (it is one of the 10 key elements of Nourishing Routes after all), it is important to restate that being more mindful still has much to offer when applied to life more generally. As I mentioned, there are vast amounts of research to show that being more mindful of our physical and psychological experiences really does enhance wellbeing. For example, when used optimally and not rigidly, mindfulness can create a sense of calm inner peace. It can also encourage us to live more compassionately with ourselves and others, as well as reduce negative self-judgement or ruminating about our worries and life stressors. These are just a few key reasons why I think that mindfulness deserves to be a key element to Nourishing Routes and becoming a Compassioneer.

Even the concept of compassion itself has mindfulness integrated into it. In order to be compassionate, we must be mindfully aware of our personal needs and values. However, when we refer to the term mindful eating, and the amount of hype that has been created around this concept over the last several years, I can't help but feel a little bit critical – especially as book after book, and course after course (usually ones that involve individuals paying a lot of money), keep popping up about the topic.

Based on the research we have to date on mindful eating and individuals' relationships to food and body, I do question the practicality and usefulness of mindful eating when it is conducted in a routine way. Part of me knows that aiming for a complete mindful eating approach to food could be pro-voking more harm than good. For example, how does it make individuals feel about themselves if a meal they recently ate wasn't in a mindful way, yet they still enjoyed it due to watching their favourite programme on TV with a friend? Does this make the act of eating non-mindfully a bad thing? Again, judging someone's eating as either good or bad in relation to how mindfully they ate would be falling in the trap of classifying things in black or white terms – which very rarely exist in the real world.

So what is the ultimate goal of mindful eating?

In many cases, mindful eating stems from a desire to control the amount of food we eat, what we weigh and our physical appearance. Even though mindful eating could technically include being aware of our social and emo-tional desires for food (which are equally as valid as genuine hunger) most courses and information on mindful eating focus on its relationship with weight, and how mindful eating has the potential to 'cure' obesity, as well as help individuals eat more 'clean', cut out 'unhealthy foods' and achieve an 'ideal weight'. In this sense, it appears that we have confused the term mindful eating with mindful dieting…

Some (questionable) experts in mindful eating claim that, ideally, we should:

❊ Only eat when we experience hunger

❊ Stop eating when we feel full

❊ Notice each and every sensory aspect of food, how it looks, smells, feels and tastes, or even sounds as you eat it

❊ Chew food a certain number of times to fully appreciate it and trigger the right signals about feeling hungry or full to the brain

❊ Never eat around distractions, such as the TV, in a deep conversation with friends, or when reading a book

❊ Plan what you eat in advance

❊ Log what you have eaten in a diet or fitness app

Following these mindful eating tips will apparently help you become a happier and healthier you. Unfortunately though, me and many individuals who have tried mindful eating while following the above rules will disagree – especially if you have experienced an eating disorder or another form of disordered eating.

The thing is, when the concept of mindful eating becomes yet another rule to apply to what we eat and base our self-worth on, then this is not going to place us on an authentic path to wellbeing, or becoming more self-compassionate for that matter. Instead, we risk getting caught up in a negative cycle of self-judgement, perfection seeking and perhaps feeling guilty for nor eating mindfully enough. If we 100% applied the concept of mindful eating to our lives, we would also be ignoring how we are all social and emotional creatures, who often eat for many reasons other than feeling physically hungry or full.

To help resolve some of the misperceptions around how to eat more mindfully, perhaps we could view eating mindfully as being aware of our social and emotional needs to eat – not just the physical ones.

What would happen if we said to our friends that we weren't going to enjoy a slice of cake at our own birthday party because we didn't feel hungry or because we thought there would be too many surrounding distractions preventing you from eating mindfully? This might be OK, but not if you wanted to eat cake because it was an important tradition to you as well as being an opportunity to socialise with individuals you love and care about. Mindful eating could also be isolating for many other social activities, such as turning down opportunities to eat with friends and meeting our needs to be part of a supportive network – just because our physical bodies are telling us that we don't need to eat.

Some individuals might disagree and say that we should only really eat when we are hungry or full, and that doing otherwise is only going to add to individuals' growing waistlines. Maybe this bears some truth, but in my view we have to look at the research evidence. When we do this, research findings show how trying to be more consciously aware of what and why we eat for lengthy amounts of time can lead to a negative relationship with food and body. In theory, applying the concept of mindful eating to meal times can be a way of enjoying food and feeling fuller for longer, but when applied with the desire of controlling weight (as is often the case) the impacts of mindful eating appear much more negative than positive. For example, mindful eating for weight loss is sending the same message to our brains as going on a diet does, which includes the information that we are about to limit our food intake.

There is currently evidence that trying to be more mindful of everything you eat for weight reasons can lead to cycles of binge eating and unhealthy fluctuations in weight. Also, because we may restrict what we eat in a way that isolates us from social situations while ignoring our emotional needs, then food becomes even more desirable and something to obsess about. Even if in some circumstances mindful eating can allow us to enjoy food in all its glory, restricting food intake through mindfulness is definitely not a key to wellness – only more disordered thoughts and feelings about food and body.

Take another example: what are the benefits to being able to chew food a certain number of times in order to enjoy it and feel fuller for longer? This might work, but how practical or emotionally healthy is it to be doing this at every eating occasion? Also, what happens when your friends offer for you to join in with them eating popcorn with the distraction of a movie even after you have already eaten? Do you turn down these opportunities because you identify with the label of being a mindful eater?

If any of you have tried to fully embrace the concept of mindful eating, you may have some similar experiences, and be wondering how you can still apply some of the concepts of mindful eating while still having a positive non-obsessive relationship with food and body.

For this question I would firstly recommend remembering that we are all social and emotional creatures, and that it is OK to eat a cake or a food you might not classify as particularly 'healthy' regardless of how hungry or full you feel. We do have the right to eat just because it fits in line with our cultural, social or emotional needs, even when it is not in the best interests of being optimally nourished in a physical way.

Secondly, you can apply mindful eating in a more practical way that doesn't involve slipping into the tight grasp of dieting mentality. For example, it is likely to be more feasible to engage in mindful eating where and when is most practical for your lifestyle. This might simply involve taking time away from your work desk to eat lunch in a place that you enjoy, or taking time to notice that you need to eat a little bit more and more frequently in order to keep your energy levels up. It could also involve turning the TV off in the background when eating with a friend or partner, rather than eating in isolation so you can fully concentrate on everything you eat. Mindful eating in a flexible rather than rigid way can additionally come in the form of noticing when you haven't had as much to eat as your body needs, as it is just as important to ensure our bodies remain nourished rather than remain in a state of hunger or fullness.

Just because we are physically satisfied or feel full doesn't necessarily mean that we have given our body what it needs. This might be the case if you have experienced a physical illness or an eating disorder, and the body's hunger and fullness signals are not quite functioning in an optimal way. In such a case, we can use our knowledge and intuition to eat that little bit more even when we might feel full or not in the mood to eat.

Thirdly, rather than planning and logging every morsel of food you eat, use the concept of mindfulness to ask yourself what type of food you are in the mood for. What will satisfy you – not only in hunger terms, but also your social and emotional needs. If this means eating a bar of your favourite chocolate while watching a favourite TV programme rather than a dry oat-cake on your own before it gets 'too late' at night, then so be it.

A final point to mention is that it is important to realise that your self-worth doesn't need to be based on exactly what, how or how much you eat. Eating mindfully can allow us to experience more of the sensory pleasures of food, as well as eating what we most feel like, but it doesn't require us to become critical of ourselves. In fact, mindfulness is one of the three key elements of self-compassion, and self-compassion by definition involves being aware of all our physical, emotional and social needs in a self-accepting, loving and non-judgemental way. In this sense, we don't need to control what we eat through mindfulness, but what we can do is allow mindful eating to help us recognise that we are complex social beings who have permission to feel loved and cared for regardless of what we put into our bodies.

Based on the above concepts, I would like to turn our attention to the concept of kindful eating.

What is 'kindful' eating?

Some might describe this approach as 'normal' eating, if such a phrase exists, but in basic terms it means being able to eat without negative self-judgement, and notice how we feel about what we eat – not just noticing what we eat.

'Kindful' eating is another level up from mindful eating. In fact, it is more or less the same as compassion-eating which we recently discussed a few chapters ago. Like compassion-eating, 'kindful' eating appreciates that eating mindfully can be of great benefit to our wellbeing in the right dosage and situations, but it additionally acknowledges the importance of not paying our 100% attention to food.

Eating 'kindfully' is about eating in a way that not only nourishes the body, but also eating in a way that nourishes our social and emotional needs as well as our personal values. For me and perhaps even you, part of this could include the value of not wanting to harm other animals through the food you choose to eat. However, regardless of what food it is that we might be eating, 'kindful' eating accounts for the fact that not everything we eat will be the most nutritious or even ethically sourced thing in the world. As you have probably already gotten to grips with, there are no good or bad foods in the world, but it is important to having an overall balanced diet that allows us to enjoy food, socialise with others, love our bodies, act in line with our values and reach our full potential in the most compassionate way possible.

When we eat 'kindfully' we no longer need to obsess about where our next meal is going to be, what we are going to prepare, or how we might feel after eating. Food doesn't become your only life mission to control, but it does play a role in your life mission to become the real you, find meaning in your existence while making a positive difference to the lives of others and the world in general.

Ultimately, 'kindful' eating is a founding principle for developing self-compassion, which, as we promote through Nourishing Routes, is a key foundation for a lifelong journey to positive wellbeing and becoming a Compassioneer – where we can nourish, flourish and thrive.

Compassioneer activity: Goals for being a more 'Kindful' Eater

As I stated at the beginning of this book when addressing our personal goals for living more compassionately and becoming a Compassioneer, why we create and pursue goals is just as important as the actual strategies we use. Within the context of 'kindful' eating, if you would like to become a more 'kindful' eater it is firstly a useful activity to identify your current mindful and 'kindful' approaches to food, as well as the reasons why a more 'kindful' eating approach is valuable to adopt for your own sake – rather than to meet some external standard or someone else's expectations.

To pursue this task, you can grab a pen and paper and answer the questions below before embarking on a journey to become more mindful with your eating:

* Ask yourself how you currently eat – do you eat mindlessly, mindfully, or does what you eat control how you feel about yourself?

* In what ways are you a 'kindful' or 'non-kindful' eater?

* Would you like to become a more mindfully 'kindful' eater?

* How would being a more mindfully 'kindful' eater contribute to your wellbeing, and why is it important to you at this time in your life?

* What ways can you begin to become a more mindfully 'kindful' eater in a way that suits your current lifestyle?

* Are there any barriers to doing this, and if so what are these?

* How can you overcome these barriers?

❋ How will you know if you have become a more mindfully 'kindful' eater, i.e. what indicators will alert you to having developed a more positive relationship with food?

❋ By becoming a more mindfully 'kindful' eater, how much would this mean to you and your wellbeing on a scale of 1 to 10, with 1 meaning not a lot, and 10 meaning a lot?

❋

"You are not a number on a scale. You are not a Calorie count. Your body, mind and soul are much more meaningful and beautiful than insignificant numbers"

Calories: Numbers We Shouldn't Count On

The humble Calorie. An invisible unit of energy, yet something power-ful enough, depending on how we interpret them, to control our eating behaviour, undermine our sense of self-worth and overturn rather than promote our wellbeing.

At one time, my whole life and eating behaviour completely revolved around Calories, but as I know realise how insignificant they really are in the grand scheme of our compassionate lives, I have a few questions for you to ask yourself about Calories:

❋ *"Why is it the norm to look at the back of every packet of food we consume to check its Calorie content?"*

❋ *"Is it really helpful to talk about a food we enjoy without soon going into a lengthy discussion about how it contains 'x' number of Calories and how if we eat too much of this or that, then we will all be doomed to obesity, diabetes and an early grave?"*

❋ *"Is it really necessary to calculate every unit of energy from all food we put into our bodies to the extent where we begin to worry if our fitness app hasn't been filled in for the past 6 hours?"*

❋ *"Are Calories really an accurate gauge to measure how healthy a particular food item or meal is?"*

❋ *"Why is it that so many individuals revolve their whole day around how many Calories they should and should not eat?"*

We will be answering most of these questions through this chapter. But, before we go to critically analyse the humble Calorie, I must say a few positive words about them. In their defence, Calories are quite literally the driving forces behind all living things. They provide the fuel for our bodies to conduct its every function, from physically moving, making new cells, forming hormones, keeping the heart pumping, sustaining brain activity, staying warm and maintaining an optimal body temperature. Without Calories, we literally wouldn't be here on this planet.

I am not here to criticise the Calorie in its scientific or practical use for some individuals who use them to guide choices that might enable to theme to nourish their body more optimally. Instead, I am considering the more societal and psychological issue of how Calories can come to define more than just energy for our bodily functions.

The vast majority of individuals now have the ingrained habit of looking at nutritional labels to determine what they 'should' and 'should not' eat. Of course this might be beneficial if we are on the lookout for whether a certain food or meal contains nourishing, harmful or ethically questionable ingredients, but where is the real value in calculating Calories? Many of us, without a second thought, pay more attention to the Calorie content of foods rather than the actual nourishing nutrients within them or the pleasurable and socially appropriate activities that they promote.

By doing this we learn to see food as something we should eat less of, rather than in terms of what is to be beneficially gained. As an analogy, Calories are sometimes viewed in a similar way to adding points to a driving licence (i.e. pounds to our waistlines), rather than tokens that will help us to win a prize (i.e. optimal nourishment, happiness and health). But perhaps our perspective should be turned on its head a bit.

When it comes to counting Calories, the way that this tedious activity is promoted suggests that the quantity of what we eat is much more worthy of our attention than its quality. It can also make us equate food with energy balance, which in general terms is translated into our body weight and physical appearance. Although weight can play an important role in wellbeing, as we have already mentioned, it is by no means the only factor that defines it.

Before going into a bit more detail about the impractical implications of trying to accurately count Calories, firstly, let's define the term Calorie more specifically.

By scientific standards we can define a Calorie as the amount of energy that is required to raise the temperature of one gram of water by the equivalent of one degree centigrade. According to this equation, when a particular food or food product is burnt (literally to smithereens), the heat it releases can be assessed in a way that allows the energy (the Calorie content) of the food to be assessed. The first experiments that used this type of assessment used a food incinerator known as a bomb calorimeter with around 4000 foods. I wasn't there at the time, but I'm confidently guessing calculating the Calories in these foods took an extensively long time. Perhaps like many individuals, the researchers carrying out this experiment must have been a pretty determined bunch of Calorie counting fanatics.

The experiments were conducted in a way that allowed the Calories in a certain food to be assessed, as well as where they came from, whether that be from fat (containing around 9 Calories per gram), protein (around 4 Calories per gram), or carbohydrate (around 4 Calories per gram). Based on these experiments, and according to the law of thermodynamics (that all energy can be converted to another form), the heat (energy) released from foods is equivalent to the amount of energy that will be available to the body when it is consumed.

Simple, right?

Unfortunately, not very simple at all. You see, despite the vast number of highly scientific experiments that have been conducted, it is unlikely that one specific food of the same variety, weight for weight, will contain the exact same number of Calories. Firstly, this is because estimations of the Calorie content of foods are just that. Estimates. What experiments can't always account for is that different foods naturally vary in Calories depending on whether they were grown in different soils, in different climates and for different amounts of time. Then there are other important factors to consider, such as how food is cooked and how each unique person digests it to release dissimilar amounts of energy to the body utilising it.

I also need to mention that the actual Calorie amounts that are used to estimate the number of Calories from each gram of fat, protein, and carbohydrate in food are not representative of the fat, protein and carbohydrates in different types of foods. For example, there is actually some deviation with the carbohydrates, proteins and fats containing more or fewer Calories depending on whether they were obtained from animal products (usually more) or plant based products (usually less). However, because we tend to prepare meals using foods from both groups, modern Calorie estimates do not account for this variation, as it would seem that any differences would average themselves out. Perhaps in a perfect world they would, but in terms of accurately counting Calories, this mission is merely impossible.

When different foods are combined together as a meal or snack, the Calorie estimates are usually based on the average proportions of each of the different foods it contains. But it is very unlikely that a meal or snack bar contains the same quantities and proportions of ingredients that it says on the label. That is just the natural laws of physics when food is prepared, so proportion estimates might be pretty good ones, but never accurate. This may seem like pretty obvious information, but many individuals (including my past self) are under the impression that the Calorie content they read on a nutrition label is the exact truth, and the same goes for the proportions of fat, carbohydrate and proteins within a particular food too.

Another flaw to highlight is the whole notion that Calories within a food burned outside the body (e.g. in a calorimeter) release the same amount of energy as when Calories are burned inside the body (e.g. during digestion). This isn't true at all, as no matter how accurate a calorimeter is, it is no substitute for being able to have an accurate insight into the complex workings of the human digestive system, which works so uniquely within each person. For example, not all individuals use energy in the same way, and this can be independent of our physical activity level. Some individuals have naturally more efficient metabolisms that allow them to expend more Calories by staying warm, fuelling digestion, fighting infection, or dispelling excess heat rather than having to use it for movement or storage.

For other individuals, the medication they take or suffering from a certain condition can also alter the way they metabolise Calories in food. Again, this highlights that Calories on a packet do not equal the Calories burned and utilised inside our bodies. For example, depending on personal circumstances, or even times of day and what a person has recently eaten, not all Calories or nutrients are absorbed in our digestive system. This means that we all inevitably excrete a small number of Calorie-containing substances in our urine and faeces (sorry for the finer details). This is a process that has again not been accounted for when devising nutritional labels – again making the energy in equals energy out equation less simple than it sounds.

Even with the above information to hand, the fact remains that many individuals continue to rigidly count Calories while ensuring that they eat or even eliminate an exact number of them every day – without fail. This is an aim that is usually based on trying to meet the average guidelines set by certain nutritional standards. However, as you probably have already realised, trying to reach an exact target in terms of Calories is probably of little use when we need to consider how every individual, regardless of their gender, is inevitably unique with their own metabolism that uses up Calories significantly more or less than another person.

Despite the range of inaccuracies around Calories there is a common belief that we can rigidly control out Calorie intake and output so long as we have enough self-regulation power, with many individuals counting and logging them obsessively. The countless number of fitness and Calorie tracking apps on phones can help to verify this craze for monitoring invisible numbers, and at the time of writing this book many Westernised nations appear to be quite obsessed with them,

What is often less talked about in terms of Calories is how the way they are often used, thought and spoken about can increase the likelihood of enduring poor physical and psychological wellbeing, including low self-esteem, poor body image, and the development or exacerbation of an eating disorder or other forms of disordered eating. By drawing upon a few of my own

✳

personal experiences, I shall now shed a bit of light on how and why this can occur.

A darker side to counting Calories

Britain and other westernised nations contain numerous communities of Calorie counters. Yet, this wouldn't be apparent to the eye, since we are living in an era where we are repeatedly reminded that we are too over-weight and at risk of multiple weight-related health problems. But, stopping to think for a moment, it is these very messages that can create a vicious circle of Calorie counting and negative thoughts about the self. In other words, Calorie counting can lead us far away from the goal of becoming more compassionate.

The more we are made to feel that we are defined by our weight and health status, the more likely we are to engage in restrictive dietary behaviours that can, inadvertently, have the long-term influence of promoting weight gain and even worse self-esteem and self-worth. On the other extreme end of the Calorie counting spectrum, an obsession around counting Calories can also significantly heighten the risk of suffering from an eating disorder, such as anorexia or bulimia nervosa.

I am not necessarily condemning anyone who counts Calories if it enables them to genuinely feel free and more empowered when making nourishing food choices. Instead, I am referring to the negative implications of when we feel that the Calories we consume need to define what we 'should' and 'should not' eat at the expense of our self-worth and ability to eat in a com-passionate way. I can guarantee that obsessive Calorie counting is no way to eat in a way that allows you to be in tune with your physical, social, emo-tional and other psychological needs. If we consider how Calorie counting can take up a considerable proportion of brain space that limits our freedom to think about food in its true nourishing form, we can notice how they can hinder our ability to socialise and gain real nourishment and enjoyment from what we eat. In plainer terms, counting Calories is not the ideal way to nourish our minds or our bodies.

Even if we are aware that counting Calories, or any form of number relating to macro- or micro-nutrient content, can lead us down a dark and lonely road, it can still seem hard to avoid this path when we are repeatedly faced with messages that emphasise how we 'should' all be counting Calories. If you have ever experienced what it is like to have an obsessive fascination with Calories, then you might be able to empathise with how hard this habit is to break, as well as how detrimental it can be. On the one hand, feeling that you are 'in the know' about the number of Calories contained within your food can promotes a sense of security. Safety seems to occur in the numbers.

However, even after meticulous calculations of what food was purchased, how it was prepared, and how many Calories we consumed, this is just a false sense of security. I would like to ask you, where is the self-compassion from knowing that we are 'good' or 'bad' at making calculations and controlling our weight? I haven't spotted it yet and don't expect to in the near or distance future with this form of black and white thinking.

To look at the bigger picture, I think that mother nature would be quite saddened to see that our intuition to naturally choose food according to its appearance, smell, taste, appetite and the social opportunities it involves has been obscured by superficial numerical figures. By counting Calories, are we willingly wasting a natural human skill that would be of much more benefit to our overall wellbeing if we were to utilise it more?

Before rambling on to answer this question, I am probably failing to mention that we no longer live in such times where we can choose to intuitively eat in a way that allows our food choices to be governed by our body's real needs. Instead, the modern age sees us influenced by a bombardment of food advertisements, and oversized portions in strategically placed eating outlets that become apparent in the absence of true hunger. It is now quite rare to physically view food in its natural form in order to make those all-important intuitive decisions, and instead we are faced with a packet, a superficial photograph and, for Calorie counting, a nutritional table of numbers. There are not many things that are beautiful or appetising about that.

Calorie counting as transactional thinking

If we learn from society that that any form of self-control regarding food is desirable, and that counting Calories is one form of this, then becoming preoccupied with them becomes very attractive. As a consequence, Calories are often unfairly idealised as a means of control, rather than nourishment, along with similar concerns such as weight reduction in a world that feels uncontrollable.

As an example of such a distorted relationship with numbers, we can sometimes view Calories as being alike to something that we need to earn in order to 'spend'. To describe this in relation to how we use money, our consumption of Calories becomes alike to the transactions that take place when purchasing a particular product. How many Calories or pound coins can I spend today? How many Calories have I got left over? Have I eaten few enough Calories to treat myself by eating more Calories later on?

But why should we have to view pleasure, such as that from food, as something that needs to be earned and counted in the form of Calories? Although this type of transactional thinking may be appropriate for budgeting monetary resources, having to always ask ourselves these questions when it comes to food and Calories may lead to a disordered relationship with food.

Can Calorie counting lead to disordered eating?

At the more pathological end of the Calorie counting spectrum individuals with eating disorders can probably empathise with how this activity can have severely negative impacts on their happiness and health. For example, individuals can get caught in a vicious cycle of 'overspending' their Calories and consequently feeling guilty about it in a way that eventually leads them to binge on food or want to restrict it even more as a maladaptive way of regaining back control.

Some individuals experience the feeling of being locked in a trap of obsessive Calorie counting and restriction, or binging and purging on the numbers they wish to control, while their bodies and minds become severely beaten to the point where their physical and psychological health significantly deteriorates. From this perspective the way we have been taught to count Calories can have a very opposing outcome to what they are designed to be used for – to keep us alive, happy and healthy.

As you have already probably grasped from reading this book so far, our happiness and health are not solely reliant on what we do and do not eat – especially in terms of Calories. For example, would you want to deny yourself opportunities to take part in social occasions that have the potential to positively boost your mood and sense of belonging just so that you can avoid eating more Calories? If we are truly being self-compassionate, then the answer will be no.

But a crucial question you may have here is whether there is any research evidence to support or not support the idea of Calorie counting. Surely there must be some evidence that it helps to regulate our weight if such a large part of our culture and process of nutritional labelling involves adding up the Calories?

One fact that might be a little hard to swallow is that Calorie counting has NOT been shown to be effective for promoting long-term health. There is no sufficient evidence to prove that counting Calories enables individuals to become physically or psychologically healthier for extended periods of time. Instead, as I have mentioned, there is more evidence to suggest, especially from that related to eating disorders, that counting Calories is usually part of a negative dieting psychology that perpetuates the love-hate relationship many of us have with our food and body.

Obsessively counting Calories is one of the main barriers faced by many individuals struggling to recover from an eating disorder. I can completely resonate with this, and these abstract numbers are what placed huge limitations on how much I felt I was 'allowed' to eat without feeling guilty, gluttonous and a worthless as a person. I can vividly remember standing in the supermarket aisle or a health food store and picking up unappetising snack bars and various other 'healthy' items while trying to find the one with the fewest Calories or 'cleanest' of ingredients. It didn't matter to me whether the food would taste nice, satisfy my appetite or meet my nutritional needs.

As long as the food would fit in line with my 'Calorie quota' for my snacks (which back then was a measly amount) then only then would it be suitable to purchase without the risk of feeling overly anxious and guilty soon afterwards.

This was a completely detached and very non-compassionate way of relating to food. By focussing on Calories I wasn't able to be mindful of my physical, emotional and social needs or, importantly, how to satisfy them. I'm also certain that the stress of trying to find a snack containing the 'right' number of Calories was more toxic than exceeding my Calorie quota or eating some unnatural ingredients or additives.

A past but not a future of counting Calories

Because Calorie counting is such an ingrained part of many individuals' behaviour, it can be difficult to remember or even contemplate a time when we didn't count Calories. But, until food industries and governments controlled what we ate, there really was no such thing as counting Calories for most members of the public. Food was just food, enjoyment and part of our social and cultural norms. There was probably much, much less of the negatively judgemental and immoral symbols we often attach to food in modern times.

Long ago we may have had an idea about some of the natural health and herbal properties of food, and an intuition about how eating it would either promote or diminish our wellbeing, but in scientific terms we had no need to count or become obsessed by Calories and specific nutrients. However, this doesn't eliminate the fact that many of us remain fixated by the Calories of the backs and fronts of food packets. Knowing the Calorie content of a food item can now easily overrule our natural intuition about what to eat by allowing our food choices to be motivated by how much energy our food contains over its quality. In practice this might mean choosing a Mars bar over an avocado, or a packet of biscuits over a roasted vegetable sandwich. Similarly, it can also mean depriving ourselves of enjoyment by picking a snack that meets our Calorie goals, but not much else in terms of authentic satisfaction of our physical, emotional and social 'hunger'.

If you can resonate with some of the above points, you may want to know what you can do to try and place less emphasis on Calories so as to improve your relationship with food and yourself.

If you have used a Calorie system for so long, then I can completely understand that it might seem difficult to reduce your reliance on it at first. It can feel like the impossible task of trying to unlearn a well-spoken language, or erasing specific parts of our memories. However, even if you can't fully stop counting Calories or being aware of them, there is definitely significant value in taking an emphasis off Calorie counting and instead focusing on the quality of what you eat as well as the many other positive and important roles food has in your life.

In time, focussing less on Calories means much more time to use food in the way it was meant to, including for energy, enjoyment and social bonding. This inevitably means being able to eat more intuitively according to our body's physical, psychological and social needs – not numerical rules and inaccurate guidelines.

But what are the practical steps we can take in order to take our focus away from counting Calories?

Compassioneer Activity: Steps Towards Taking Your Focus Away from Calories

❉ **Identify and note down your current Calorie counting behaviours**

Perhaps it is not yet a wise move to go completely cold turkey by deciding to never look at or count Calories again. Such a move might trigger a wave of anxiety rather than a sense of freedom. Alternatively, note down the Calorie counting behaviours you currently engage in, and also when and where they take place.

❉ **Don't try to be precise**

If you are all too familiar with counting the exact number of Calories you eat, you could firstly try to take a more estimative outlook. For example, if you know that your usual mind-morning or afternoon snack bar contains 187 Calories, round this down to the nearest 50 Calories. The same goes for main meals, but you could choose to round up or down to the nearest 100 Calories.

❉ **Get rid of those food weighing scales**

OK, so getting rid of food scales isn't about specifically counting Calories, but it is usually related. Obsessive Calorie counting very often goes hand in hand with weighing the amount of food you eat. By not using a scale or even a measuring jug when deciding what or how much to eat, this encourages you to make an estimation on what feels intuitively right for your rather than what you think 'should' be right according to society's guideline or someone else's standards. Unless you are following a particular baking recipe, weighing can draw you away from being able to eat intuitively, and only adds to eating occasions becoming anxiety provoking and stressful if you worry about not being able to weigh things exactly.

❉

If you feel that getting rid of your weighing food habit isn't going to happen overnight, then try to do it in steps, such as only weighing food for one or two meals of the day.

Perhaps you could start by choosing to use your own hand to measure out a portion of cereal, pasta and rice etc. You could alternatively use your own eye to gauge how much milk to put in drinks or cereal. Don't worry if you can't do everything at once. Little steps are still worth just as much in terms of long-term process. Eventually you can build up to not having to weigh out any part of your meal at all. Believe me, it will feel so much more liberating then waiting for food to be an exact number on a scale before you eat it.

❊ Limit how much time you spend logging food

Instead of logging how many Calories you eat each day, try to write out what you eat without the Calorie number next to it. Rather than judging your daily intake by its Calorie content, instead think about all of the positive things about what you have eaten that day in terms of its quality and also how it has made you feel. For example, was that avocado on toast full of nourishing fats and skin revitalising vitamins?

Perhaps eating a certain food or meal may not have been necessary, such as if it was to fill an emotional void, but think about this occasion as something to simply take note of and learn more about yourself from. Don't beat yourself up about what you eat, simply view it as a way of getting back in tune with and reflecting on the connections between our thoughts, feelings and behaviours. If you do find that you frequently eat or restrict food in response to certain emotions or feeling stressed, ask yourself whether there are any other practical ways to help you cope with negative emotions or life stress other than food – e.g. a creative activity or meeting up for a cup of tea with friends.

You could also or alternatively write out a food list of what you have eaten each day, but instead of focussing on Calories, you can note down around three to five things that you have enjoyed or felt grateful for in the last 24 hours or past week. These don't need to be food related, as long as they allow you to think more positively about your life and whole self.

❊

✴ **Choose food to eat in line with what you feel like, not the Calorie label.**

Try to buy the foods you love and that bring you the most satisfaction and nourishment in terms of what you really feel like and enjoy. Do you want to eat something hot, cold, spicy, fresh, sweet, savoury, crispy, soft etc.? Try to think of eating as a multi-sensory experience. It is not useful, or even healthy, to buy a food just because it is labelled as 'low Calorie', or because its Calorie content fits in line with your daily target.

Rather than going straight to the back of a food packet or looking at an online menu to find the Calorie section, firstly ask yourself whether what you are truly looking for is something that is going to nourish you psychological and socially – not just physically. Even if you go for a food with a higher Calorie content than usual or originally intended, think of this as a self-compassionate way of eating intuitively by satisfying your mind and body's physical, psychological and social needs.

To get back in tune with eating in line with what you really want and feel like, when you pick up a food that is in a packet, take a little more time to mindfully think about the item before looking at the Calorie label. Feel the wrapper, look inside at the actual food it contains and appreciate its smell, colour and texture if you can. Can you imagine tasting it, enjoying it and feeling satisfied?

✴ **Question food items that are labelled as 'low Calorie'**

Next time you see a food product that is labelled as 'low Calorie', or low in any nutrient for that matter, ask yourself whether your body would actually benefit more from the higher Calorie version. For example, perhaps it is likely that the 'low Calorie' food item has been bulked out with poor quality ingredients and has alternatively been marketed as low in Calories, all natural or gluten free to portray a false sense of healthiness to the consumer. Remember, food companies are well trained in deceiving customers to buy their products, regardless of whether the foods they sell contain any real health benefits.

❈ Limit pre-Calorie checking when eating out

If you are about to go out for a meal, try not to reduce your anxiety about needing to count Calories by looking up the nutritional information on the food company's website. I can understand that this method can offer useful information regarding allergens for those of us who have special dietary requirements, while giving us a general idea of the types of meals on offer. But, most of the time, making a meal choice in advance based on its Calorie content is unlikely to give you true satisfaction when you order.

Ideally, go with the flow by going out for a meal spontaneously with friends, family or a partner, while picking out what you really want and feel like on the menu. If it is a meal you genuinely love and don't get much chance to cook at home, then go for it and enjoy all of the tastes that you experience – regardless of how many Calories you think it contains.

❈ Create more of your own meals and snacks

Instead of relying on ready-made meals or snacks that usually label the Calorie content, try to create more your own meals and snacks without counting or weighing the ingredients precisely. As well as taking the focus off Calories, what you make will also probably be more tasty, satisfying, nourishing and cheaper too. I personally love to make homemade snack bars out of dates, nuts and nut butter, then take them to cafes for me to nibble on with my tea or a cappuccino. Trying to make your own food can also help you to feel like you have effectively accomplished something, or at least made a go at it, no matter what the end result.

❈ Mix it up a bit!

If you are used to following more or less the same meal and snack routines, then it will inevitably be hard not to count the Calories, since you are already likely to know what the nutritional label says. To beat getting stuck in this rut, you might like to try setting yourself the goal of incorporating one new food or meal, even if it is one that you would normally view as being a 'high Calorie' one, into your weekly meals and snacks. For example, if you have chicken and potatoes each night, why not swap the potatoes for pasta, and add a homemade tomato sauce, lentils and roasted vegetables. You could also try to refrain from buying as much pre-made food in packets for a while, as this can help to reduce the temptation to begin counting Calories obsessively.

✲ Be more spontaneous

If your friends or family ask you out to a restaurant (perhaps one that you have not been to or have previously looked at the Calorie content of the meals they have online), say YES! You might feel anxious in the moment, but perceiving the meal as a social occasion rather than as a detrimental barrier to your Calorie schedule, you will eventually come to appreciate the meal time for what it truly is – a chance for social as well as physiological nourishment.

When getting to the restaurant, you could also try to view the food menu in terms of what you can have, rather than what you think you can't. For example, rather than going through a procedure of eliminating all the dishes you usually forbid yourself to eat, look out for nourishing ingredients that you actually enjoy (or remember enjoying) eating. Remember, tackling such barriers is nourishment in itself for the whole mind, which will ultimately reflect positively on the body.

On a final note regarding taking steps to stop or reduce Calorie count-ing, there are many steps, in addition to the ones I have suggested above. Importantly though, all steps taken can be tailored to suit your own life-style preferences. For myself, the journey towards not counting Calories took quite a while, and I can't say that numbers don't pop into my head occa-sionally. But, that's all they do – just pop up and then fade away. Calories no longer control what I choose to put into my body, or my life in general.

Even though there are so many messages out there that promote Calorie counting, for myself and many others individuals, breaking away from this ingrained behaviour has been a positive step forward to learning to live in harmony with food and their own bodies.

By learning to truly trust your own intuitions, while not placing a weighty focus on Calories, I have every bit of Calorie-free confidence that you too can learn to thrive and enjoy life while feeling liberated to eat the food that enables you to optimally nourish your mind and body.

Creating a Compassion-Eating Meal Plan

Perhaps the title of this little chapter sounds a little bit contradictory. Haven't we just been talking about the importance of letting go of control around food, Calorie counting and instead stepping into a more intuitive and flexible way of eating? Surely a meal plan is just another way of being tied down to something where we feel forced to follow some form of rules or rigid structure – even if they are our own?

You wouldn't be misguided to ask these questions. Most meal plans do revolve around a rigid structure that allows little room for deviation, or colouring outside the lines of the rules that a certain lifestyle (usually a faddy diet plan) has prescribed. However, this is NOT the case with the Nourishing Routes ethos or my approach to meal planning.

From my own recovery from an eating disorder, getting to a place where I no longer 'needed' any meal plan in order to optimally nourish my body became possible by following a more compassionate lifestyle. However, at the very beginning of this journey, creating a meal plan was essential to my recovery and placed me in a position where I could ensure that my body was getting more rather than less of the energy and nutrients I needed. Without a meal plan to begin with, I would feel too compelled to fall back into a more restrictive way of eating, usually as a way to cope with the negative emotions that I was being bombarded with on a minute by minute basis.

Although I knew that eating more intuitively on a physical, psychological and social level would be one of my main goals to reach in terms of my recovery, I also realised that my body just wasn't ready for that – not yet anyway. At that point, my body literally didn't know whether it was hungry or not hungry, and trying to recognise such signals seemed like a complete impossibility. This is not surprising, as years of restricting food and having a negative untrusting relationship with food does take its toll on how the body and mind are able to pick up and react to certain signals that ensure our survival.

Whether you currently have an eating disorder, disordered eating, a negative relationship with food, or are just trying to improve the way you are able to optimally nourish your body, you might have experienced a sense of mistrust with food and your own body at some point in your life.

Through years of dieting, depriving your body, excessive exercising, or experiencing cycles of binging and restriction, your body has likely become very confused. By that I mean that your body possibly doesn't know whether there is a feast or a famine on the way. Also, knowing what hunger or fullness really feels like, or being able to eat the types and quantities of food that you truly enjoy, with full permission to do without feeling guilty, might seem very foreign to you.

From research in the field of eating psychology we know and understand that individuals who have gone through periods of restriction, bingeing or yoyo weight cycling tend to feel very confused when it comes to intuitive eating. For example, as we just mentioned, you may not truly know what it is like to feel truly hungry or full anymore. Similarly, you may not know what type of foods your body and mind are craving, or why this might be. There might also be a worry that experiencing a craving for food will send you into a cycle of wanting to restrict what you eat, or no longer being able to leave a packet of biscuits open after eating just one…

Getting to the main point of this chapter, a meal plan from a Nourishing Routes perspective is not a way of enhancing the control you want to feel over food. It is also not following anything rigid that allows little room to 'colour outside the lines'. This would just be exacerbating a problem you are probably wishing to find freedom from.

Alternatively, a meal plan the Nourishing Routes way is a compassionate path to finding freedom and getting back to a place of trusting your body around food, and your body trusting food. As we discussed a few chapters ago, it is about placing 'compassion-eating' and 'kindful' eating back on the menu. It is also about discovering the foods that you know you genuinely enjoy and feel nourished from, as well as being adventurous with new foods or eating routines you are not familiar with. It additionally involves ensuring that you take time to consider what you really feel like eating and what you know will truly nourish your body physically, psychologically, socially and even emotionally. Developing a meal plan in this way can also fit alongside meeting various dietary requirements, whether that involve an allergy, intolerance, or ethical form of living where you don't consume animal products.

A meal plan for myself meant seeking out the foods that I really wanted to eat and allowing myself them – no matter what rules or restrictions I had previously placed on myself. I made a commitment to finding foods that would suit how I wanted to make myself feel, not how I wanted to look. This meant additionally reducing Calorie counting and rigid planning too.

By continuing creating a rigid meal plan a day in advance, I wouldn't have been able to eat intuitively or compassionately. Instead, becoming more open to the idea of a compassion-eating meal plan meant taking a mindful note of how I felt before, during and after eating. This simply involved asking myself, honestly, if I feel like eating something sweet, savoury, hot, cold, spicy, sour, fresh, crunchy etc. It definitely did not involve judging whether I would feel guilty, ashamed or unworthy of pleasure after eating. I would deal with and overcome that unnecessary part of eating when it occurred, rather than planning ways to avoid it through choosing 'safe' foods. To this, I allowed any feelings to pass and fade away with the knowledge that, regardless of how horrible or guilty I felt, that I would still take time to nurture and nourish myself in the way that my body and mind so strongly desired. Pleasure no longer came to mean bad, gluttonous, fat, unworthy, or unlovable.

A compassion-eating meal plan for me was about developing trust and allowed me to know that I would eat around six to seven times per day (it still usually is), no matter what. Instead of compensating for what I would eat or already had eaten, I made a commitment to never deliberately skip or compensate on a meal or snack. I also began to incorporate 'fear foods' such as those that I had previous viewed as 'dirty' 'bad' or 'too high in Calories' into my daily diet. A compassion-eating meal plan didn't dictate exactly what I ate, where, how much and when. Instead, it simply provided a flexible framework that gave me permission to eat in a way that would enable me to get back in touch with my natural physical, psychological, emotional and social hunger.

As we discussed earlier, food is so much more than the nutrients and Calories it contains, so finding a way of eating that allows you a flexible amount of space to respect the many functions food plays in our lives is vital to our happiness and health.

So, what does a compassion-eating meal plan actually look like in practice for yourself?

Let me start answering the above question by saying that a compassion-eating meal plan doesn't look anything like a meal plan that has a main goal of weight loss or even weight gain. It will never involve measuring your self-worth or progress based on numbers, whether that be Calories, nutrients or body weight. A compassion-eating meal plan using the Nourishing Routes philosophy is a much more empowering approach to nourishing the whole mind and body, and involves the following steps:

❉ Making a list of the foods you currently restrict or have a poor relationship with, but want to gradually incorporate into your life.

❉ Writing down all of the foods that you genuinely enjoy the taste or sensory experience of, and ensuring that most of your meals or snacks contain at least one of these foods.

❉ Choosing foods that are in line with how you want to make yourself feel – that could be more energised, strong, empowered, feminine, masculine, full of vitality or relaxed for example. At the same time, choosing foods that make you feel deprived, unhappy, depleted of energy and sluggish can be taken off your regular menu. Of course, sometimes we will eat foods that make us not feel our best, but as long as we choose those foods because we truly enjoy them, or because it is part of our

❉

cultural values or a social occasion, then there is more than enough room for these types of foods to be a feature in our lives. We are all human after all, and there is no perfect meal plan of foods that make us feel nourished 100% of the time.

* Making a list of meals that you know you can easily prepare with your financial and time resources, and making these a regular appearance in your meal repertoire.

* Ensuring that there are no two days where you eat exactly the same things as the day before. The Nourishing Routes way of compassion-eating meal planning encourages you to feel OK with breaking free from rigid routines and making life more exciting with a wide variety of recipes and room for experimenting with new foods.

* Setting out a number of times that you want to eat per day as a minimum (e.g. 3 meals and 3 snacks), and allowing yourself room to eat in between your usual food times if your day doesn't go as planned. This means using meal times as a guide rather than a definitive rule around when you should and should not eat. Time doesn't really account for much when it comes to compassion-eating, as long as you find the time to nourish your mind and body as much as possible.

* Allowing occasions where you can spontaneously go out for a meal, no matter what time, and still fit in your other meals and snacks for that day – even if you say yes to having a starter and dessert with that meal too.

* Having a day in the week where you experiment with trying a new food, type of meal, or recipe.

* Having times in the day or week when you challenge yourself to a particular food, or meals that you normally deny yourself or associate with feeling guilty, fat or wanting to restrict or binge eat. In this case, having a compassion-eating meal plan allows you to let these feelings pass if they do arise, as you know that you have set out with the intention

that you will continue to nourish (and not punish) your mind and body regardless of how negative you feel.

❋ Making a commitment that you will make time to nourish your body with food, and try not to miss meals or snacks throughout the day.

Unlike a usual meal plan, there is no need to pre-plan exactly what, how much or when you will eat when having a compassion-eating meal plan. This means that using the tools that we covered in compassionate-eating and 'kindful' eating is vital.

From my own experience, writing a compassion-eating meal plan that didn't involve an extremely specific structure felt very foreign to me at first. I couldn't really grasp the concept that it was OK not to know everything that I was going to eat that day in advance, or track the number of Calories in each meal or snack I would be consuming. However, I eventually learned that allowing flexibility with my food choices, including spontaneous occasions of eating outside the house or usual meal and snack times, was an essential part of leading a happy, healthy and ultimately more compassionate lifestyle. It was what I needed to nourish my body and mind, rather than fulfilling some specific Calorie quota that a dietician gave me (who really had no clue of what real recovery from an eating disorder or a negative relationship with food is).

Most professionals in the health and wellness sphere still promote Calorie tracking and specific forms of meal planning for losing weight, gaining weight, reducing your risk of experiencing a chronic illness or to aid individuals recovering from an eating disorder. However, from evidence and personal experience, a meal plan that does not allow much room for Calorie counting or any form of rigid structures is much a more empowering and self-compassionate route to take when it comes to investing in your happiness and health.

By creating your own flexible meal plan that includes meals and snacks, and allows you to regain a positive and trusting relationship with yourself and food, you may gradually realise that the foot you have been holding on the control pedal for so long begins to release. Where you may have always

❋

felt a need to weigh out food or calculate macronutrients and Calories, this obsession will likely be replaced with a passion to seek opportunities to enjoy foods you enjoy, as and when you like in a way that fills you with contentment – not guilt or any other forms of self-sabotaging thoughts and behaviours. On a last and vitally important note, when we eat with a compassion-eating meal plan as a guide, we are empowering ourselves immensely to become the Compassioneers we were born to be.

PART 4:

Compassion with Your Body

"Your body isn't beautiful because it looks slim, curvy, fit, athletic or any other glorified shape. It is beautiful because it is a miraculous wonder of the universe"

Every Body is a 'Good' Body

When did we come to the view that it is so important to be really slim, fit, muscular, or have a perfectly 'clean' diet? Why, somewhere along the line, did we begin to not accept that we are perfect and good enough just the way we are – our bodies included? You might not know the exact point in time that this type of thinking ventured into your mind, but you might be familiar with some of the following thoughts in relation to changing your body in order to feel better about yourself:

I would be a 'better' person or would have a 'good' body if I had:

❋ Slimmer thighs

❋ A slimmer waist

❋ Less fat on my body

❋ Bigger and more toned muscles

❋ A firmer or more perky bottom

❋ Clearer skin

❋ Larger breasts

❋ A broader chest

❋ Less wrinkles

❋ A more nutritious 'clean' diet

❋

Even if you do attain any of these things, none of them really define who you are, how healthy you are, or how 'good' of a person or body you are. Striving for them might say more about your sense of self-worth and ability to show self-compassion though.

There is a crucial fact about our own bodies that we can't ignore. This fact is that what it weighs or physically appears like doesn't really account for much in terms of our overall health, happiness and wellbeing.

What really does matter though is how we are made to think and feel about our weight and physical appearance, and the impacts this has on our ability to be the best version of ourselves – in whatever size or shape that may be. This piece of information is related to one of the key elements of Nourishing Routes, which is Health at Every Size. However, even though there is growing research in this field to show that what individuals actually weigh is insignificant in comparison to other key areas of our lives in terms of promoting health, there are many contradictory messages that we are bombarded with every day. You may be very familiar with some of these yourself, with some including messages that state something along the lines of:

✴ Being overweight is killing people

✴ Losing weight will help you live longer

✴ Weight gain is self-inflicted and anyone can lose weight if they gain more self-control over their food intake and exercise more

✴ Accomplishing weight loss will last in the long term and inevitably lead to a positive body image and overall happiness – a slimmer, healthier and happier you

But in truth, there is much more research to support how, on average, individuals who are classified as overweight live longer than 'healthy' weight or 'underweight' individuals. There is research to suggest that individuals who are 'overweight' tend to be less happy and experience more poor psychological health issues than individuals who are a 'healthy' weight, but this is likely because individuals who are classified as being overweight often experience

✴

302

weight stigma and other related inequalities that contribute to the way they feel. It is also interesting to bear in mind that:

❊ No piece of research has ever found that losing weight directly prolongs life or leads to increased happiness in the long-term

❊ Weight is not solely dictated by our ability to self-regulate or place more control over what we eat

❊ Regardless of 'trying' to lose weight, there are many other factors that predict individuals' weight – which usually fluctuates around a 'set point' depending on both genetic, social and other environmental factors

❊ Losing weight is not associated with increased body dissatisfaction. There is more evidence to suggest that increasing weight loss leads to worse body satisfaction, poorer health and regaining more weight than was initially lost in the long term – leading to a vicious cycle of yoyo dieting

An overarching problem with the many untruthful messages about how our physical bodies relate to health and happiness is that they support the idea that there should be a distinction between 'good' and 'bad' bodies. Those that are 'good' become associated with the unrealistic ideal that everyone should be slim or of a healthy weight in order to experience happiness and health. A similar problem lies in how these messages actually make individuals feel worse about themselves, placing them in a vulnerable position that makes them even more likely to invest in the diet and fitness industry to eradicate their 'bad body' problems. As we have already discussed in detail, this is not the type of investment that is really going to lead to authentic happiness and wellbeing.

Nourishing Routes philosophy and being a Compassioneer goes against the grain of these unhelpful and derogatory messages that exploit more individuals than they benefit. Instead, the Nourishing Routes philosophy supports the need to remember that every body, not matter what size or shape, is completely worthy and deserving of love and respect right now. This means that our self-worth does not need to be based on our weight, how much exercise we do, what we look like, our grades at school college or university, our employment status or even our financial income. Each and every one of us lives in a body that is unique, with you as a person having your own personality and character strengths that no one – other than you – can replicate.

We can apply this way of thinking to how we think about health and happiness. Although much of the media and many research articles based around achieving happiness and health can suggest that diet and fitness is essential, the real fact is that your postcode, or where you live and your social status, has a much greater impact on your long-term happiness and well-being compared to what you eat, weigh or how much you exercise. This is because most of us live in a very unequal society comprised of immense wealth and privilege at one end of the spectrum, but poverty and oppression at the other. These stark inequalities are what lead to a vicious cycle of chronic stress, metabolic dysfunction, mental illness, poor quality diets, diminished levels of physical activity and resulting chronic diseases such as cardiovascular disease and diabetes etc.

Very robust research has been showing these findings for decades. Yet we are continually persuaded that it is our individual responsibility to look after our own health – mainly through dieting and exercising – rather than focussing on the societal structure as a whole which is leading to inequality. This might seemingly save the government money through transferring this responsibility onto individuals, but in reality there are much greater costs to contend with if governments, organisations and media outlets continue to use this as a model to promote optimal societal happiness and health.

Inequality can even result from and be exacerbated by the diet and fitness industry. As I have talked at length about before, we live in a time when there are so many unnecessary expectations placed on us at the expense of our self-worth, but for the gain of someone else's financial profit.

It is generally more affluent individuals who are able to buy into the latest diet or fitness trend, as this becomes a symbol of their wealth. However, with most individuals trying to live up to expectations around diet and fitness, it is a common case that individuals strive for some of the least important things in life – leading us further away from an ideal state of happiness and health. The trick lies in how profit making organisations manipulate their customers (i.e. us) to feel as though they are lacking in something (usually a product or certain body type) and get into the habit of black and white, all or nothing thinking. In relation to the body, this might involve thinking that:

✣ *"If I can't achieve 'x' body type, then I am an unworthy or unsuccessful person."*

✣ *"If I can't lose of gain an ideal amount of weight, then no one will love me and I will die alone."*

✣ *"The reason I feel sad or anxious is because I am fat, too skinny or ugly."*

By being manipulated into thinking these types of thoughts we slowly but surely begin to strive to meet others' and society's expectations – not our own. Yet the outcomes we try to attain in order to achieve this a so called 'good' body only scratches at the surface of who we really are, and more often than not we still believe that our bodies just aren't good enough as they are.

The promises of the diet and fitness industry that we buy into, whether we are rich, middle class or poor, can lead individuals already experiencing inequality into a cycle of further stress and poor physical and mental health. Many individuals commonly receive the message that they should lose weight or exercise more to avoid chronic illness or becoming a burden on societal resources. This isn't only contributing to undermining their self-worth, but also keeps them spending money, unnecessarily, on various products and resources that really don't lead to happiness and health. More time might be spent on perfecting a person's appearance and food intake rather than spending time with family, being creative, or gaining the confidence to pursue ambitions that would allow them to fulfil their dreams and purpose in the world.

The message of 'not being good enough yet' sometimes takes a different form for wealthy individuals, who are sent the message that looking beautiful, being slim, and eating 'clean' is what will make them a successful, worthy and attractive person who can uphold their high social status (which might

✣

be under threat by other more attractive successful competitors). On the exterior, such individuals may appear slim, beautiful, happy and healthy, but an assessment of their levels of stress, mental health and sense of self-worth might tell us a different story.

A continuing theme throughout this book has been that improving the physical body in any way rarely enables us to unlock the code to experience real happiness and health in a way that is self-compassionate. Living up to external expectations and not viewing yourself or your body as good enough right now is also hugely disempowering to your confidence and self-worth. Yet, this is what most of our western society still promotes as a one-way ticket to happiness and health, rather than the many beautiful avenues and blissfully Nourishing Routes you can venture on in. This needs to change. Now.

So, if you still think that becoming healthy or attaining a 'good' body or being a successful person involves holding your nose drinking green smoothies, regularly weighing yourself, counting Calories, feeling lethargic from a juice cleanse, or grinding your teeth and clenching your fists in order to stay on a treadmill for longer and lift more weights that you did yesterday, then it might be worth trying to think again.

You might also want to reconsider the preconceived idea that making yourself feel guilty after eating something you enjoy or not doing as much exercise than you normally do is benefiting your body or mind. Alternatively, feelings of guilt can actually be more toxic for the body than any type of food or lack of exercise ever could be, as guilt is ultimately perceived as a stressor – potentially leading to chronically toxic chemicals to be released from our adrenal glands (e.g. adrenalin), which plough through our bodies to try and alleviate that stressor – eventually leading to inflammation, fatigue, and ill health, physical and psychological wellbeing. At this point it is useful to remember that, as human beings, we were designed to make food and movement social and enjoyable parts of our lives – not as a measuring stick to judge our self-worth by.

I can tell you right now that you are worthy and amazing in this very moment – every single inch of your body that can be seen and even the parts that are not seen. Whether you believe this yet though is another matter, but it is a matter that you can resolve by choosing to embark on your own Nourishing Routes and being more open to the idea that self-compassion and becoming a Compassioneer really is a possibility for you.

We need to remember that every body is a good body now, while saying a fond farewell to body loathing. It may seem a little patronising to mention, but it really boils down to the basics of appreciating the miracle that we already are. Even in terms of the amazing way we are able to uniquely perceive the world around us, how our legs enable us to walk through life and the way our hands allow us to experience touch and express and fulfil our creative potential. Our taste buds and sense of smell are also there to help us eat nourishing foods that we can thoroughly enjoy.

To really love our bodies and express body positivity we must firstly learn to love ourselves, which you have probably realised. We need to bear in mind that body positivity isn't temporary either, and that it is a lifelong journey of developing a secure and trusting relationship with ourselves that we can learn to always treasure and nurture.

Although I could simply advise that we all should need to start appreciating, looking after and loving our bodies as they are right now, this may be much easier said than done for individuals like yourself who may have developed a harsh relationship with their body for a number of years – perhaps too many to even remember.

Speaking from personal experience and research, the route to complete body positivity is not a straight road and does not involve any quick fixes. If you have led a life of perfectionism, trying to meet others' expectations, aiming for being the best, and pursuing the next best diet or fitness fad, then loving your body and who you are right now might not come so naturally.

There is also the fact that there will always be occasions when we experience a situation or a personal thought that instigates negative thoughts and feelings about our body into self-destructive action again. For example, you might overhear a person speaking about how 'fat' or 'skinny' they feel, even though it seems clear to you that you are either bigger or smaller than they are in terms of body size. Similarly, there are also times when you put on clothes and they simply don't fit in the way that they once used to. These are just simple everyday events, but nevertheless occasions that can send us over the tipping point.

My advice to you from this point onwards would be to aim for progress and not perfection in terms of accepting your body as 'good enough' now, while aiming to stop judging yourself unnecessarily when and where possible. The aim with body positivity, as we will go into much more detail throughout this part of this book, largely involves treating your whole body in the way you would treat a cherished friend. Trying to become more attuned to your natural instinct to care for your body in the way it would want you to is also vital, which might involve resisting the urge to punish yourself with rigid exercise and fitness regimes or toxic thoughts of guilt and poor self-worth. In addition, finding ways to allow your body to relax and feel nourished, energised and nurtured is absolutely essential. You are unlikely to achieve all this at once, but steady steps over a period of time can make a huge difference.

I am completely being honest when I say that you are beautiful in your body just the way it is right in this very moment. If we try to firstly jump the gun by striving for a better body, before we can learn to accept and be more compassionate to ourselves, then I'm afraid that the output will be a bit of a messy one. In contrast, if we reverse the calculation and allow self-love to come first, we inevitably and very naturally start to develop an eagerness to want to care for and nurture our body in the best way possible.

Instead of developing a rigid exercise and fitness regimen with the main aim of 'improving' the body, we become more focussed on feeling happier, healthier and getting involved in the creatively enjoyable activities that bring us joy and fulfilment.

What we eat becomes more about eating the foods that nourish us physically, psychologically and socially, rather than depriving ourselves of pleasure and essential nutrients in order to lose weight, strip fat, become slimmer, gain more muscle, get extremely fit or meet someone else's ideal standards of beauty. Such detrimental pursuits rarely lead to authentic happiness and health because they don't really resolve any of our insecurities that remain skin deep.

On your own journey towards leading a more self-compassionate lifestyle with your whole body I would like to offer you the opportunity of engaging in a bit more genuine self-care. Instead of taking time to think about how you are next going to make a change to your diet or exercise regimen, take a moment to question where this urge is coming from. Is it to become happier and healthier? Or, is it to reduce feelings of guilt and feel able to meet expectations to have a 'better' body or 'cleaner' diet in order to feel more accepted by ourselves and society?

If it is the second option, I would highly recommend reminding yourself of all the amazing things your body can do regardless of what it has eaten or how much exercise it has done. This can simply involve writing down three things that are quite miraculous about your body. Look at this list, then close your eyes and think about what you have written.

Accept that you have been blessed with these three positive attributes, and that they contribute to creating your own uniquely beautiful body – independently of what you look like, weigh, eat or how much exercise you are able to do. Your body is one of the many miracles you can use to flourish and thrive throughout the wonder that is your life.

Compassioneer Activity: Sending Yourself Some Body love

To give yourself and your whole body some of the time, attention and compassion it deserves, I invite you to develop your own body love ritual. Compassionately driven rituals, no matter how short or simple, can create meaningful and lifelong positive habits that have an empowering impact on our lives. The body love ritual that I am about to introduce you to certainly delivers just that, while being oh so simple to carry out on a daily basis.

All it involves is having a body (so hopefully a tick there), and also some moisturiser or body oil. It also simply involves noticing each and every body part without negative judgement as your hand comes into contact with it – giving loving care, attention and positive words in an authentic way. So, without further ado, let's begin:

* At a convenient time in the morning or evening, give yourself around five minutes to find a quiet, calm and safe space where you can be in the moment with yourself and your thoughts.

* Get out some of your favourite moisturiser or body oil (I sometimes like to use coconut oil), and put it to one side while you carefully and lovingly undress yourself.

* Beginning this activity requires you to enter a space of non-judgement, so as you undress, do this knowing that you are about to enter a loving space where no one or no thoughts can harm you – not even your own.

* Set out with the intention that no matter how much your urge is to give negative body hatred talk to yourself, you will resist doing this for the moments that you are immersed within this activity

✤ Once you are fully undressed, get out your moisturiser or body oil and rub a decent amount into your palms while gently warming it in between them and your fingers.

✤ First start with your lower feet, calves and thighs. Place the moisturiser softly on your ankles and calves and rub into them as you would if you had a strong desire to care for them and give out love. As you do this, work up towards your thighs while saying to yourself:

"My legs are so important to me. They have been here since I was placed on this planet, and they have allowed me to step into life and towards my goals. My legs have enabled me to embark on all of the journeys I have ever been on. In the past and present, I may not have been kind to my legs in the way that I deserve. However, now is different.

"Now I know that they are beautiful. It doesn't matter what shape they are, whether they have cellulite or any other 'imperfections'. My legs are amazing just as they are. They are part of my identity and are my tools to get through life and achieve my dreams.

"No matter what I may have thought or said in the past, I choose to fully accept my legs as they are right now. I give love to each leg in the way that I would give love to a close friend.

"My legs are not my enemies, they are my allies and will forever support me on my journey towards leading a more compassionate lifestyle filled with happiness, health and wellbeing."

✤ As you say these words to yourself, close your eyes and breathe a little more slowly than before. Allow your body and mind to experience to full sensation of how the moisturiser feels on your skin, as well as the thoughts and feelings that are flowing through your mind. If there are any negative thoughts about your legs not being beautiful or worthy of your care and attention, don't judge them for being there. Just let them arise and gradually float away.

❋   Now move on to your middle body, starting with your stomach. Move your hands slowly in circular motions, and take care not to be too harsh with your technique. Similar to before, say to yourself:

"My stomach, back and breasts are so important to me. They are me, and I deserve to love me. My stomach carries out so many amazing functions that I can't even grasp just how miraculous it really is.

"Regardless of how large or small my stomach is, I am grateful for the way it protects my organs, digests my food, and sends out the vital nutrients to the rest of my body so that I can survive.

"No matter what negative things I have previously said or thought about my stomach, or what anyone else has said, I know in this moment that my stomach is worthy of my love. Without it I wouldn't be here, and if I wasn't here, then no one else would be able to take my place in order to do the many amazing things that I was born to do.

"My back has held me up in this world, and it has kept me strong when I have felt like holding my head down and not carrying on with my mission."

If you are a woman, you can also say:

"My breasts, regardless of how big or small, have also been there throughout my life – contributing to the way my body is able to optimally function by helping to produce the many vital hormones it needs to thrive.

"My breasts may even have the opportunity to provide another life with nourishment, but even if they don't, my breasts are part of me and my identity and I deserve to love me.

"If I have had any current or negative thoughts about my stomach, breasts or back, I am now in a privileged position to simply accept that they happened, but are now about to drift away."

Now venture on to your lower and top arms, starting with one and then the other as you gently rub in the moisturiser or body oil that you love. On this occasion say to yourself:

"My arms are two miracles. They allow me to express my creativity, whether that be through writing, typing or drawing and painting. My arms have allowed me to reach out into the world and grasp at my dreams.

"My arms, no matter how big, small or 'flawed' I may perceive them to be, have been vital to my survival. Without my amazing arms, how would I have been able to eat and nourish my body? Without my arms it would also be extremely difficult to show love to another person. My arms allow me to hug other people and provide loving support. It is this type of loving support that I was born to and deserve to give to myself.

"For all the negative thoughts and words that have been expressed about my hands and arms, I will now let them go. As I watch them drift away, I know that I am grateful for my arms, and will try my best to send them authentic love and care."

Finally, when you have completed the above steps, stand for a few moments and take in all the physical sensations, psychological feelings and thoughts that you are experiencing. If any of them are negative, let them be and eventually float away. Meanwhile, imagine that you have just given a massage to your friend or a close partner, and send your body the same love as you would do to them. After doing this, say thank you to yourself for being willing to take the time to invest in you. Remember that you fully deserved this loving experience to take care of each part of your amazingly beautiful and miraculous body.

Worrisome Weight Stigma

With the common mantra that our 'health is our wealth' we have to contend with the how these terms have come to be equated with looking slim, attractive and picture perfect. To appear otherwise, or to be classified as being overweight, is alternatively associated with negative attitudes and stigma that can have long-term negative impacts on a person's life and ability to be compassionate to themselves and others. as well as their ability to reach their full potential.

This is completely unacceptable. A person's weight, at least not unless it severely affects their physical or psychological wellbeing, should not dictate their ability to live happily, love themselves and thrive. When the media display someone as being a bit on the heavier side of a 'healthy weight', what they often portray is someone who appears lazy, poor, unattractive, jobless, incompetent, socially awkward and generally less likeable in comparison to someone of an ideal weight.

It is also sad that children as young as three describe other children who are 'overweight' as mean, stupid, lazy and ugly – with these views persisting across childhood, adolescence and even adulthood. Young children and adolescents who are 'overweight' are also often subjected to name calling and even physical harassment for way that they look, which is unlikely to be an ingredient that leads to self-compassion, happiness and positive mental and physical health. Alternatively, it draws away from a life that is able to be lived to the full as a Compassioneer.

Weight stigma unfortunately plays an unnecessary role in many aspects of our everyday lives, including education, healthcare and employment, where it can also lead to unfair treatment and discrimination. For example, weight stigma has been described as one of the last remaining acceptable forms of discrimination.

This can be seen when individuals who are deemed to be 'overweight' lose out on being employed for a new job, gaining a promotion, or being given a higher wage. There are even cases where health professionals inappropriately communicate with individuals who they perceive to be 'overweight', who are also significantly more likely to be denied appropriate treatment compared to individuals who are regarded as being a 'healthy weight'.

Our society has taught us that being overweight or obese is something to dislike and avoid at all costs – even to the point where individuals become willing to take a very negative perception of others based on their weight and physical appearance. This can make individuals who are overweight more likely to be out-casted by their peers, which can have long-term negative impacts on the way they learn to socialise, experience stress and cope with negative emotions. In this way, individuals can begin to use food to temporarily help alleviate or avoid facing their negative experiences and feelings. There is even emerging evidence that weight stigma, whether that be at work, school, or in other public settings, encourages individuals who are overweight to eat more on the days when they experience it. This isn't surprising when we look at other research evidence that shows a strong link between stressful experiences, maladaptive eating behaviour and weight gain.

Research has repeatedly shown that overweight individuals are much less likely to be chosen in a job interview over a slimmer candidate. They are also more likely to be earning a lower wage, regardless of their educational background. Even if they do get the job, it is not uncommon for overweight individuals to be taunted by colleagues or become subject to undermining conversations that revolve around the need to diet and lose weight. All of these issues can significantly contribute to the way individuals who are deemed to be 'overweight' experience inequality, a low social status and poorer life circumstances that lead to ill physical and psychological health.

More recent research has shown that individuals who experience weight stigma have a lower life expectancy than individuals who don't, independently of what they actually weigh, eat, how much they exercise and other health-related behaviours. What this really means is that how people think and feel about their weight and appearance is more influential over our wellbeing than any direct physical implications of weighing a specific amount. So, a key question is, is it really fair or helping the inequitable society we already live in? In the context of Nourishing Routes, is it ever going to help individuals to lead more compassionate lives so that they can really flourish and thrive?

Even if you answered no to the above questions and are angered by the stigma that individuals who are viewed as being 'overweight' face, it is still hard to get away from the fact that many of us are bombarded with explicit images and messages that equate being 'overweight' as something that classifies someone as a bad and unworthy person. Most of us, whether we know it or not, have a bias to negatively judge individuals who appear 'overweight'. Yet the main reason for such individuals' poorer life circumstances, including health, is not down to their weight or the personal characteristics they were born with – it has much more to do with the way society views and treats them as a consequence of looking the way they do.

How is it that we can justify weight stigma if it is likely having the opposite impact than intended? Will discriminating against or victimising someone really make them more likely to become motivated to lose weight and become healthier (if that is even necessary), or will it drive them further down a stressful spiral of self-hate and poor self-control when it comes to dealing with negative life events and using emotional eating as a coping tool?

It is perhaps a little bit ironic then that weight stigma, regardless of how it is inflicted, can increase a person's stress, lower their self-esteem and diminish their ability to optimally nourish themselves. Individuals subjected to weight stigma on a regular basis are also more likely to embark on restrictive diets, which can inevitably lead to vicious cycles of binging and weight fluctuation – hardly a recipe for improving health and wellbeing!

There is currently very little evidence to suggest that being overweight, or at least not an ideal BMI, makes a person lazy, gluttonous, or unworthy of

❋

being decently treated by society. Yet these are the exact words that we associate with being overweight on a regular basis, whether that be through the media or our own friendship circles. The reality is that there are many individuals who, despite being classified as overweight, have experienced success in sport, business, politics, academia, volunteering, creativity and many other fulfilling life goals.

Another key issue that I have with weight stigma is how it contributes to the general population experiencing poor body image, disordered eating, and generally a poor relationship with food and themselves.

With so many negative messages about the consequences of being overweight – even that directed to parents of primary school age children when they are weighed in class – it is hard to escape that nagging feeling that we 'should' all be doing something to avoid being overweight. For many individuals this simply means eating more nourishing foods or doing a little bit more physical activity. However, for some vulnerable individuals, it could mean growing to dislike their body, going on restrictive diets and pursuing punishing exercise regimens.

All in all, our fear of becoming overweight can fuel disordered ways of thinking about ourselves rather than growing to love and show compassion our bodies just as they are. We now judge ourselves on how big or slim we look, rather than all the amazing things our body can do regardless of the numbers it happens to weigh on a scale.

So what can we do to tackle weight stigma in our weight obsessed society?

A great first step to tackle weight stigma, in line with the philosophy of Nourishing Routes, would be to help individuals, as early in life as possible, to love and show compassion to themselves just as they are. If we can enable individuals to become more self-compassionate, and view their body as more awesome and amazing rather than just a symbol of weight, appearance and what others negatively judge them by, we can help them to use their body in ways that allow them to flourish and thrive as human beings.

❋

We could also help the situation hugely if we choose not to engage in negative talk about weight. This means avoiding the need to criticise or negatively comment on our own or other people's body weight and physical appearance, which is a topic of discussion we will soon touch upon a little later in part three of this book. By doing this we set a new norm – a norm that reduces the need to unnecessarily worry about weight or appearance too much, as it is no longer a popular topic that influences how we are critically judged by other people and society in general.

Part of being more self-compassionate and reducing weight stigma additionally involves taking a focus off being overweight. Yes, for some individuals their weight may negatively be contributing to their physical and psychological health, but in most circumstances an individuals' weight is not the first issue that should be resolved. Also, communicating to individuals that they are contributing to a growing and costly issue through the use of stigmatising images and documentaries about the negative aspects of being 'overweight' is unlikely to really help empower individuals to become more compassionate, happy and healthy. All in all, these stigmatising images, videos and messages need to be minimised as much as possible, while instead placing a focus on developing individuals' compassionate relationship with their whole body – regardless of what it weighs or looks like.

Gaining Nothing From Feeling Fat

Our capacity to develop a positive relationship with food is inevitably interlinked with the way we think and feel about our bodies. Unfortunately, this often equates to what we eat being associated with feelings of being 'fat', which by society's standards is something we disapprove of and should avoid at all costs. If I had a penny for every time I heard the phrase "I feel fat" after someone has eaten a certain food or meal, I would surely have enough money to buy the whole tea menu from every existing cafe known to mankind. That might me great for me, but definitely not for anyone else.

The thing is, we can't really 'feel' fat – fat is a molecule, not a real feeling or an emotion. Yet we continually use the phrase as a substitute for how we are feeling. What we really mean with our words though, is that we feel useless, unworthy, unlovable and as though something is crucially missing from our lives. Instead of simply stating that we feel upset, angry, guilty, ashamed, lonely, or low in self-esteem, saying that we feel fat seems to act as a widely accepted substitute for what is really going on inside our minds, which is the real issue that needs to be tackled.

Fat is something that many of us have, at some point in our lives, viewed as an evil thing that we should take care to avoid – no matter the harm that we might place on ourselves by doing so. However, continually using the phrase of feeling fat is not helping our own or anyone else's wellbeing. In reality, it only exaggerates our own and society's inaccurate and sometimes self-destructive opinion on what the word fat symbolises.

If we really think about it, we can't physically transition from feeling different extents of fatness from one day to the next – that would defy the laws of physiology. Yet many of us wake up feeling much fatter than we did yesterday, or even a few minutes previously. For example, we can be unexpectedly struck by sensing (inaccurately) that our legs and thighs are overwhelmingly big. Similarly, we may wake up feeling fine in our own bodies, only to then try on a piece of clothing later in the day or step on a scale and resultantly feel absolutely awful about ourselves. We then falsely attribute this negative feeling to being 'fat', when the likelihood is that there is a deeper insecurity within us that hasn't yet been brought to our attention or resolved.

Looking at this issue from a more realistic perspective, fat itself is not the main factor causing our distress. What is more likely to lead to distress is how we continually and negatively evaluate and judge our bodies throughout the day. Perhaps you looked at yourself in the mirror and felt inadequate in relation to how you think you 'should' look, or even let down by not having achieved a particular goal for the day. Instead of looking at where those feelings of inadequacy really came from you might instead place the blame on being fat, which integrating this experience as a negative feeling. You might also ask yourself:

"If only I could reduce or eradicate fat from my life, or at least lose weight and become slimmer, then perhaps I would be much happier and successful?"

I think you might already know what my views are on the above question.

Unfortunately we can't resolve life's problems simply by learning to feeling less fat or by losing weight. That is not what living compassionately and becoming a Compassioneer involves, so continuing to think like this will not result in developing an authentic sense of self-esteem, happiness or health. There is a much bigger picture to be explored here, but thankfully one filled with compassion rather than negative judgement.

Trying to 'fix' our problems by aiming to sculpt and shape our bodies in a certain way, or even eradicate fat altogether, can lead to engaging in activities that don't really nurture our bodies and minds in an optimal way. We can also start to develop maladaptive coping mechanisms that involve having a negative relationship with what we eat, how much we exercise and our overall body image. Similarly, we may spend less time focusing on activities that do have a genuine positive impact on our self-esteem, such as quality time with family and friends and engaging in the hobbies we enjoy or are truly passionate about.

However, there is some truth in the importance of identifying and resolving why we define how we feel based on our sense of 'fatness'. For example, if we take the time to challenge the reasons behind feeling fat, then this can help us to develop a more compassionate and understanding relationship with our bodies so that we can make positive transformations in our lives.

Breaking Free from Fat Talk

Expanding on some of the previous topics around weight stigma and feeling fat, it is important to understand the benefits of being able to break free from negative talk around fat.

To begin thinking a little bit more about some of the collective issues we have just discussed, ask yourself when did it become normal to relate to who we are, or perceive ourselves to be, as fat?

In any Oxford dictionary, the word fat is actually a noun, not an adjective. Yet fat is the very word many of us use to describe how we look, feel and act:

❋ *"My thighs and hips are fat"*

❋ *"I just feel so fat"*

❋ *"He/she is so fat"*

❋ *"Stop acting like a fat idiot"*

❋ *"Our nation is becoming fatter"*

Whether you have heard or even said these statements or not, it is hard to ignore how the term fat has become so ingrained into everyday language – often not for the purpose of describing what fat actually is.

However, fact of the matter is that no one can actually be fat.

It makes me really sad to see and hear the word fat violently thrown around and shoved into the mouths of individuals who, when psychologically

❋

swallowing it, integrate the idea that merely feeling or identifying as being fat is something to be deeply ashamed of.

When we hear that the nation is becoming 'fatter', is this really motivating individuals to become healthier in body and mind? Or, is it actually promoting the view that our society is made up of individuals who are already fat and, through their own fault, are becoming even fatter?

Fat has even become a word that we now use to mask our real feelings and emotions. For example, instead of accurately defining our emotions, the word fat substitutes this quite easily, as everyone seems to recognise that fat is innately bad...

With fat stigma and associated inequalities playing out in our everyday lives, it is not hard to see why we don't want to be associated with fat. In word association tests, the very idea of fat is linked with notions of ugly, grotesque, incompetent, lazy, and gluttony. By realising these negative associations, fat inevitably becomes a devalued term, and used to describe a vast range of negative feelings. Unsurprisingly, fat has become something we all try to consciously or even unconsciously avoid. This can often be in an obsessive manner that leads to even more conversations about avoiding fat or looking down on individuals who are viewed as fat. This means that we have created a society that thrives upon fat shaming, self-criticising ourselves, highlighting the immense risk of becoming 'overweight', and creating 'superfoods' or specialised cosmetic procedures used to eradicate fat.

But why have we come to give fat such a bad name? Also, why should we let such a simple word take over our thoughts, feelings, self-esteem and ability to be compassionate to ourselves? To answer this we must firstly begin a story about how the revolution of the diet and fitness industry grew to make absolutely huge amounts of profit by equating eating less fat with weight loss and feeling great about it. Although we have moved away from this overly simplistic and false equation, the way we describe individuals who are overweight to this day still involves use of the F-word along with negative connotations about what it means to be fat.

While an individual or nation cannot literally be fat, the risk of becoming fat is persistently highlighted as being extremely costly for individuals and society. We have been made to believe that we are in a never ending war with fat, and that we should avoid it, reduce our consumption of it, or significantly most of our fat from our own bodies in order to win.

However, I don't agree with this way of thinking and I certainly don't encourage the idea that we should be spreading any more erroneous messages that frame the word fat or any related terminology in a victimising way – regardless of whether such messages are in the form of a news headline, journal article, or part of an everyday conversation. In my view, I believe that using the word fat as a way to describe poor physical and psychological wellbeing can be very disempowering to individuals, leaving them feeling unable to gain support for their real life concerns and act in a way that can genuinely help them to improve their overall happiness and health. However, at least for the time being, our very ignorant way of using the word fat is part of a growing rather than a shrinking problem for the wellbeing of individuals and society.

If we continue to use the word fat in such a negative way this might exacerbate the disadvantages and inequalities face by individuals who are viewed as being 'overweight'.

So how can we take action to help reduce the stigma around weight, feeling fat and the negative consequences this can have on our whole lives and minds as well as our bodies? Well, a crucial step involves breaking free from fat-talk. This involves choosing to not engage in negative discussions about weight or fat, whether that be aimed at others or ourselves. Instead, we can begin to question when and why we use the word fat. Can we ask ourselves, why am I using fat to describe an emotion or body feature? Is this really necessary?

When recognising that we might use the word fat to describe how we feel, we can question why we prefer to use this term instead of using other relevant terms that can more accurately express our emotions. By doing this, we can become much more aware of how the use of the term fat is so common yet often irrelevant to most circumstances. For example, unless we are

✳
324

describing how much fat a food contains, or how much body fat we have as a proportion of our body weight, fat to describe a whole person is just not very accurate. Instead, it is quite dehumanising while unlikely being very compassionate at all.

If we use the word fat to describe something we don't like, whether that be about ourselves or another person, we are still contributing to the negative stigma and inequalities that currently linked to this type of terminology. Alternatively, we can use our creative language skills to use a diverse range of different terminology to express what we really mean. If we really feel ashamed or guilty about something, admit to yourself or someone else that this is how you feel. That way we can gain support for what we really need. Also, as easy as it is to use the term fat in every day conversation with friends and family, try to draw their attention away from the word fat. This might involve standing up for your values when another person begins to talk about fat in a negative way in relation to another person or themselves.

Don't worry, I am not advocating that you go out into the world giving everyone a telling off for saying the F-word. However, I am simply suggesting that you critically question the use of the word fat as part of our everyday language. Without becoming critical, it will be difficult to truly become more empowered to develop a positive relationship with your own body as well as grow to become a Compassioneer, who doesn't use the term fat to sum up their self-worth.

Not everyone you speak to might be as open to viewing the word fat as unnecessary, but suggesting this idea as just one point of view is still an important first step in making positive changes. We may not change the world, or even our own minds, overnight, but if we take small steps towards questioning this stigmatising norm, perhaps we can allow the idea to provide much food for though.

So what are some of the practical ways that we stand up to and challenge weight stigma, feelings of fat and talking about fat?

❋ **Challenge your reality:**

The social norms we come into contact each and every day, whether that be an image on the front of a magazine or a news article proclaiming the next new diet fad, can have a marked impact on how we view the world and ourselves. However, just because this is what we see or hear doesn't mean that this is what is, or has to be. We have the power to choose whether we believe in or adopt those messages. We can also speak compassionately to ourselves when we see or hear a message that makes us feel bad or fat. That feeling doesn't necessarily speak the truth about us as a person, as beauty and good in the world comes in many different forms – not just a certain socially constructed body shape, dieting technique, or exercise regimen. When we challenge our current reality, we ultimately become empowered to question and pursue the way we would really like to lead a compassionate and fulfilling life.

❋ **Break free from the scales:**

Finally get rid of those body scales and say good riddance to them for good! They absolutely don't deserve your time or your company. Remember that your weight doesn't define how much of a beautiful or amazing person you really are. What you weigh is hardly an indicator of your overall happiness and wellbeing, it is just a measure of your own impact on gravity. Weight doesn't even measure anything like your body's muscle composition, how physically fit you are, or, even more importantly, how you are feeling and all the amazing things you are able to offer the world.

Do you really want to let a number on a scale dictate how you should feel, what you wear and what tasks you feel able to accomplish for a particular day? Only after I learned to love myself and my body have I found the answer.

The truth of the matter is that counting and obsessing over numbers on a body scale really won't do us any favours in terms helping us to nourish, flourish and thrive. This fact would appear to go against many advanced technologies and mobile apps there have been developed to help us monitor our weight more accurately than ever before. If anything, weight monitoring physically and psychologically holds us back from doing what we were born to do, especially if we fall into the trap of thinking that we can only be 'good' individuals, or take action on something we want in life, when we have reached our optimal desired weight.

I can't restate enough that what you weigh is totally insignificant compared to the deeper real life issues that affect our happiness and health. If you base your self-worth on a number, this is not a compassionate route or effective way to get through life.

So, to firmly restate, you are not a number on a scale. You are worth so much more than what you weigh, and no matter how your current weight compares to a past weight or a future desired weight, no amount of weight change is ever going to help you achieve your full potential in order to nourish, flourish and thrive. Only learning the art of self-acceptance, love and compassion can do that. With that said, the time is now to ditch those scales forever.

❊ **Limit self-comparisons with others:**

We are all unique and therefore have a beautiful individuality that makes us all able to offer something positively unique to the world. Yes, we may come in all shapes and sizes with slightly dissimilar genetic codes, but this is part of the beauty within us – not the problem. Just because your jeans or dress size may be larger than your friends' doesn't make you bad or less of a person. In fact, you can become a stronger and more compassionate person by realising these subtle differences are insignificant in comparison to the many other amazingly unique things you have to offer the world.

❊ **Enjoy the way your body moves and how it functions:**

Part of feeling fat can stem from negative emotions and how we think our bodies look. Feeling fat is rarely based on what the body actually does. By feeling fat, we limit our focus away from the awesome things the body can actually physically and psychologically accomplish, whether that be thinking creatively, giving someone a hug, writing about your experiences, getting stuck into some DIY, or cooking a tasty meal – amongst many other things. Remember, the body is a wonderful and ingenious creation regardless of how fat you feel, so try to make time to appreciate how it feels to have the privilege of navigating how it functions, moves and the exciting places it can venture to.

❋ Spend more time with people who have a positive relationship with their food and body:

In a self-obsessed world it is easy to get caught up in many conversations about diets, appearance, exercise and punishing regimens to become a so called better person. I literally hear them all of the time and it really is a disheartening experience. I want individuals to love themselves right now, not only hope to do so when they have embarked on a faddy diet and lost weight! In the long run surrounding yourselves by individuals who pursue these things are likely to be detrimental to your sense of self-esteem.

The more and more time we spend with certain individuals or groups, the more alike to them we become – whether we are conscious about this or not. To step away from negative social circles, try to engage better with individuals you feel have a more positive and compassionate relationship with their food, mind, body and the planet, as well as individuals who don't solely value their self-worth on their appearance. The more we do this, the more we can feel confident that stepping into a place of self-compassion with our body is a completely acceptable and worthy activity to pursue.

❋ Understand that feeling fat, not having fat, is the real limitation:

Considering that having a bit more fat on your body compared to another person is unlikely to affect your ability to flourish, unless it severely affects your physical or mental health, we still spend a great deal of time worrying about the consequences of feeling and being fat. However, remember that size is one of society's most accepted and well ingrained prejudices that still unjustly exists. If barriers in your life or reductions in your self-esteem do seem to occur due to feeling fat, remember that this is not your limitation, but society's own subtle way of continuing to advocate discrimination and inequalities while making a profit out of them.

❋ Disengage from negatively judgemental talk about fat:

We might not always realise it, but as well as talking negatively to our own selves about our body and what we eat, many of us also comment on what others eat and look like, or how 'good' and 'bad' certain foods are that ourselves or others are eating. By doing this we are promoting the view that our self-worth is based on things that don't really have much value in terms of happiness and health. They also alert other individuals that they should also be taking more care of what they eat and look like in order to avoid feeling negatively judged.

If we can learn to talk to people, or about people, in ways that don't centre on body-related issues in a negative way, we can draw a more positive focus towards other more meaningful aspects of human beings. For example, we can we talk about how caring a person has been rather than their how their new clothes suit their body shape.

What about the character strengths of a person who is hardworking and determined to help others too?

By speaking less of other people in terms of their eating, body weight or overall appearance, we can help our culture develop more positive ways of striving for self-happiness and health, which ultimately involve viewing the positive aspects of a person's whole character and what they have to uniquely offer the world.

All in all, I would like to sum up by saying that we don't gain anything by accepting that it is normal to feel fat. Instead, we lose out on the opportunities to positively regard our character strengths and the truly important things that will enable us to flourish as compassionate human beings. By learning to speak about ourselves and others in a more positive way, rather than in relation to what we eat, weigh or look like, we can set our focus on realising our true potential – the fact that you are not just what you eat – and definitely not just fat.

❋

"Don't punish your body by forcing it into rigid fitness regimes that bring more pain than gain. Nourish your body by lovingly engaging in pleasurable movement that fills you with joy"

Compassionate Physical Activity

Let's hit the ground running.

Most of us are aware that being more physically active is a way of increasing our physical and psychological health. There is a wealth of evidence showing that the way and how much we move is associated with increased strength of our bones, cardiovascular fitness, a reduced risk of several chronic diseases, resilience against stress and anxiety, greater levels of happiness and many other key indicators of wellbeing.

However, what many of us don't realise is that the way exercise is associated with health is not as straightforward as it appears, and that the way we think and feel about exercise, similarly to food, can sometimes lead to more harm than good. The reason behind this lies in the relationship we have with exercise, and how it links into many other key elements of health and wellbeing. Believe it or not, exercise isn't just about burning off what we have just eaten, or trying to attain optimal physical fitness. Thinking about exercise in this way is very one-dimensional and over time it can reinforce the idea that a healthy lifestyle involves basing our self-worth on what we can physically achieve and the physical dimensions of our body. This perspective can even lead to self-destruction in terms of our psychological wellbeing, where our main goals become aligned with trying to meet some ideal societal standard of what health and fitness is deemed to look like. For example, the common goal by individuals pursuing exercise is less about feeling more physically and psychologically energised, but more about needing to burn 'x' number of Calories, burn 'x' amount of fat or become lean and trim.

From a more compassionate perspective that also considers elements of positive psychological as well as physical health, the way we exercise and think about it promotes a burst of mood-uplifting endorphins in the brain. The effects this has can uplift our mood, make us more social and willing to connect with other people and kick into action our natural ability to think creatively. Physical activity, whether than be a light walk or an intensive run, can also increase the likelihood of coming into contact with mood-boosting sunlight, other individuals to socialise with and surroundings of natural beauty and green space – all of which are positive determinants of health and happiness.

With the above examples in mind it becomes a bit clearer that the links between exercise and health don't simply arise from the physiological changes, whether that involve burning off Calories or losing weight directly from walking, running swimming, jumping or whatever movement a particular exercise might involve. Instead, there are critical mind and body connections to consider, including the concept of pleasurable movement, which is one of the 10 key elements of Nourishing Routes.

But how might certain types of exercise actually lead to more harm than good – if that is even possible?

To answer this question yourself, your thoughts might initially latch on the idea that excessively exercising can have damaging wear and tear effects on our muscles and joints. Also, you might come to the conclusion that without adequate nourishment from food, excessively exercising can lead to feeling depleted of energy and experiencing nutritional deficiency, bone loss and an increased risk of chronic illness.

You would be right with these assumptions and research has provided some key pieces of evidence to suggest that there is a 'tipping' point when exercise, especially for some vulnerable individuals, starts to have a more detrimental rather than incremental impact on health. An example might be for individuals with an eating disorder or form of malnourishment. Any vigorous amount of exercise for such individuals has been linked with unhealthy weight loss, further nutritional deficiency and even heart attacks. However, you don't have to be underweight to experience the harms of exercise, and society still promotes the idea that any form of physical activity, no matter how vigorous, is what we should be aiming for in order to be happy and healthy.

Look in any women's or men's health and fitness magazine, and you will be bombarded by articles alongside excessively Photoshopped images that suggest that we should all be getting on board with the latest fitness trend – even if this means becoming exhausted, not enjoying the activity and, perhaps most annoyingly, burning as many Calories as possible, losing weight and buying into ridiculously expensive equipment and clothing.

Apart from such messages often being based on the idea that we all need to improve ourselves before we can even begin to love ourselves just the way we are, they fail to mention that they erroneously promoting a 'one-size fits all' model. They also miss out on the complex mind and body connection that crucially interlinks exercise with happiness and health.

To expand on a few of the points mentioned earlier in this book, the link between exercise and health is not just a physical one. In order to gain any benefit, it needs to holistically take place under ideal psychological and social conditions.

In real terms this means that physical activity needs to be enjoyed, and be in line with what a person's real values and goals are. All too often individuals jump onto an exercise trend because they think it will make them appear fitter, slimmer and fashionable, which are goals more suited to the needs of trying to meet other people's expectations. Such goals also tend to revolve around an insecure desire to gain approval from others, rather than the acceptance and self-love from ourselves that we already deserve.

Crucially missing from common messages about exercising is that individuals engaging in it need to be able to enjoy it, while doing it because they already love their bodies and want to nurture it – not necessarily the other way around. Without enjoyment, how realistic will a certain form of exercise be in the long term? Can you really imagine a 90-year-old man or woman pumping heavy weights in a gym or pounding away on a treadmill aiming to burn a certain number of Calories?

OK, there may be some individuals who do this, but for the vast majority of individuals such forms of exercise would not be enjoyable, sustainable, or even for the benefit of their overall wellbeing.

There is also the concern that some forms of exercise, especially those that involve frequently going the gym or entering athletic competitions, inevitably involve coming into contact with other individuals who:

* Are insecure about their bodies

* Follow strict rules in relation to what they eat and their rigid exercise routine

* Try hard to look 'good' while exercising in order to look more attractive or better than others

* Push themselves beyond their limit in a way that negative impacts their physical health and ability to optimally nourish themselves

* Are not willing to show themselves self-compassion

* Are currently experiencing a disordered relationship with food and body

* Are suffering from exercise addiction or an eating disorder

Not everyone who goes to the gym or exercises competitively fits into the above list, but the key point here is that such environments aren't exactly an ideal setting or community to be in if you have your own personal issues around food and body to battle. For example, by being integrated into an obsessive fitness community, you might easily integrate the negative idea that it is OK to hold negative views about yourself and push yourself the limits more and more – no matter what the physical or psychological costs.

Looking at exercise from a more holistic and compassionate perspective, how can we choose a form of exercise that will promote our wellbeing, while also enabling us to positively tap into our mind and body connection?

A key point to remember is enjoyment. If we go into an activity that we think we will enjoy, even if it just involves a light bit of walking (which has still been shown to have various health benefits), then we are more likely to make time for and stick with the activity.

The frame of mindset we have while exercising is also crucial. If we try to push ourselves to work harder and faster through telling ourselves off, or trying to attain some perfectionistic standards in what we do, then the only main thing getting stronger will be our own inner critic. Do you really want to become your own worst enemy rather than an encouraging friend?

It might seem OK for a coach to shout at a person so that they exercise even harder, but what happens when that coach isn't there? In fact, whether we are shouted at by ourselves or a coach, research has shown that this can reduce our overall motivation to exercise, and that any form of physical activity we do aim to pursue won't be carried out for the long term.

This brings me to the point of intrinsic motivation. Intrinsic motivation is the drive we have to carry out activities, either because they are inherently enjoyable, or because they are linked to some other personally important goal that we have (ideally a goal that isn't related to trying to please others). An example is a mother or father who wants to exercise to help improve their mood and fitness so that they can be more energised parents who can remain active with their children and create loving bonds with them. Similarly, an individual might go to yoga because they enjoy being able to feel how flexible their body can be and the limitations they can push – without the need to be the best or strike a perfect pose.

Alternatively, if your exercise routine is based around trying to be perfect, burning off Calories, punishing yourself, becoming more physically attractive, or proving your own self-worth, then you are probably going to end up running around in circles.

In my own personal experience, the type of exercise I have found to be the most helpful in terms of recovery and living more compassionately is yoga and walking with my dog. These types of activities do not have the focus of weight loss, pushing yourself or trying being perfect, which has been hugely beneficial in terms of learning to love my body the way it is. They also allow me to meet and mingle with positive individuals in my life, as well as come into contact with places of natural beauty, calm and tranquil spaces as well as with lots of mood-uplifting green space.

Most of the time, the forms of physical activity I do are free flowing, without a particular routine to follow, and do not even allow me to break a sweat. They don't require expensive equipment or gym wear, and are also are very gentle while allowing me to feel in the present moment and reframe any negative thoughts into a more positive perspective. I also allow myself days to skip my normal routine, such as when staying at a friend or going on holiday. I don't let my exercise rule my social life or sense of freedom. This approach to exercise is completely different to the way I used to be obsessed with trying to walk, run or remain active as much as I found physically possible – just to burn Calories and avoid feeling guilty or lazy for having not completed 'enough' physical activity.

I am not advocating that my way of exercising is for everyone. It also might not make me an Olympic athlete any time soon! However, by tailoring my exercise routine around my own personal needs and goal to live more compassionately, I have become much more relaxed and happy in my own skin, which has really helped me to control my anxiety, say goodbye to depression, bid a relieving farewell to an extremely negative relationship with food and body. I know all too well how detrimental setting myself a rigid exercise routine to follow and a specific number of Calories to burn off leads to much more harm than good – along with a bag full of self-hate rather than self-compassion.

So how can you engage in exercise that involves pleasurable movement and is both self-compassionate and beneficial to your psychological as well as physical wellbeing?

Compassioneer Activity: Creating a compassionate exercise routine

A first point of call to developing your own routine of pleasurable movement is to pinpoint why you want to engage in more physical activity, join a gym or try a certain type of exercise class. Is it for your own health and goal achievement, or simply to prove a point or appear fitter and more attractive to someone else? If your answer aligns more with the second part of the question, then my advice is to create a list or a mind map of all the reasons why carrying out exercise will benefit your wellbeing – not how you look or how others think about you – just your own wellbeing in terms of physical, psychological and social benefits.

Now you have your goals set out a bit more clearly a next step is to write a list of forms of physical activities you think you would enjoy, are willing to try out and can see yourself pursuing for several years – not just a few months, weeks or days. The main goal here is to choose an enjoyable activity that suits your level of fitness while being both enjoyable and sustainable

After picking an activity – preferably just one to begin with – carve out one or two times in the week where you will spend time getting involved in it. At first this might simply involve researching the activity a little bit more, seeing if you will require and particular equipment, searching for local practitioners or classes (e.g. yoga or Pilates) and if it is something that will suit your budget and amount of spare time.

It is also important to remember to be flexible. No, I don't mean being able to stretch like a professional gymnast, but I do mean becoming flexible in terms of letting yourself go with the flow without being too rigid and strict with your exercise routine. In practice this means feeling OK about having days without exercise, or not exercising at specific times when other activities get in the way. Being flexible also means allowing room for imperfections,

✤

not pushing yourself to the limit and being open to changes in your mind and body rather than forcing them to happen with any rigid goals in mind.

Finally, a step that really helped me was to note down my thoughts and feelings before during and after exercising. For example, at the end of each yoga session (even if that involved simply using a yoga mat in my own room with a yoga YouTube video) I would ask myself whether I felt satisfied, energised and willing to engage in another session in the future. Similarly, when walking my dog, I would ask myself did I like that route I ventured on, or did I walk in a way that allowed me to use more energy rather than enjoy natural green space.

When I had my answers to these questions, I could then tailor my activities in a way where they became more enjoyable and something that I genuinely looked forward to rather than forced myself to do. Another very helpful activity was to tell myself that it didn't matter how much progress I made in yoga (if any at all), how far I had walked, or how many Calories I burned off (which I eventually decided didn't need tracking using a fitness app or a pedometer!). Instead of basing exercise on a need to avoid guilt or not feelings good enough, I made a firm decision to only exercise when I felt like it would be pleasurable and in my own best interests both physically and psychologically – not because I needed to prove myself to someone else or even my own unrealistically high standards.

Getting to the main take-home message of this chapter on physical activity with the aim of pleasurable movement, I would like you to realise that exercise can be a self-compassionate activity rather than a way of engaging in self-punishment or negative self-comparison. Just like the relationship between what we eat and wellbeing, the links between exercise and wellbeing are much more complex than we might initially believe. It is therefore in our own best interests that we begin to learn about, appreciate and practically explore these complex relationships in more depth. I would also like you to recognise what types of activities you find fun and genuinely enjoy in the long term, without placing any unnecessary expectations on yourself in a bid to gain self-acceptance or approval from others.

If you can set yourself up on the self-compassionate starting line when engaging in any form of physical activity, then there really are no limitations to where you can propel yourself forward along your journey towards happiness, health and living more compassionately. Just remember that it isn't how hard or long you exercise for that links physical activity and health, but the way we can tailor how we move in a way that allows us to experience pleasure, find freedom, express self-compassion and tap into many other essential elements of wellbeing that contribute to our own Nourishing Routes.

Bodily Compassion Over Comparison

It is hard to find a person who does not know what it feels like to dislike their own body or negatively compare it to other people's. Sad as this seems, many of us feel caught up in a culture that shallowly judges people based on their body size, weight, skin texture, facial features, muscularity, or any other aspect of their physical appearance. Many of us also have experiences on a daily basis of comparing ourselves to other people, especially in terms of our appearance and body weight.

But not negatively judging or comparing ourselves can seem like a huge challenge when a large part of our society continues to equate beauty and success with appearance. Failing to be as attractive, thin, curvy or muscular has unfortunately been viewed as a symbol of laziness, poor self-regulation, gluttony, or lack of that 'get up and go'. But, there is no truth in this belief, and believing it is likely to be detrimental to our ability to flourish and thrive as human beings who can live compassionately with ourselves and others...

We may rationalise the pursuit of a 'better' body as being related to enhancing our health. We just want to be healthier, live longer, feel fitter. Surely making our bodies better would be a step in the right direction? However, when we get to the bottom of most motivations for 'bettering' the body, you will find that they centre on trying to meet the expectations of others and society. In some sense, by beating up our bodies for not being quite good enough yet, we set out along a path of battering rather than 'bettering' our bodies. We can feel as though we are lacking some essential element that makes us a 'good' person, and so choosing to evaluate ourselves in relation to others based on how we look becomes the norm, even though this can be both psychologically and physically destructive.

Body dissatisfaction is increasingly prevalent among both females and males in the UK, Europe and the USA, and is estimated to occur regularly in around 80% of individuals on a daily basis. If this isn't shocking enough, then there is also the fact that body dissatisfaction is a significant predictor of eating disorders such as anorexia, bulimia, and other forms of disordered eating behaviours, which are literally destroying people's lives every single second of every day. Body dissatisfaction can also lead to anxiety and depression, as well as negatively impacting a person's quality of life.

When we look at research on the issue of body satisfaction it is quite clear that most individuals striving for a better body are less content with themselves as a person and regularly compare themselves to others. What is perhaps even more interesting though, is that even when goals for a better body are reached, body satisfaction and self-worth tends to decrease rather than increase. By embarking on a journey to pursue a better body we inevitably become beings of social comparison rather than compassion. By definition, body dissatisfaction is underpinned by feelings of inadequacy in comparison to others – particularly in relation to appearance.

We might start with our own positive intentions to improve the body, but rarely do these function independently of how we are faring in relation to others' bodily 'achievements'. Suddenly, seeing those with 'better' bodies than ourselves is perceived as a threat and it even becomes anxiety provokingly stressful to realise that we are not the best and that there is still far to go in terms of reaching the goal we started out with. For example, some individuals strive for a slimmer body, but for many vulnerable individuals this can quite easily lead to engaging in disordered eating and exercise behaviours. At the same time, such individuals place themselves under constant restrictions and scrutiny that considerably undermine their self-worth. However, no one can achieve the perfect body. This myth does not exist, and our view of perfection constantly changes just as different trends and cultural norms also change. Yet, literally millions of women and men set out to pursue that very goal – constantly comparing themselves to other people along the way.

It saddens me that this is the case. In someone's eyes there will always be someone better than how individuals see themselves. If we continue to take this pessimistic perspective, though, we will never realise just how beautiful, good enough and worthy of love we are right now. We will never be satisfied with what we already have, and our sense of self-worth will mostly centre on gaining the approval of others and meeting a certain unrealistic ideal rather than developing ourselves in ways that allow us to lead a more compassionate, happy, healthy and fulfilling life.

But is there a light at the end of the tunnel through all of this? If we currently live with regular self-comparison and body dissatisfaction, are we destined to do these things forever? The answer to these question depends partly on how willing you are to see the true realities behind why you are striving for a better body. It also depends on how willing you are to open yourself up to being more self-compassionate – realising that we are beautiful, worth taking care of, and ultimately human beings who are not destined to be perfect or have the 'best' body.

There is lots of research evidence currently showing how becoming more self-compassionate can alleviate the negative effects of body dissatisfaction, and can even prevent it from happening or escalating in the first place. Self-compassion acts as a positive emotional coping strategy that involves being sensitive to our own feelings and having a desire to alleviate our own suffering. It also involves the ability to become kind and understanding towards ourselves when we hear our inner critic (falsely) tell us that we are inadequate, useless and unworthy.

Self-compassion is a little bit like a best friend or a hero that lies within ourselves – someone who can step in to save the day and our sanity. It saves us from falling into the trap of a downward spiral of self-comparison, while helping us to realise that we are all humans who are perfectly imperfect. Self-compassion also helps us to recognise that life is a journey of self-discovery that cannot be adequately sustained on the self-hate that grows like weeds when striving for the 'perfect' body, diet or whatever else we have been made to believe will make us more accepted, successful and loveable.

How does self-compassion relate to issues around the bodily self-comparison?

What research is currently showing is that self-compassion not only plays a positive role in boosting happiness, optimism and experiences of positive emotions, but that it also helps to diminish body dissatisfaction and related issues like associated disordered eating behaviours.

By becoming more self-compassionate we can learn to accept our negative views about ourselves as being part of a wider issue, and that it doesn't reflect who we are or the potential we have as human beings. I can assure you that each and every part of your body doesn't deserve to be constantly compared to other bodies, or the next best standard of how a person's body should look like. True acceptance and feelings of worthiness can only come from within – not self-comparison and meeting others' expectations. This also makes a perfect reason for us to avoid surrounding ourselves with toxic relationships that often lead to negative self-comparisons or not feeling good enough about ourselves.

Compassioneer Activity: Breaking Free From a World of Negative Self-Comparison

Below are a few simple steps and reminders that you can carry out or contemplate to help you break free from a world of negative self-comparison.

* If you have one or multiple social media accounts (e.g. Facebook, Instagram, You Tube, Twitter), unfollow accounts or individuals whose news feeds and/or pictures make you feel inferior, lacking in self-worth, guilty, or relatively unsuccessful or unattractive. Similarly, stop buying or throw away any magazines that lead to similar feelings or a need to strive to some unrealistic expectation or social norm.

* The same as the above piece of advice applies if there is a person in your life who negatively compares you with other people, in which case start by spending less time with them. You could also tell that person how their tendency to compare you with others is making you feel, and that you would appreciate it if they could try not to do this. More often than not people who negatively compare you with others have a long list of their own insecurities, but if they continue to make you feel inferior to others and unhappy in yourself, then it is probably time to cut ties with them.

* If you find yourself in state of comparing yourself negatively with others remember that you are too unique to compare in an accurate or fair way. No one can replicate you or offer what you can offer the world other than you. You may not have a certain talent or gift that is as 'good' as someone else's, but equally they don't have yours either. You can fill the gaps in the world that they might not be able to. Remember that you have just as many unique talents and gifts as anyone else, no matter how different or seemingly insignificant, that are equally important and make you a successfully thriving human being.

❀ Remember that there is an endless list of potential comparisons you could make, and that no one is perfect. Even if you aim to become similar to or better than someone you have compared yourself to, and achieve this goal, this doesn't put an end to self-comparison. This is only a route to continued self-comparison and dissatisfaction where you never feel quite good enough. True acceptance and feeling 'good enough' happens when we can love ourselves as we are right now, regardless of whether we have achieved a certain goal or ideal standard or not.

❀ Self-comparison is an energy depleting activity that only leads to a road further and further away from leading a compassionate lifestyle. Self-comparison is definitely not the driving fuel behind becoming a Compassioneer. The more we negatively compare ourselves with others, the more we learn to dislike rather than love ourselves.

❀ Become more aware of your own character strengths and positive attributes. To do this you can simply note them down or remember when someone has provided you with a compliment, praise or token of appreciation.

❀ Don't look for happiness in self-comparison and striving to be better than someone else. You will naturally grow and develop personally by pursuing personally valuable goals that are related to leading a more compassionate lifestyle – e.g. through taking time to relax, helping another person or volunteering for an organisation that has an ethos in line with your own values. These activities also provide opportunities for you to realise your own unique strengths and how you have the amazing capacity to positively contribute to the lives of others as well as the planet.

❀ When there is an opportunity for self-comparison, such as when competing in a race, aiming to get a promotion at work, or a striving for a higher grade at college or university, try to take the focus off what other people might or have already achieved. Instead, place your focus on what you would feel happy with achieving in relation to your own standards – what you know in your heart will make you happy in the long-term.

❀

❄ Find a positive form of distraction when you feel that your inner critic of self-comparison creeps in. Instead of getting caught up with these negative thoughts, engage in a creative, energising or relaxing activity that highlights some of your own personal strengths. This can be as simple as going for a walk, writing a poem, painting, running, practicing yoga. It can be absolutely anything, whatever makes you feel energised and able to express your own personal qualities and strengths.

❄ Find inspiration from others and celebrate their successes with them. Accept that you might find this uncomfortable at first without feeling jealous or engaging in negative self-comparison, but say to yourself that part of connecting with others in this way is part of being a compassionate human being who is able to learn from others too.

❄ Aim to primarily compare yourself with you. Only you can understand what is positive or negative in terms of your own personal development. You can also use this understanding to know when the time comes to celebrate and praise your own personal development – no matter how small that development might appear in relation to what others have achieved.

Trust Nobody But Your Own Body

Humans, and therefore our bodies and minds, have evolved over literally millions of years. We have our very own automatic high tech mechanics that allow us to eat, digest food, obtain energy, regulate our temperature, keep our hearts beating, and ultimately survive to the best of our abilities – even in the most harsh and hostile of conditions.

Yet, many of us find it difficult to trust our own bodies. Many of us believe that eating too much food or eating certain types of food at certain times of day will lead our whole bodies and minds to spiral out of control. By out of control, I am talking about the fear of losing or gaining an unwanted amount of weight, or acting in a way that involves binging on or restricting food.

Part of this problem boils down to black and white thinking – a topic that we have already mentioned at the beginning of this book, but a topic that is crucially important when it comes to understanding our ability to trust our own body. Black and white thinking promotes the idea that one action will lead to a negative domino effect, where we will lose all sense of control and sense of self-regulation. Either eating that one biscuit will turn into a whole tin of demolished biscuits, or that one time skipping a meal or snack will lead to a whole period of restriction, bingeing and yoyo weight cycling. It is unsurprising, then, that many of us experience physical anxiety and raised blood pressure when thinking of and being around food.

We are bombarded with messages day after day about how we need to take care not to lose control of our minds and bodies, and instead push all of our physical and psychological resources into ensuring that we optimally self-regulate ourselves. We apparently need to be oh so very careful to avoid eating too much at a meal, or heaven forbid give into temptation of eating sugar and saturated fat – evil devils in the dieting and fitness world.

We have been falsely told that we are all destined to 'fall off the wagon', 'veer off track', 'commit a sin' or become failures at regulating our bodies to the extent where we lose control of our bodies and become classified as not being the 'ideal' weight or image of beauty. Falling off the wagon has been equated with having no willpower and losing control at every opportunity around food. In other words, we are taught to be wary of our urges to eat and that, if we don't, our body will take on a whole personality of its own, eat everything in sight, or encourage us to engage in behaviours that lead to self-destruction and becoming 'fat' or 'overweight'.

Let me tell you now, your body wasn't built to go on self-destruct mode. The diet and fitness industry however have scared us into believing this. If you did trust yourself around food, would you go to the extent of investing money or other resources in their latest programs and products? Probably not, which gives even more reason for them to use scare tactics around not being able to trust our bodies. The diet and fitness industries then, instead of being viewed as the villains they often are, become viewed as heroes who can provide us with the sense of control and security that we feel we do not already naturally possess.

In reality, the messages we are sent about our bodies losing control contribute to the main problem of losing control in the first place – not ourselves. By entering a place of distrust and fear with food and what we eat, internally this results in a state of anxiety and stress. Suddenly, thoughts around food and body become obsessive. Fear naturally leads to thinking about the object of fear, and if this is food and weight, then it is inevitable that trying to avoid food and weight gain become our main obsessions and goals in life. This isn't something that randomly happens, but our bodies and minds have also evolved to react in a certain way when they feel that we might encounter a period of scarcity – yet another reason why diets and restrictive forms of eating do not work.

In a bid to avoid losing the control we have been deceived into thinking we don't already possess, we enter into a negative relationship with our food and body. Over time this can be hugely detrimental to our wellbeing, whether this involves disordered eating or months and even years of yoyo weight cycling. Perhaps even worse is what distrust around food and our bodies does to our own sense of self-esteem, worth and compassion. If we have grown to fear the very things that make us who we are, then t can make us feel wholly unworthy of self-love. Why love something that we have been taught to view with an eye of caution?

These are not outcomes anyone would wish for in a bid to promote health or happiness, yet it is subliminally promoted by the media and even our own family and friendship circles every day.

How can I begin to develop a more trusting relationship with my body?

What we need to do in order to develop a more trusting relationship with our own body is to turn the idea of distrust on its head. Instead of trusting the diet and fitness industry, or other people's comments about what we eat and our bodies, what we should really be trusting is food, body and our own intuition.

If left to live in peace without messages about distrusting food and body, we would probably be much more likely to eat in line with our natural hunger, emotions, and social lives – allowing our real essential needs to be met. Instead of worrying about how our body will react to eating a bar of chocolate, slice of cake, a spoonful of sugar, or a heavy meal, our focus would be on enjoyment till we are fully content.

Intuition is really key here if we are to develop trust with our body. Trust, like you would expect to occur in a relationship, involves communication. Intuition also involves communication, but a form of communication that requires you to speak to and listen to your body and how you think and feel about it.

When was the last time that you asked yourself what your body really wanted? What type of food did it want, rather than what type of food you thought it 'should' have? Ask your body how it would like to feel and become optimally nourished physically, psychologically and socially. I'm going to make a confident guess that it probably wouldn't respond by saying *"I want to feel restricted"*. It would probably say something along the lines of:

"Please trust me and feed me in a way that will nurture and optimally nourish me. Do not restrict me. I will use the food you give me in a way that will allow you to flourish and thrive. All you need to do is intuitively trust me."

Arguably the most important relationship we will ever have in this world is the relationship we have with ourselves, including our own body. We have to get real with the fact that this is the longest relationship we will ever have in life and, if we can't break free from it, we may as well learn to nurture or heal the relationship we have with our body as it is now. Also, as I recently mentioned, trust is a vital element in this relationship, so why go out of our way to harm our body by not being open or willing to place trust in ourselves?

If you can venture into place of trust with yourself and your whole body, not only will this empower you on your own journey towards living more compassionately, but it will also help lead you to a positive place where your body and mind takes back its own control. This control, by default of our human nature, is a compassionate form of control – the control we have evolved to use in order to enable us to survive, flourish and thrive. I therefore invite you to begin to step into a more trusting relationship with your whole self and body. There really isn't anybody else who we could trust yourself better other than you for the ultimate benefit of your own happiness, health and being able to live life as a true Compassioneer.

PART 5:

Final Steps Towards Becoming Yourself and Living as a Compassioneer

"Knowing that your body holds beauty, meaning and purpose is a gift. Believing and acting like you know that is a priceless treasure with unlimited potential"

Breaking Free from Triggers
and Toxic Relationships

As our culture is literally obsessed with the way our bodies look in relation to certain standards it can sometimes be hard to escape negative – and often 'triggering' – messages and comments about them. We will answer what triggering messages and comments are very shortly, but firstly I will mention that it can be hard for many individuals to escape the cultural and environmental reminders that we are apparently not good enough if we do not mould ourselves into an ideal body size, weight or shape. These messages and reminders can seem especially potent and toxic if you currently have a negative relationship with food and body, and/or suffer from an eating disorder.

But what do I mean by messages and comments that are 'triggering'?

Triggering messages and comments are the words, phrases or actions of others, or aspects of our culture and the environment, that lead us into a negative mindset about the way we look and perceive ourselves as individuals.

Triggering comments can take multiple forms. They could be conversations about weight and the way we look, the way our clothes feel and the excessively advertised dieting sections we walk by in the supermarket. However, their potency mostly depends on how we interpret them and apply them to ourselves. For example, a simple comment such as:

"Your face looks a bit more filled out than last time I saw you"

can be triggering if it is interpreted as meaning, "Oh, don't you look a bit fatter today." This is likely to be especially so for individuals who are sensitive to comments and conversations regarding weight and body size.

In our society it is hard to ignore how gaining weight or becoming 'overweight' has been almost aggressively associated with being an unworthy, unlovable, unsuccessful and useless person. We have already discussed how detrimental this is, as well as how there are many opportunities where we are coerced to jump on board with the latest dieting trend or take extreme methods to alter our body weight and appearance.

Even when already leading a healthy lifestyle, or when in recovery from an eating disorder or healing a negative relationship with food and body, messages about embarking on a detox, buying into a juicing programme, joining a new gym offer or purchasing the latest weight loss pill can all signal alarm bells. These bells usually ring the tune that we are simply not good enough in our own skin – unless we succumb to the pressure of buying into the diet, fitness and beauty industries. I find it hard to contemplate the sheer mass of weight-loss products that now overpower the shelves of so-called 'health' stores. Quite honestly, each time I see another advert or product that promotes these negative triggering messages it makes me feel like ripping up one of the advertising signs – or bashing my head against a wall.

The widespread norms and expectations about how we should lead a life of weight manipulation exacerbate the way individuals negatively talk about themselves and others. This includes the volatile way many popular magazines focus in on weight loss stories and celebrity body changes. Such norms also stimulate our own social circles to have whole conversations (sometimes for hours on end) about what we should and should not eat in order to achieve a better body. It is now normal to talk about: going on a drastic diet on Monday, joining the gym to shed fat, skipping meals and detoxing to lose weight, limiting your Calorie intake to live longer, or eat 'cleaner' and cut out sugars, fats and carbs to avoid chronic disease. The list unfortunately goes on, but these triggering messages and comments appear to be completely acceptable – at least for now...

The fact that we live in a world that makes it OK to view individuals as unworthy or unlovable because of their weight, appearance or what they eat makes me quite angry. Apart from knowing first hand just how triggering certain comments about weight, food intake and body shape can be, I feel deeply sorry for the individuals who have had so much precious time and life zapped away from them by feeling the need to talk about and manipulate their food intake, weight and appearance. This is not just in terms of weight loss, but also weight gain. For example, telling someone that "you would look better if you were heavier" or "you would be more attractive if you had a bit more meat on your bones" still sends the message that our identity and self-worth should be based around weight and appearance. If you have already begun to see the bigger picture of wellbeing while reading this book so far, you probably understand that there are many Nourishing Routes to happiness and health – not just our weight and appearance.

It saddens me to listen to some of my family and friends talk at length about how they are being 'good' for not eating much or skipping meals, or how they feel guilty and need to excessively exercise at the gym to 'burn off' a 'naughty' slice of cake or several biscuits they have recently eaten. Sometimes certain situations literally send chills down my spine. As a recent example, I was faced with someone who I didn't know commenting on the size of my bum and also calling me relatively fat to someone else they knew. Initially this brought back a very unpleasant memory of me feeling horrible about my whole body while contemplating the idea that I would be a better person if I didn't eat as much or lost a significant amount of weight in order to feel good again.

Although I would never venture down a road of food obsession and weight manipulation as a coping mechanism for the way I have been made to feel in triggering situations, being around individuals and messages that promote the idea that we should place a focus on our body weight and food intake does make me experience a wave of anxiety. Thankfully though, I know through living a more compassionate lifestyle that real health and happiness does not lie in the falsified realm of weight loss or having a perfect diet. I also know that most individuals who speak negatively about their own or other people's body or food intake don't want to make them feel bad about themselves. Instead, most individuals who make such comments are caught

❖

up in their own bubble where talking negatively about food and body is the norm for them and the people they associate themselves with.

What can I do to avoid or become stronger against triggering comments and messages?

So how can we become knights in shining armour within our body-obsessed world where triggering comments and messages are still out on a mission to take away our compassionate armour? How can we make our armour even stronger? Below are a few simple and practical tips on how you can do exactly that:

✳ **Realise that most individuals, no matter how triggering their comments may seem, don't set out with the intention to hurt or trigger you through the comments they make about weight and body:** Most individuals are simply trapped in a diet and body obsessed world where their own identity and self-worth are largely based on these insignificant things. Rather than viewing these individuals in a negative light when they spark a triggering situation, we can show some compassion to them by realising that their words are probably a reflection of their own insecurities and that they probably need help and support too. They are in this battle with us rather than against us.

✳ **Make connections with individuals and engage in activities where weight and body will unlikely be the main focus of conversation:** All too often individuals join weight-loss groups as a way of trying to gain more self-esteem about themselves, but this can amplify negative conversation about how weight and body have been sources of shame throughout a person's life. A more empowering option would be to engage in activities that involve developing a new skill, finding new meaning in your life, or rekindling a new hobby. By doing this, not only will probably learn to love whatever activity you decide to engage in, but you can also build a sense of self-worth that is not dependent on weight while speaking to other individuals about more important issues than body weight or appearance

✳

❋ **Avoid (as much as practically possible) watching programmes about the latest diet or weight loss strategy:** Although doing this can raise awareness about just how diet obsessed our culture is, I have found that watching them can still make us wonder whether we really would be better individuals by focussing our attention on what we eat, weigh and look like as the main route to wellbeing. As I know this to be a complete unreality, I find it much better to invest in TV programmes, movies and activities that I find humorous, or tap into other lifestyle topics that I have an interest in.

❋ **Find opportunities to love yourself as you are now:** When I am met with yet another triggering situation, I remind myself that we are all worth so much more than what others think about the way I physically appear. I remind myself that, as compassionate human beings, we have a much deeper and meaningful purpose than to manipulate our weight and what we look like. Part of this purpose can involve taking action to help reform our weight and diet obsessed world. For myself, this means pursuing what I am passionate about in the form of my blog posts, website and supportive mentoring coaching while raising awareness of how we can be more compassionate individuals – no matter what we eat, weigh, look like or even how much we exercise.

❋ **Remember, no matter how triggering your situation may be, it can be an opportunity for personal growth rather than personal demise:** For every situation that we are able to rethink and place into perspective in a more realistic way, then the more we can learn how strong we are. We can also eventually come to terms with the fact that we have so much more meaning and purpose in the world than our weight and body shape, or the way that we eat and exercise. Perhaps this can involve developing a personal life mission to help reform the way society gradually learns to promote a holistic and empowering routes to health and happiness through living more compassionately.

❋

Growing Your Own Tribe
of Compassioneers

To have the greatest chances of success in terms of becoming our very own Compassioneer, we need to grow our own tribe of passionate Compassioneers. Just like many other things in life, being a Compassioneer is best experienced with the company and support of others.

In the case of your own Nourishing Routes, the best way to be a Compassioneer is to share this experience with individuals and communities who accept your values and also take their own actions that are in line with leading a more compassionate lifestyle. This doesn't mean going out into the wilderness and setting up an actual tribe of people who self-sustainably live off the land and handmade campfires, although I certainly wouldn't try to stop you if you were really thinking about it. What it does mean though is that part of our own journey towards living more compassionately involves surrounding ourselves by individuals who can help us, especially those individuals who are willing to lead their own compassionate lifestyle. At the same time, we can take action to reduce time spent with individuals who, no matter how hard we try to help them or ignore them, make us feel drained of energy, lead us to act out of line with our values, inferior, and also feel as though our compassionate lifestyles are not worth pursuing. These are the types of toxic relationships and triggering situations that we are better pulling apart from.

Another key reason for growing your own tribe of Compassioneers is the fact that human beings have evolved to live in tribes and supportive communities. The tribe we connect with and surround ourselves by will ideally be the compassionate community that helps us to feel safe and understood, while allowing us to experience an authentic sense of belonging, support and purpose. Just like a close family member or friend, individuals who we identify with as being in our own tribe can act as positive role models and positively contribute to our self-esteem when we are not feeling or acting in a way that brings us the most joy, happiness and health. In other words, growing your own tribe of Compassioneers is a key foundation that can help us to grow into becoming more compassionate beings – our own Compassioneers.

In relation to Nourishing Routes, surrounding yourself with a tribe of like-minded individuals, or individuals who are open to the concept of living more compassionately, can help to reinforce the idea that we are worth loving, and also that we have so much love to give to ourselves and others. As we have frequently spoken about within this book, compassion really does breed more compassion, so what better way to do that than surrounding yourself with individuals who also live and breathe your own values and life mission.

So how can we begin to build a tribe of Compassioneers?

A first point to remember when aiming to grow our own tribe of Compassioneers is that we probably already know individuals in our lives who we can classify as being a Compassioneer. Perhaps you see them regularly or very infrequently, but communicating a simple message to them about your own mission to live more compassionate can be a great starting point. Perhaps the Compassioneer you have identified might give you some words of wisdom that you can apply to your own life, or simply just restate that your goals are definitely worth pursuing. I can guarantee that sharing your own mission to become a Compassioneer will not be something to be laughed at. Instead, speaking from my own personal experience, you will probably be met with inquisitiveness, support and opportunities for other individuals to share their own positive views and motivating stories.

Alternatively, we may look towards individuals like our friends and family to share our mission with. Perhaps they too also want to get involved and see what their own Nourishing Routes journey will look and feel like. There can never be too many individuals striving for a more compassionate way of living, and the more individuals you can journey with, the more support and encouragement you will get. There will probably also be times when you may have to reach out a helping and reassuring hand to others on their own journey, which provides a perfect opportunity for you to give back some of the compassion you are gradually learning to give to yourself.

Other Compassioneers you can include in your tribe might be individuals with whom you don't have physical contact. For example, you may know of individuals on social media (e.g. Instagram or Facebook) who can act as a positive role model. Including them in your tribe might simply mean following them on social media (while unfollowing those who make you feel unlovable or disjointed from your compassionate mission). You could even write them an email to say how much they have inspired you to lead a more compassionate lifestyle, such as how they have helped you to learn to love yourself more or engage in activities that also help others and the planet. Once again, providing this appreciation is yet another activity that can enable you to show compassion to others, as well as gratitude for what they have been able to positively contribute to your life.

An additional way you can begin to grow your own tribe of Compassioneers involves spreading the world in your own uniquely creative way. For me this initially involved setting up my own Instagram account, blog, website and Facebook page, where I could log my thoughts, feelings and just about anything that I felt passionate about sharing. Not only can doing this help express our creativity, but it can also help us to gain support from others.

A few final words of wisdom are about fear. More specifically speaking, try not to fear the idea of building your own tribe of Compassioneers. I can completely understand how scary it might seem at first when embarking on your own journey, no matter what this looks like. But rest assured you will feel more comfortable as you go along and meet many other people along the way. You will be surprised by how many people really resonate with your beliefs and goals, and the likelihood is you will probably be an inspiration for many others. This is yet again an example of how compassion can breed even more compassion, and that each of us can play a vital role with even the simplest of actions.

Guaranteed there will be many individuals out there looking for a person like you to be inspired by. This might seem hard to believe, but there really is something magic and special in all of us that at least one other person will strongly resonate with and feel inspired by. Think of how amazing it could feel to be a person who can help someone to embark on their own Nourishing Routes journey to becoming a Compassioneer.

This may sound a bit biased coming from the author of this book, but going on my own Nourishing Routes journey really has been one of the best and most fulfilling things I have ever done for my own happiness and health. So, by openly sharing your own compassionate mission, there is no doubt that you will be helping others to feel empowered and inspired to follow in your footsteps, experience the benefits for themselves, and perhaps even go on to spread their own compassionate mission to other potential Compassioneers. This positive cycle is never ending.

The Compassioneer Pledge

One of the most crucial steps towards become a Compassioneer involves making a pledge. We briefly discussed earlier how important it is to pursue our goals for reasons that are based on our own intrinsic values and personal needs, rather than other peoples' expectation or trying to gain some form of external validation and approval. This is what a pledge is all about. More specifically though to Nourishing Routes, a Compassioneer pledge is based on the idea that our journey towards leading a more compassionate lifestyle relies on the need to make a commitment to ourselves, and not necessarily anyone else.

When our goals are in alignment with what will bring us the most authentic happiness and health, then this is when the magic starts to happen. This is why I have developed an all-encompassing Compassioneer Pledge. This is a pledge that you can choose to sign up to or not, and is also a pledge that does not revolve around meeting anyone else's goals other than your own. It also doesn't involve 'failing' or 'falling off the wagon', as we realise that, as Compassioneers, our journey is about progress – not perfection. All we can do is aim to try our best with each Compassioneer pledge and remain open to all of the opportunities, events and feelings that we experience along our own Nourishing Routes.

The Compassioneer Pledge is made up of 16 simple and actionable points, which each relate to one or more of the 10 key elements of Nourishing Routes. This means that they are evidence based and tailored to leading a more compassionate lifestyle, while also not being too specific so that you can practically relate them to your own personal circumstances, goals and life mission.

By committing yourself to the Compassioneer Pledge, I can guarantee that this is one of the best decisions you will ever make, and if there was ever a 'best' time to do it, then the time is now. Are you ready? If the answer is yes, all you have to do is keep on reading with an open mind and compassionate heart.

As a Compassioneer I pledge to:

1) Forgive myself if I have ever physically or emotionally abused my mind or body. I also forgive myself if I have ever physically or emotionally hurt someone else, and will forgive others who might have done the same to me.

2) Accept, appreciate and love my body the way it is, while feeling grateful for all the amazing things it can already do to help me function, keep me alive, and live compassionately.

3) Not view food in black and white terms of 'good' or 'bad', or make myself feel ashamed and guilty after eating certain types or amounts of food.

4) Nourish my body in a loving way, where food symbolises enjoyment, culture, connecting with others and wanting to energise rather than deplete my mind and body.

5) Not punish myself by starving myself of nourishment or engaging in excessive and rigid forms of exercise or self-harming behaviours as a way to avoid not feeling 'good enough'.

6) Spend more time for me, away from work or other commitments, while realising that this is important in order to relax, feel energised, express my emotions and unleash my creative potential.

7) Fill my life with activities that I enjoy and can be passionate about.

8) Find ways of helping others, whether that be through regularly volun-teering, supporting someone going through a difficult time, or eating

in a way that minimises the exploitation of other humans, animals and living beings.

9) Take time, where possible, to mindfully notice my own thoughts and feelings without negative judgement.

10) Not engage in negative self-comparison with others, while instead realising that I am beautiful, good enough and worthy of love in my own body – especially because I have my own unique personality and gifts to share with the world that no one else but myself can offer.

11) Know that I am worth much more than how much or what I eat, how much I weigh, the amount of physical activity I do, or my physical appearance. I know that real beauty and happiness grows from the inside out.

12) Take time in my day to notice and feel grateful for all the beautiful and amazing things and people I already have in my life, no matter how small or simple they may seem.

13) Set goals and act in ways that align with my beliefs and personal values, as opposed to trying to meet some ideal standard or someone else's expectations.

14) Critically question messages I see or hear that make me think that I am not good enough as I am, or that I need to be a certain weight or become more physically attractive in order to be worthy of love and success.

15) Surround myself and make friends with other compassionate individuals who respect and support my personal values and goals, while helping me to realise that I am good enough and worthy of love just as I am.

16) Take whatever steps I can to live a more compassionate lifestyle and ultimately find my own Nourishing Routes to happiness, health and fulfilment in life.

Final Thoughts But New Beginnings

I can't complete this book without wishing you all the best of luck with a life-changing journey on your own Nourishing Routes. I also need to restate that I wholeheartedly believe that you have the natural instinct, courage, strength and potential to follow your own Nourishing Routes in order to become your very own Compassioneer. Just remember, this gift and way of nourishing, flourishing and thriving is within your genes, and that you are totally worthy of giving and receiving love – including your own.

With some of the advice and practical guidance in this book, along with your own personally driven goals and values, I hope that you can now trust your inner compass – the natural instinct you possess to now venture on an empowering journey towards leading a more compassionate lifestyle. You could also be compassionate by passing this book onto someone else, so that they too can grasp the opportunity to realise and follow their own Nourishing Routes. By pursuing this journey, you have an unlimited amount of potential to love food, mind, body, others and even the whole planet in every magical moment. You are a true Compassioneer.

"Even in a universe filled with stars, we can cherish the fact that no star will ever shine the way we will"

If You Were Inspired by this Book and Resonate with the Nourishing Routes Philosophy:

Visit my website, blog or make your very own Compassioneer pledge at:

www.nourishingroutes.com

Pass this book on or recommend this book to a friend, family member, or someone you think will benefit from the Nourishing Routes philosophy.

Follow me on Instagram:

@Nourishing_Routes
nourishingroutes

Join the Compassioneer Community on Facebook:

Name: Nourishing Routes

Sign up for my uniquely tailored 8-week online Compassioneer Academy.

Within this safe, inspiring and empowering space you can join many other Compassioneers while following step by step guidance on how to apply the philosophy of Nourishing Routes to your own life with the aim of loving food, adoring your body and becoming yourself. The link to sign up for the Compassioneer Academy can be found on my website.